Understanding Ireland's Economic Growth

Edited by

Frank Barry
Senior Lecturer in Economics
Department of Economics
University College Dublin

First published in Great Britain 1999 by
MACMILLAN PRESS LTD
Houndmills, Basingstoke, Hampshire RG21 6XS and London
Companies and representatives throughout the world

A catalogue record for this book is available from the British Library.

ISBN 0–333–73362–2

 First published in the United States of America 1999 by
ST. MARTIN'S PRESS, INC.,
Scholarly and Reference Division,
175 Fifth Avenue, New York, N.Y. 10010

ISBN 0–312–21971–7

Library of Congress Cataloging-in-Publication Data
Understanding Ireland's economic growth / Frank Barry.
p. cm.
Includes bibliographical references and index.
ISBN 0–312–21971–7 (cloth)
1. Ireland—Economic conditions—1949– 2. Income distribution–
–Ireland. I. Barry, Frank, 1956– .
HC260.5.U53 1999
338.9415—dc21   98–44641
                                                      CIP

This book is printed on paper suitable for recycling and made from fully managed and
sustained forest sources.

10 9 8 7 6 5 4 3 2
08 07 06 05 04 03 02 01 00 99

Printed and bound in Great Britain by
Antony Rowe Ltd, Chippenham, Wiltshire

Do mo thuismitheoirí

Contents

Preface

This book was commissioned when I delivered a paper to the Royal Economic Society Conference in Stoke-on-Trent in March 1997; the paper charted the massive recent jump in Ireland's share of EU-bound foreign direct investment. It was becoming clear to the world just then that something quite dramatic was happening in Ireland; living standards had converged rapidly on the European average while employment, traditionally the weak point in Irish performance, had grown even faster than in the US in recent times, and far faster than in the UK or overall EU.

Alongside this economic success, so long in coming, there seemed to be a strong popular interest in other aspects of Ireland. This was reflected in a huge increase in tourist numbers. Irish dancing had joined Irish literature and Irish music, both traditional and not-so-traditional, in attracting international attention; the Irish film industry was booming; even the Irish soccer team had found some equally long-awaited success, while the Eurovision Song Contest, its hour come round at last, seemed to slouch frequently towards Ireland.

Sunder Katwala, Macmillan's commissioning editor, felt that the time was ripe for a book on the changing Irish economy. As the sunshine on that mid-March morning appeared propitious, I agreed. The colleagues whom I approached responded with enthusiasm and so the book came together rapidly, with substantial cross-fertilisation of ideas as the chapters were being written. My thanks to all the contributors for making the editing of this book such an easy and pleasant task. My thanks also, for assistance with the data, to several past and present employees of Forfás (Finbarr Tumelty, Aidar Meyler and Denis Slater), to William Beausang of the Department of Finance, and especially to Fergal Shortall of the Economic and Social Research Institute.

FRANK BARRY

Notes on the Contributors

Frank Barry is a Senior Lecturer in Economics at University College Dublin. He holds an MA from the University of Essex and a PhD from Queen's University in Canada. He has held visiting positions at the Universities of Stockholm, California and New South Wales, and served for a time in Asia with the Harvard Institute for International Development. His publications are in the fields of macroeconomics and international trade.

John Bradley is a Research Professor at the ESRI in Dublin, having previously worked in the Central Bank of Ireland. He has published extensively on the economics of the island of Ireland – with a particular focus on North–South interactions – as well as on the economic implications of Structural Funds and the Single Market for the periphery states of the EU. He currently directs an ACE-Phare project comparing the transition of Central European economies to EU membership with the cohesion process within the existing EU.

Tim Callan is a Research Professor at the Economic and Social Research Institute, and was awarded the D.Phil by Oxford University for his work on the international transmission of economic disturbances. In recent years he has specialised in the research areas of poverty and income distribution.

Joseph Durkan is a Lecturer in Economics and Director of the Centre for Health Economics at University College Dublin. Prior to joining UCD he worked in economic consultancy for a number of years, before which he spent 15 years with the ESRI, mainly on forecasting, and some six years in Africa. His research interests range from macro-economic policy to health economics.

Doireann Fitz Gerald is a graduate student at Harvard University, currently working in the area of economic history.

John Fitz Gerald is a Research Professor with the ESRI. He began his career in the Department of Finance where he worked on economic forecasting and modelling. He moved to the ESRI in 1984 where he has published studies of the impact of 1992 and the EU Structural

Funds on the Irish economy as well as a study on the *Economic Implications for Ireland of EMU*. He is a joint author of the ESRI's *Medium-Term Review: 1997–2003*.

Aoife Hannan is a graduate student at the European University Institute in Florence. She formerly worked as a quantitative analyst in the Irish financial sector and as a researcher at University College Dublin. She has published on trade integration and unemployment issues, and is currently interested in economic geography.

Colm Harmon is a Lecturer in the Department of Economics at University College Dublin. He completed graduate study at the University of Keele and has held previous appointments at the National University of Ireland (Maynooth) and as a visiting research collaborator at the Industrial Relations Section of Princeton University. His main area of research is in microeconometric analysis of labour market issues, with particular reference to the economic returns to schooling. He is co-editor of a recent edition of the journal *Labour Economics* on this topic.

Patrick Honohan has worked on financial sector, macroeconomic and fiscal policy issues both in Ireland – at the Economic and Social Research Institute, the Central Bank of Ireland and as Economic Adviser to Taoiseach Garret Fitz Gerald (1981–82 and 1984–86) – and at the International Monetary Fund and the World Bank. He received his PhD from the London School of Economics and has taught economics there and at the University of California, San Diego, the Australian National University, and University College, Dublin.

Brian Nolan is Research Professor at the Economic and Social Research Institute, and studied economics at University College, Dublin, McMaster University and the London School of Economics. He formerly worked at the Central Bank of Ireland. For the last decade he has been engaged in a programme of research on poverty, income inequality, tax and social security policy at the ESRI. With Tim Callan he is editor of *Poverty and Policy in Ireland* (1994), and with Christopher T. Whelan is co-author of *Resources, Deprivation and Poverty* (1996).

Eoin O'Malley is a Senior Research Officer at the Economic and Social Research Institute, Dublin. He has been a consultant to the National Economic and Social Council, the European Commission and various

Irish government agencies. His research has explored aspects of Irish industrial development including its performance through history, the impact of EU membership and the Single European Market, the contribution of foreign-owned industries in Ireland, the regional impact of industrial change and the experience of specific industrial sectors.

Eric A. Strobl is Lecturer in Economics at University College Dublin; he previously taught at the University of Dublin (Trinity College) from where he received his PhD. His research interests are in the fields of labour economics, law and economics, and regional economics.

Brendan Walsh has been Professor of National Economics at University College, Dublin, since 1980. He graduated from UCD in 1961, obtained a doctorate in economics from Boston College in 1966, and taught in several US universities before returning to Ireland to take up a post at the Economic and Social Research Institute in 1969. He has served overseas as an economic advisor with the Harvard Institute for International Development – in Iran in 1975–76 and in the Gambia in 1989–91. He has written widely on the Irish economy, and is a member of the Royal Irish Academy.

Introduction

Frank Barry

Ireland's economic performance over the last decade has been spectacular, not only in terms of its own historical experience but in an international comparative context also. GNP figures are not much distorted by the transfer pricing behaviour that bedevils some Irish statistics: Irish GNP expanded by almost 70 per cent in the 10 years from 1987, during which time the US expanded by only 27 per cent, the 15-country EU by 24 per cent, and the UK by 20 per cent. Ireland has had a long-standing problem with low levels of job creation. By 1997 there were 23 per cent more jobs in the economy than in 1987. The US created 17 per cent net new jobs over this period, the UK 5 per cent and the EU15 only 3 per cent.

This economic success has led Irish living standards to converge on average European levels. Irish GNP per head in 1987 stood at 59 per cent of the EU15 average, largely unchanged from its 1960 position. Ten years later it had risen to 88 per cent.

The present book presents the reflections of a group of Irish economists on the processes that led to this success. There is widespread agreement by now on the factors that have a role to play in the story, though the emphasis placed on the various components will differ as always with the storyteller. Generally included are the long-term consequences of the fiscal stabilisation of the late 1980s, the European Structural Funds, the increased educational attainment of the workforce, continued Irish success in attracting FDI inflows, and the wage moderation and peaceful labour relations that have characterised the last decade. As we will see though, there are disagreements over the factors that precipitated some of these beneficial developments, as well as over the precise mechanisms through which the beneficial effects come into being.

These issues need to be debated if we are to understand more fully the process of Irish transformation and convergence. Such lessons will be of benefit also to international observers who hope to gain insights from a study of the path Ireland has followed. It is hoped that the book will prove rewarding to both groups of readers.

In Chapter 1 the basic facts of Ireland's economic performance over the last 10 years are presented. Here it is shown that the boom is not simply a mirage caused by the transfer-pricing behaviour of the foreign-owned sector, as some commentators initially claimed. The most obvious proof of this is in the record levels of job creation. The chapter also identifies the sectors in which job creation has been most substantial. Most of the new jobs, as elsewhere in the industrialised world, are in market services. Unlike the experience elsewhere in the EU and OECD, however, manufacturing-sector employment has also risen, in both indigenous and foreign-owned sectors.

The relative roles of domestic demand and international competitiveness, and the question of how these sectoral developments are related to each other, requires the elaboration of a model of the economy. Chapter 2 represents a new step in this direction. Drawing on recent developments in the fields of economic geography and endogenous growth theory, this chapter reappraises the arguments of economists and economic historians over the path to development for an economy like Ireland. Ireland at independence (in 1922) is modelled as a regional economy (in which the size of the labour force is dependent on migration patterns) with an agricultural export base. The economic success of such an entity (entailing growth in the size of the economy as well as in income per head), it is argued, depends on achieving competitiveness in internationally-traded sectors other than agriculture. *Laissez faire* cannot achieve this because capital accumulation in an agricultural region displaces labour. The protectionist policies of the 1930s–1960s fostered import-substituting industrialisation; this failed to raise international competitiveness, and so the economy ran into balance of payments constraints. The early era of outward-oriented interventionism (from the 1960s to the mid-1980s) saw the economy simultaneously becoming competitive in the market for FDI while losing competitiveness (reflected in declining market shares) in traditional sectors that were opening up to international competition. It is this latter trend that has been reversed in the 1990s.

While Chapters 1 and 2 point out that internationally tradeable segments of market services have expanded considerably over the last decade, Chapter 3 focuses exclusively on manufacturing. The strong growth in the foreign-owned sector is shown to arise not just from growth in the levels of FDI available, but from a dramatic increase in the share of these flows that Ireland is capturing. Indigenous industry, after a long period of decline, has also been performing strongly since the mid-to-late 1980s. Its loss of domestic market share has been halted, and its exports and export market shares have risen. These effects coincided with an increased focus on the part of the industrial development agencies on the development of a strong indigenous sector. Furthermore, there would have been a high quality pool of firms remaining after the shake-out of the 1980s. The overall macro-environment had also become much more benevolent, in terms of cost-competitiveness (including substantial cost reductions by international standards in formerly heavily state-regulated utilities such as electricity and postal and telecommunications services) and in terms of physical infrastructure. The chapter also reveals the increasing backward and forward linkages of both indigenous and foreign firms, a corresponding increase in R&D expenditures, and a gradual but perceptible movement of indigenous industry into modern sectors.

The next four chapters analyse the improvement in the general economic environment. Patrick Honohan, in Chapter 4, reviews the fiscal crisis that ended with the successful stabilisation programme of the late 1980s. This is the aspect of recent Irish experience that has drawn most international attention until now, and the chapter corrects a number of erroneous interpretations that have begun to become embedded in the international literature. In a short period of time Ireland went from crisis to near fiscal balance, and the improvement has been sustained; a decade after the stabilisation programme was introduced the debt-to-GDP ratio has just about halved. Honohan details the context in which the reforms took place, and how precisely they were effected. He also considers the role of the interest-rate and exchange-rate policies followed at the time. The Irish stabilisation, unlike many such programmes pursued elsewhere, was not exchange-rate based. Nevertheless, the fiscal crisis was not allowed to spill over into exchange-rate or financial crises. One of the lessons learned from the comparison with earlier unsuccessful attempts at stabilisation concerns the limitations of tax increases as a means of correcting deep fiscal imbalances. When the tax-based strategy was tried the knock-on effects on wage demands proved recessionary, which made the task of balancing the budget more difficult. One of the legacies of the adjustment, he argues, has been a more realistic and restrained set of national pay agreements. This issue will surface again below.

One of the fortuitous circumstances concerning the stabilisation programme of 1987–89 was the fact that large FDI flows were entering the country at the time in the lead-up to the Single European Market. Thus manufacturing employment was already on the rise, while the doubling of the EU Structural Funds allowed a resumption of deferred public infrastructure projects from 1989 onwards. This illustrates the difficulty in disentangling the effects of the various factors that contributed to Irish success.

Chapter 5 looks in detail at these aspects of the European dimension: the Single Market and the Structural Funds. While the coming into effect of the Single Market has lagged well behind the timetable implicit in the Cecchini Report, with Monti (1996) reporting an estimated effect on EU GDP of around 1 per cent, in contrast to the Cecchini predictions of 4.5 per cent, there can be little doubt that the effects have been positive for Ireland. The *Survey of Current Business* published by the US Department of Commerce ascribes much of the increased US FDI inflows into Europe from the late 1980s to the development of the Single Market, while Ireland, as shown in Chapter 3, captured a sharply increased share of these inflows. Even Irish indigenous industry appears to have gained, in that within the sectors deemed likely to be affected by the Single Market (because restrictive public procurement policies had been prevalent for example) indigenous industry had been relatively competitive.

It is paradoxical then that Ireland should have done so well in terms of its allocation of the increased Structural Funds available from 1989, since part of the rationale for the increased funding was the fear that market integration would widen regional disparities. In looking at the impact of the Structural Funds programmes, Chapter 5 focuses on quantitative assessments that have been carried out. This leads us to ignore issues of rural regeneration, for example, that sociologists argue to be important. We also tend to downplay the effects of some of the funding for investment in training, because of the danger of confusing inputs with output. In this again we may well in time prove to have been overly conservative. The chapter discusses the methodology behind the various quantifications of the impact of the Structural Funds, and compares the results of a number of these studies. Even the most optimistic assessment, however, some readers may find surprisingly low. This is that the combined effects of the various programmes may have raised GNP by now to a level 4 per cent above what it would otherwise have been.[1] While this is substantial it represents a contribution of only one half of one percentage point of the per annum growth rate of GNP over the 1990s. The boom cannot under these circumstances be ascribed solely to 'money from Europe'. As we make clear in Chapter 5, however, the overall effect through interactions with other contributory factors may be far higher. Thus the increased share of US FDI inflows into Europe that Ireland has been capturing since the early 1990s may not have materialised had Irish physical infra-structure not been improving during this period.

At the root of the remaining four chapters are labour-market issues. The broad historical sweep of Chapter 2 presented a model of the economy with completely open labour markets. If this were the case there would be little room for divergence between Irish and UK real after-tax wages. The entry into the Irish labour force of a more highly educated cohort could not then represent an independent stimulus to growth, because, unlike in the closed labour market case, the return to these workers could not be bid down so that a level of demand equivalent to the supply would appear. The reality is clearly more complex than this simple model though. If there were a fixed cost of migration, the Irish–UK wage gap could lie anywhere within this margin. Then the issue becomes one primarily of where internationally footloose firms will choose to operate. With low availability of high-quality workers in Ireland, production facilities will locate in the UK and Irish workers will be drawn there. A ready availability in Ireland, on the other hand, may tip the balance towards locating production here; agglomeration economies will then lock the companies in, as long as the ready supply of well-educated workers is maintained. This is the kind of macro-picture that underlies the analysis of the role of human capital in recent Irish growth. It is more complicated of course than the standard model with closed labour markets that motivates most international analyses.

Durkan, Fitz Gerald and Harmon in Chapter 6 note that the Irish rate of human capital accumulation (through education) has risen to the standards of other industrialised countries only relatively recently. This means there has been a sharp increase in the quality-adjusted labour force in recent times. The quality adjustment is done by taking account of differences in earnings ascribable to age and to education, as a measure of the productivity differences of different groups of workers, and adjusting the raw employment numbers accordingly. They show that while total employment increased by 13 per cent between 1981 and 1996, the quality-adjusted measure increased by 34 per cent. This of course was associated with rapid output growth, alongside total factor productivity levels that are high by international standards. Chapter 2 showed that labour productivity growth has been high in Ireland since the late 1960s and this was there ascribed both to pro-ductivity catch-up within sectors and to a shift from traditional low-productivity into newer high-productivity sectors. These views of the processes driving productivity growth are consistent of course since, as seen in Chapter 3, the newer manufacturing sectors are the ones that employ more highly-educated workers. A difficult question in the Irish case is whether this is a product of the supply-side of the labour market (where the increased supply of educated workers, as in most economies, will lead to the upgrading of sectors), or of the demand-side (where the ability to attract FDI, to the extent to which this is dependent on factors other than the educational system, leads to a demand for these workers, who would otherwise emigrate).

Sorting out these demand- and supply-side issues in the Irish labour market is the challenge taken up by John Fitz Gerald in Chapter 7. This seeks to identify the causes of the more moderate wage settlements negotiated since 1987, which have seen the wage share in GDP fall by around 10 percentage points in the last decade. The 'traditional' approach, used by Barry and Bradley (1991) in a study of Irish unemployment up to 1987, was to model real wage inflation in manufacturing as dependent on unemployment, productivity growth and the tax wedge, while the unemployment rate was affected by the extent of migration. This method has proved inadequate since the end of their data period however. This could be because the basis on which wages were negotiated has changed, as some commentators argue. Another possibility is that, given the increased weight of foreign industry and the associated practice of transfer pricing, manufacturing-sector productivity as it appears in the data has become increasingly inadequate as an indicator of real productivity. Even expressed as a proportion of GNP, however, the fall in the wage share is substantial, as shown in Chapter 9. Fitz Gerald takes a different tack, arguing that UK labour market conditions enter more directly into Irish wage-setting behaviour than is recognised in the traditional approach. According to this view, the fact that Irish wages are now close to UK levels removes a good deal of the pressure that had been pushing them upwards before now; the increase in female labour-force participation has the same effect.

This view then ascribes relatively little weight to the four three-year social partnership programmes that set national wages from 1987–99. Yet agreements to trade off moderate wage agreements for reductions in income taxes certainly emanated from these programmes; some commentators argue that this would not have been possible in the absence of social partnership. Honohan in Chapter 4 describes the moderate national wage agreement of 1987, which instituted the partnership approach, as a reflection not only of the weakened position of trade unions, but also of a new awareness on their part of the nature of the economic crisis and the appropriate response to it. Teahon

(1997–98) suggests that the partnership approach continues to promote a shared understanding of key economic mechanisms and relationships.

One of these key understandings that emerged from the failure of the tax-based attempts at fiscal stabilisation is that tax concessions can promote wage moderation to the benefit of business, of the currently employed and of those who will get the extra jobs that the strategy generates. Leddin and Walsh (1997) estimate that tax reductions accounted for about one-third of the real increase in post-tax income per worker over the 1987–97 period.

While the partnership approach may well promote wage moderation, however, in itself it is unlikely to promote labour-market liberalisation. There is however some evidence which may suggest liberalisation also.[2] Figure I.1 below, compiled jointly with Morgan Kelly, charts the pay achieved in Ireland by higher educational award recipients within one year of college graduation, alongside economy-wide nominal compensation per employee.[3] It is apparent that the rate of increase in entry-level pay began to fall well below that of average compensation in the early 1990s. This could reflect a trend towards increased competition in

Figure I.1   Graduate pay versus average compensation

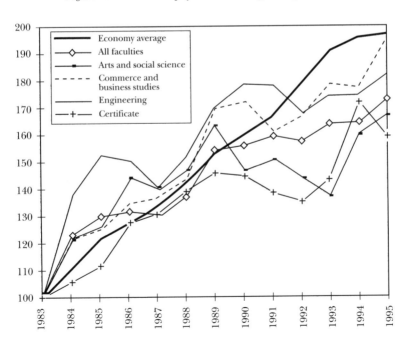

the labour market. Fitz Gerald's argument would suggest, to the contrary, that it is evidence only of the weak UK labour-market conditions of the time.

The final two chapters of the book deal with the underside of the booming economy; the continuing high levels of inequality, social exclusion and unemployment. Chapter 8 looks at the trends in inequality and poverty in Ireland over the 1980s and 1990s, and places the country in international context. In terms of pre-tax earnings, Ireland is found to have a high degree of inequality by international standards, and inequality increased over the 1987–94 period. In terms of disposable income (which is market income plus social welfare payments less income taxes) when adjusted for household size, however, the picture is quite different; Ireland had a high degree of inequality in 1987 but was no longer an outlier by international standards in 1993. Inequality increased in a number of other OECD countries during this period, but not in Ireland. Furthermore, real incomes rose substantially in Ireland over this period while inequality remained constant; Callan and Nolan suggest that this represents an unambiguous increase in social welfare.

This last point is important to the discussion of poverty also. Poverty is variously measured as relative or as basic deprivation. Looking at relative measures first, the numbers of the very poorest (those living below 40 per cent of average income) fell between 1987 and 1994; numbers living below 50 per cent were broadly stable, while those living below 60 per cent rose; even the last group though were a good deal nearer the line in 1994 than had been the case in 1987.

When poverty is defined in terms of basic deprivation, Callan and Nolan show that the numbers rose between 1980 and 1987, but fell from 1987 to 1994. There were three important differences between the two periods; (i) real income growth was negative in the first period and positive in the second, (ii) the unemployment rate rose substantially in the first period and fell in the second, and (iii) the means-tested safety net for the unemployed was raised closer to average take-home pay in the second period. As the authors note,

> While it makes sense to see poverty primarily in relative terms … this will fail to highlight the seriousness of a situation where the real incomes of the poor actually fall, as apparently occurred in the UK during the 1980s, in contrast to the substantial rise in real incomes for the poor in Ireland between 1987 and 1994.

Turning now to *relative* measures for the purposes of international comparison, Ireland for the mid-to-late 1980s and for 1993 is bunched with a group of countries that includes our Cohesion partners, Greece, Portugal and Spain, along with the UK. In fact Ireland comes out slightly better than the UK in the various measures proposed.

It is clear from Chapter 8 that unemployment is one of the most important determinants of poverty. Brendan Walsh points out in Chapter 9 that by 1997 the Irish rate of short-term unemployment, at a little over 4 per cent, compared favourably to that in many other OECD countries, as one would expect of an economic boom. The rate of long-term unemployment, however, still remains high by international standards. Even this has been dropping, though, not just as a rate but in terms of raw numbers as well, as seen in Table I.1 (note that these numbers are based on the ILO classification and are therefore different from the numbers normally quoted).

The table shows that the numbers of long-term unemployed have fallen even more than the short-term unemployed over the period (though the current low rate of short-term unemployment suggests that it is mainly frictional in nature, and so cannot be expected to fall very much further). It is apparent from Chapter 9, though, that short and long-term unemployment are very different phenomena, and that the long-term unemployed maintain only fairly tenuous connections with the labour market. They are likely to be the last to benefit from a buoyant economy, though there is evidence that the state employment schemes are going some way towards re-establishing these connections.

Table I.1 Employment and unemployment (ILO classification): thousands.

	1992	1993	1994	1995	1996	1997
Employed	1165.2	1183.1	1220.6	1281.7	1328.5	1379.9
Unemployed, of which:	206.6	220.1	211.0	177.4	179.0	159.0
reported as < 1 year	85.1	88.6	76.4	68.1	71.8	67.1
reported as > 1 year	116.5	125.4	128.2	103.3	103.3	86.3
State employment schemes	16.0	17.0	31.0	41.0	40.0	41.0

Source: CSO, *Labour Force Survey*.

In terms of the overall unemployment rate, Walsh shows two of the most important determinants to be the rate of GNP growth in Ireland and the rate of unemployment in the UK. Again this connection between the Irish and UK labour markets surfaces, making the functioning of the labour market one of the most heavily researched and yet not fully understood aspects of the Irish macro-environment. Nevertheless, for all the doubts expressed at times over the difficulty of getting the unemployment rate down when the labour market is very open, it has come down substantially over the last decade.

Dangers remain, of course, and are alluded to throughout. Chapter 4 reminds us that Irish fiscal policy stands out in cross-country comparisons as being pro-cyclical; incredibly, given the severity of the recession of the 1980s because of the pro-cyclical fiscal policies of the 1970s, fiscal policy remains pro-cyclical today. Even at the height of the boom cyclically-adjusted budget deficits are large. Chapter 4 also cautions us that within EMU most domestic macroeconomic policy instruments will have been removed, and the burden of adjustment shifted even more onto wage bargaining. The wage-bargaining mechanism is a very fragile one. Chapter 7 suggests that the catch-up of Irish to UK wages may have moderated wage demands in recent times. A less benign scenario for the future is the one, based on historical experience, that O'Rourke (1994) paints; he shows that Irish wages have exceeded UK wages at various times in the past, and that equilibrium was achieved through higher Irish unemployment. The nightmare of recent Irish economic history can yet return. Chapter 3 reminds us of how vulnerable the economy is, not just to world conditions, but to changes in the international market for FDI, and to Ireland's relative attractiveness in this regard; it advises that we use some of the proceeds from our MNC-reliant strategy to buy insurance, in the form of continuing to develop the infra-structure upon which the competitiveness of indigenous industry is dependent. We saw in Chapter 2 the extent to which the boom has been magnified by competition in formerly monopolised sectors such as air access and telecommunications. This should remind us of the dangers to economic well-being posed by entrenched interest groups; there are still many battles to be fought on this front.

A final danger, not alluded to elsewhere, relates to the saying (of Einstein's, I think) that man's imagination matures more slowly than his practical powers. The original quote relates to the atomic bomb. It applies just as well though to something closer to home that destroys the natural and the built environment. Thus rural Ireland's boom of decades means that one can no longer even glimpse the magnificent sea on the road from Galway to An Cheathrú Rua. Urban money means that the great Victorian red-brick Tara Street of my youth is no longer a street at all, and certainly neither Victorian nor red-brick, but a mere gaggle of buildings. Our economic buying power has developed more rapidly than our sense of value. We will grow to regret these things.

Notes

1. Receipts from Brussels become part of GNP (which is a measure of earned income) only when they stimulate productive activity in the economy. Thus their contribution to Irish income, earned and unearned, which is Gross National Disposable Income, is higher. These issues are dealt with in Chapter 1.
2. This is not inconsistent with the migration link. O'Rourke (1994) in a study of the historical links between the Irish and UK labour markets found, in an echo of the Harris–Todaro model, that both wages and unemployment were frequently higher in Ireland than in Britain.
3. The data source for labour market entrants is the Higher Education Authority's annual report on the First Destination of Award Recipients in Higher Education; nominal compensation data from European Economy (1997).

References

Barry, F. and Bradley, J. (1991) 'On the Causes of Ireland's Unemployment', *Economic and Social Review*, 22, pp. 253–86.

CSO, *Labour Force Survey*, various years (Dublin: Central Statistics Office)

European Economy (1997) 'Broad Economic Policy Guidelines', no. 64, statistical annex.

Leddin, A. and Walsh, B. (1997) 'Economic Stabilisation, Recovery and Growth: Ireland 1979–96', *Irish Banking Review*, pp. 2–17.

Monti, M. (1996) *The Single Market and Tomorrow's Europe: A Progress Report from the European Commission* (London: Kogan Page in association with the Office for Official Publications of the European Communities).

O'Rourke, K. (1994b) 'Did Labour Flow Uphill? International Migration and Wage Rates in Twentieth Century Ireland', in G. Grantham and M. MacKinnon (eds), *Labour Market Evolution: The Economic History of Market Integration, Wage Flexibility and the Employment Relation* (London and New York: Routledge).

Teahon, P. (1997–98) 'The Irish Political and Policy-Making System and the Current Programme of Change', *Administration*, 45(4), pp. 49–58.

1 The Real Convergence of the Irish Economy and the Sectoral Distribution of Employment Growth

Frank Barry, Aoife Hannan and Eric Strobl[1]

INTRODUCTION

In this chapter we present the basic facts of the recent Irish growth experience. The last decade has seen a substantial increase in income per head and in employment numbers, so that Ireland has converged rapidly on European and UK living standards. Furthermore, this progress was achieved with low inflation and without the sacrifice of fiscal or balance of payments stability. Productivity growth has been substantially higher than the European average since the late 1960s, due both to 'catch-up' by traditional sectors and to their replacement by more modern sectors; real convergence would have been experienced much earlier then had employment growth in Ireland proceeded at the same rate as elsewhere in Europe. This raises the question of whether, and under what conditions, catch-up could have been achieved by the traditional sectors without the amount of job-shedding actually experienced over the last few decades. Chapter 2 considers these issues. The present chapter is concerned with the less-speculative task of identifying the sectors in which recent employment growth occurred.

THE MACRO PICTURE: INCOME, EMPLOYMENT AND WAGE GROWTH

Ireland's economic performance over the last decade has been remarkable, not only compared to its own historical experience but also to the concurrent performance of the UK, EU, US and Japanese economies. Ireland's convergence to EU levels of GDP per head, measured in terms of purchasing power, is shown in Figure 1.1. While Europe was catching

Figure 1.1 GDP per capita (in purchasing power parity terms) relative to the EU average; EU15 = 100

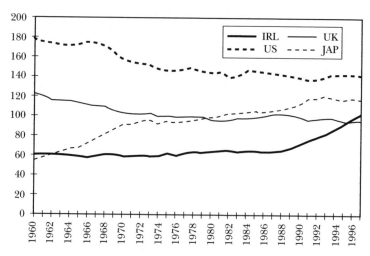

Source: *European Economy* (1997).

up to US income levels over this whole period, Ireland started to catch up to the EU average only since the late 1980s.

It is well-known, of course, that GDP represents, for Ireland at least, a particularly poor measure of national income; the reason for this is that it includes interest payments paid on the economy's foreign debt and, more importantly for Ireland, the profits that foreign multi-national companies operating in the country repatriate to their home bases. These have amounted to more than 13 per cent of Irish GDP in recent years. Gross national product (or GNP) excludes these and therefore provides a better measure of the income earned by Irish capital and labour. There are some special circumstances, however, that dictate that even the GNP measure must be used with care. One is that the prices of some of Ireland's most important exports have been declining in recent years: agricultural product prices have fallen in the direction of world prices with the scaling back of the Common Agricultural Policy, while computer and computer-product prices fall continuously at this stage of the product cycle. This means that a given volume of Irish exports purchases less imports, and so GNP must be adjusted for these changes in the terms of trade to give a more adequate measure of the purchasing power of Irish incomes. GNP stands at around 85 per cent of Irish GDP at present, while, given the worsening terms of trade over most of the 1990s, GNP adjusted for the terms of trade stands at around 81 per cent. The latter is one of the better measures of the productive earnings of the economy.[2]

Figure 1.2 shows that Ireland experienced rapid convergence on average EU living standards even in terms of this measure, and that this convergence was much more dramatic than anything experienced by the other 'cohesion', or relatively less well off, EU economies: Greece, Spain and Portugal.

The measures just cited, while clearly important, depict just one aspect of growth; that is *intensive* growth, or growth in the living standards of the resident population. In an economy as open as Ireland's in terms of migration, policy-makers have traditionally been concerned also with *extensive* growth; that is, with growth in the size of the economy (in the absolute level of GDP or GNP), in population and in numbers at work.[3] Recent Irish performance has also been remarkable in terms of extensive growth, and Figure 1.3 compares recent Irish growth in GNP adjusted for the terms of trade with GDP growth in the US, the UK and the EU15.

Extensive growth alongside substantial intensive growth requires of course that the numbers at work must have risen dramatically in recent times, and this is indeed the case, as shown in Figure 1.4.

Irish employment growth, then, has been far more rapid than in the US, UK or EU15 since the early 1990s. Nor has this simply been

Figure 1.2   The convergence experience of the cohesion economies; national income per capita in purchasing power parity terms; EU15 = 100

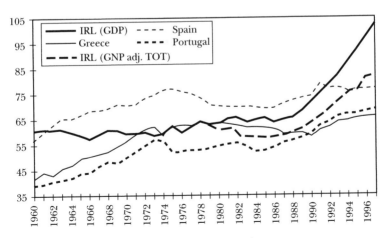

Source: *European Economy* (1997) and own estimates.

Figure 1.3   Extensive growth

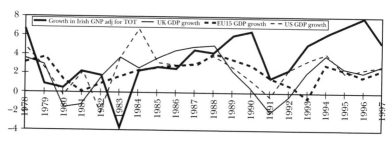

Source: *European Economy* (1997) and own estimates.

Figure 1.4   Employment growth rates, 1979–97

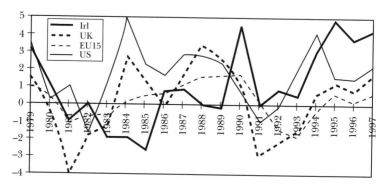

Source: *European Economy* (1997); OECD *Employment Outlook* (1998).

making up for lost ground, as Figure 1.5 shows. Concomitant with this growth in employment is a sharp fall in the numbers emigrating, so that Ireland is experiencing net immigration at present.

One sometimes encounters the claim in Ireland that workers' share in these GNP gains came in the form of employment growth rather than real wage growth. It is certainly the case that the share of wages in national income has fallen. Beyond this, however, the claim is incorrect in that average real after-tax wages have increased substantially over the last decade. For example, the real value of compensation per worker is 22 per cent higher in 1997 than it was a decade earlier.[4] In the UK real compensation grew only 16 per cent over this period, and in the EU15 it grew even less, by 12 per cent. This is pre-tax income; Leddin and Walsh (1997) calculate that after-tax earnings for a worker on the

Source: *European Economy* (1997); OECD *Employment Outlook* (1998).

average industrial wage rose by a further 9 per cent, so that reduced tax rates accounted for about one-third of the rise in real take-home pay.[5] While the most highly-educated workers clearly gained most, as shown in Chapters 6 and 8, those with jobs gained substantially, and there were many more jobs in Ireland than there would otherwise have been.

A recent report from the Economic and Social Research Institute, Bradley *et al.* (1997), demonstrates the role that employment growth has played in the growth in income per head. It notes that GNP per capita is the product of four variables: productivity (GNP per worker), the employment rate (workers as a proportion of the labour force), the participation rate (the labour force as a proportion of the population of working age) and the inverse of the age dependency ratio (that is, those of working age relative to the total population).

Changes in these variables will occasionally be related; the employment and participation rates tend to move together, for example, because of the discouraged worker effect, while the employment and dependency rates will move inversely to the extent that single people of working age emigrate in periods of poor employment growth. Nevertheless, the variables retain some independence as will be discussed in a moment. Figures 1.6 and 1.7 indicate the contribution that each of these variables has made to growth in GNP per head.

Productivity growth, we see, has been fairly stable over the whole period since 1960. It is only over the last decade, however, that all four factors have made positive contributions to income growth. Labour-force participation has grown primarily because the participation of married women has risen steadily towards European levels in recent

Figure 1.6   Growth in GNP per capita

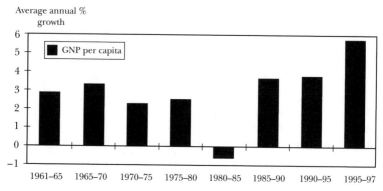

Source: Bradley *et al.* (1997).

Figure 1.7   Decomposition of GNP per capita growth

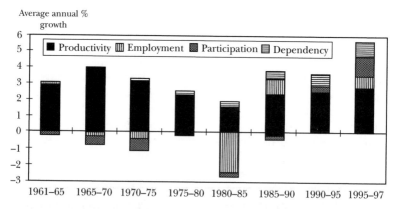

Source: Bradley *et al.* (1997).

years, while age dependency, which has led to worries about a 'demographic crisis' in the rest of Europe, has actually been improving in Ireland with the proportion of children in the population falling rapidly in the last ten years after remaining stable between the 1960s and the mid-1980s. The trend in employment, however, is the major factor that has shifted from having a negative to a positive effect. This perspective leads naturally on then to the task of identifying the sectors in which the dramatic employment growth of recent times has taken place.

THE MICRO PICTURE: SECTORAL EMPLOYMENT GROWTH

Figure 1.8 charts developments in sectoral and total employment in Ireland since 1973. Agriculture has been in continuous decline; industry and non-market services have had chequered histories, while market services has increased steadily throughout and increased rapidly in recent years.

Total employment has increased each year since 1989. The distribution of employment growth has been very uneven across sectors, however, as shown in Table 1.1. Agriculture (broadly defined to include forestry and fishing), which comprised around 15 per cent of employment in 1989, shed 29 000 jobs (a decline of 18 per cent) between then and 1997. Industry, which comprised 28 per cent of employment added 80 000 new jobs, an increase of 26 per cent; these new jobs were divided about 70:30 between manufacturing and construction. Non-market services (health, education and public administration) comprised 16 per cent of employment in 1989, and 32 000 new jobs (a gain of 18 per cent) were created in this sector; while market services, which comprised a little over 40 per cent of total employment initially, grew by a phenomenal 37 per cent. Of the 248 000 (net) new jobs created between 1989 and 1997, therefore, which represented an increase of 23 per cent, the market services sector accounted for a total of 165 000.

Figure 1.8   Sectoral employment levels

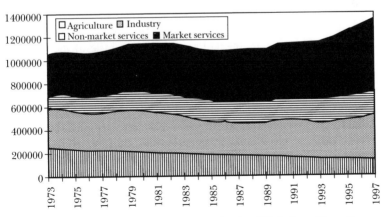

Source: ESRI/Department of Finance Databank; CSO Labour Force Survey, various issues.

Table 1.1   Sectoral employment; levels and growth

	1989	1997	Job gain	% change
Agriculture	163 200	134 200	−29 000	−18
Industry, of which:	306 400	386 400	80 000	26
mining and utilities	20 700	18 400	−2 300	−11
building and construction	70 300	96 700	26 400	38
manufacturing	215 400	271 300	55 900	26
Non-market services, of which:	178 300	210 700	32 400	18
health and education	111 800	136 500	24 700	22
public administration	66 500	74 200	7 700	12
Market services	442 000	607 100	165 100	37
Total Employment	1 089 900	1 338 400	248 500	23

Source: CSO Labour Force Survey, various years; health and education data from the Department of Finance.

We now want to look at these sectoral trends in a little more detail. We do not have too much to say about agriculture. It remains important in Ireland relative to the situation in most other European economies; we have seen, however, that employment in the sector has continued its inexorable decline, while gross agricultural product (the difference between gross agricultural output and the cost of farm materials and services) has for the last five years been below the levels prevailing in the early 1990s. Combined with the employment loss that we saw over the period, this reflects a large increase in productivity. Nevertheless, with both output and employment falling, we must conclude that agriculture *per se* (as distinct from food processing, which we will consider in a moment) has contributed little to the extensive growth that Ireland has experienced over the last decade.

Table 1.2 reveals that employment growth has occurred in all the major segments of market services. Most of it, however, unfortunately for our purposes, was concentrated in the heterogeneous 'Other, including professional' segment. However, the regional perspective that we propose in Chapter 2 suggests that attention can usefully be focused on the internationally tradeable segments of the sector. There has been growth in two important internationally tradeable segments of market services: international financial services (Table 1.3) and tourism. While growth in absolute numbers in the former has been relatively small, it is important because it is a high-pay and arguably high-productivity-growth segment.

Table 1.2 Employment in market services, levels and growth

	1989	1997	Job gain	% change
Market services, of which:	442 000	607 100	165 100	37
distribution	169 700	202 500	32 800	19
insurance, finance and business services	52 100	78 200	26 100	50
transport and communication	65 700	83 800	18 100	28
others including professional services	154 500	242 600	88 100	57

Source: CSO Labour Force Survey, various years; health and education data from the Department of Finance.

Table 1.3 Employment in financial services

	1989	1997	Job gain	% growth
Internationally traded and international financial services employment, of which:	9 699	29 556	19 857	205
Irish-owned	4 113	9 790	5 677	138
Foreign-owned	5 586	19 766	14 180	254
IFSC component	322	4 014	3 692	1 147

Source: Forfás, 1997 Employment Survey.

Employment in tourism services, on the other hand, is not generally very highly paid. The sector however has experienced rapid growth over the last decade. Data from Bord Fáilte, the Irish Tourist Board, show that the total number of overseas visitors to Ireland, and tourism revenue from out-of-state visitors, more than doubled in the ten years to 1997. Employment associated with these expenditures, whether direct, indirect or induced, grew from almost 64 000 in 1989 to 110 000 in 1997.[6]

Within the broadly-defined industry category, employment grew strongly in building and construction, fell slightly in utilities, and, against both OECD and EU trends, grew in both indigenous and foreign-owned manufacturing.

Table 1.4 presents manufacturing-sector data from Forfás that allows one to distinguish between ownership groupings. These data show that employment growth in manufacturing was confined to a relatively small

Table 1.4   Employment levels and employment growth; indigenous (I) and foreign-owned (F) industry

	1989 (I)	Growth 1989–97 (I)	% growth (I)	1989 (F)	Growth 1989–97 (F)	% growth (F)
Non-metallic minerals	8 999	−909	−10	2 890	−790	−27
Chemicals, of which:	3 100	929	30	11 148	5 675	51
pharmaceuticals	711	426	60	5 492	4 822	88
Metals and engineering, of which:	25 078	8 295	33	40 118	20 916	52
metal articles	10 702	3 235	30			
mechanical engineering	3 812	1 496	39			
office and data processing	1 448	304	21	6 472	11 710	181
electrical engineering	4 095	1 963	48	12 107	5 046	42
instrument engineering	1 049	564	54	6 983	4 379	63
Food, of which:	29 692	2 380	8	8 621	−329	−4
dairy products	8 215	−794	−10			
other food products	1 641	742	45	1 920	887	46
Drink and tobacco	1 964	−384	−20	5 692	−1 552	−27
Textile industry	3 484	−477	−14	6 164	−1 703	−28
Clothing, footwear and leather	10 720	−3 350	−31	4 415	−2 262	−51
Timber and furniture	8 641	788	9	685	280	41
Paper and printing	12 167	−46	0	2 169	132	6
Miscellaneous industries, of which:	6 329	2 128	34	4 882	294	6
processing of plastics	3 584	1 136	32			
other manufacturing industries	2 192	1 007	46			
Total indigenous manufacturing	110 174	9 354	8			
Total foreign				86 784	20 661	24
Total indigenous and foreign (Forfás)				196 958	30 015	15

Source: Forfás, unpublished employment data.

Table 1.5   Manufacturing employment; levels and growth

	1989	1997	Growth 1989–97	% growth
Indigenous manufacturing (Forfás)	110 174	119 528	9 354	8
Foreign manufacturing (Forfás)	86 784	107 445	20 661	24
Total indigenous and foreign (Forfás)	196 958	226 973	30 015	15
Unclassified	18 442	44 327	25 885	140
Total manufacturing (LFS)	215 400	271 300	55 900	26

Source: Forfás, unpublished employment data; CSO Labour Force Surveys (LFS) various years.

number of sectors. Of the 10 major sectors, both ownership groupings (that is, indigenous and foreign) shed jobs in 4 sectors and raised employment levels in another 4. The sectors in which both groups shed jobs consisted of two largely non-tradeable sectors – non-metallic minerals and drink and tobacco – and two easily-entered low-wage sectors: textiles, and clothing and footwear.[7] Interestingly, of the 4 sectors where both groupings expanded in employment terms, two were the most modern sectors, chemicals and metals and engineering, while employment gains in the other two were marginal.

The Forfás data suggest that manufacturing-sector employment stood at 226 973 by 1997. More comprehensive data from the Labour Force Survey set the number at 271 300, however, showing a substantial increase over and above that appearing in the Forfás data set; Table 1.5.

CONCLUDING COMMENTS

After experiencing little or no convergence between the 1960s and the late 1980s, Ireland has progressed rapidly towards average European living standards over the last decade. This convergence is reflected in all the various measures of per capita income. Numbers at work also expanded considerably over this period, most notably in the market services sector. Within manufacturing, employment in both the indigenous and foreign-owned sectors expanded, against both US and EU15 trends. Furthermore, as discussed in detail in Chapters 2 and 3 below, the economy achieved substantial success in export markets during the recent successful decade of economic growth.

Notes

1. We are grateful to Fergal Shortall of the Economic and Social Research Institute for help with the data.
2. While useful as a measure of earned income, GNP adjusted for the terms of trade underestimates Irish income because it excludes EU transfers to the economy. Most of these are included in Gross National Disposable Income (or GNDI) which currently stands at close to the unadjusted GNP figure.
3. For example, if one were to focus just on intensive growth in the 1840s and 1850s one would overlook the catastrophic effects of the Great Famine, since the living standards of the remaining Irish population improved substantially; Ó Grada (1994).
4. These measures use the private consumption deflator. The source is European Economy (1997).
5. The standard and top rates of income tax both fell by around 10 percentage points between 1988 and 1998, and the thresholds at which they applied were raised in real terms.
6. These numbers do not include employment estimated to come from the recycling of taxes paid by tourists, which is thought to add another 8 per cent to these figures; on this see Deegan and Dineen (1997).
7. Non-tradeability is reflected in a fairly successful defence of the home market against competing imports; Barry and Hannan (1996).

References

Barry, F. and Hannan, A. (1996) 'On Comparative and Absolute Advantage: FDI and the Sectoral and Spatial Effects of Market Integration', Centre for Economic Research Working Paper WP96/19, University College, Dublin.

Bradley, J., Fitz Gerald, J., Honohan, P. and Kearney, I. (1997) 'Interpreting the Recent Irish Growth Experience', in *Economic and Social Research Institute Medium-Term Review: 1997–2003* (Dublin: ESRI).

Central Statistics Office, *Labour Force Survey*, various years (Dublin: CSO).

Deegan, J. and Dineen, D. (1997) 'The Tourism Dimension to Irish Economic Development', in F. O. Muircheartaigh (ed.), *Ireland in the Coming Times: Essays to Celebrate T.K. Whitaker's 80 Years* (Dublin: Institute of Public Administration).

European Economy (1997) *Broad Economic Policy Guideline*, no. 64, statistical annex.

Forfás *Employment Survey*, various years (Dublin: Forfás).

Leddin, A. and Walsh, B. (1997) 'Economic Stabilisation, Recovery and Growth: Ireland 1979–96', *Irish Banking Review*, pp. 1–17.

Ó Grada, C. (1994) *Ireland: A New Economic History 1780–1939* (Oxford: Clarendon Press).

2 Irish Growth in Historical and Theoretical Perspective

Frank Barry

The nature of the Irish economy, and the definition of Ireland's economic problem, were shaped by a combination of events that occurred in the nineteenth century. One of these was the large-scale emigration that the Great Famine induced. This left as its legacy a willingness and an ability on the part of the population to migrate when economic prospects elsewhere seemed brighter. Ireland henceforth functioned more as a regional economy, whose population expands or contracts as economic conditions dictate, than as a national economy whose population size is determined largely by demographic factors. As Krugman (1997) points out, national productivity determines the well-being of a national economy, regardless of the sectors in which the economy specializes. The size of a regional economy on the other hand is crucially determined by its export base (or more generally by its international competitiveness); if exports collapse, for example, regional income falls, expenditure on non-tradeables declines, and workers emigrate.

The second crucial event of the nineteenth century that is important to our story is the de-industrialisation of the country that followed in the wake of the industrial revolution. Irish industry heretofore had been quite successful, relying on low wages for competitive advantage. Agglomeration economies grew in importance as the industrial revolution proceeded, however, which favoured British industry. As transport costs declined, sectors which had been largely non-tradeable and therefore protected became internationally tradeable, Irish industry went into decline, and the economy became an agricultural hinterland of Great Britain.

The problem for an agriculturally-based regional economy is that capital accumulation tends to displace labour and so *extensive* growth in overall GDP or in population is difficult to achieve. Positive externalities also appear to be less prevalent in agriculture than in some other sectors, which reduces the likelihood of real convergence in *intensive* terms (that is, in terms of income per head) in such a region.

25

The Irish economic problem, in the light of these events, we define as the need to achieve competitiveness in internationally-tradeable sectors other than agriculture. Other successful late-industrialisers, from Germany in the wake of the British industrial revolution (Pollard, 1985) to Japan and the East Asian NICs since the Second World War 'climbed the ladder of comparative advantage' through the development of low-wage sectors; this strategy then offered room for advancement through human-capital accumulation, learning-by-doing, reverse engineering and so on. Since the emigration option in the Irish case placed a floor below which wage levels could not fall, however, this path to economic development was largely blocked.[1]

This chapter develops these hypotheses and charts the route to success that Ireland eventually discovered.

OPTIMISTS AND PESSIMISTS IN THE STUDY OF IRISH ECONOMIC HISTORY

Ireland in the early nineteenth century had a fairly large industrial sector by the standards of the time. In 1784–86, for example, Ireland exported nearly twice as much industrial produce to Britain as vice versa, while in the 1841 census one-fifth of the working population was reported to be occupied in textile manufacturing alone. As the effects of the industrial revolution spread, however, industrial activity declined over most of the country. British industrial exports to Ireland surpassed those flowing in the opposite direction in the late 1790s, and were always greater thereafter.

The first sectors to be affected by the concentration wrought by the factory system were textiles. The Irish woollen industry contracted, as did smaller British regional centres, in the face of the growing dominance of Yorkshire, while an equivalent pattern emerged for cotton which became concentrated on Lancashire and Glasgow. Linen did better since one of the centres on which it was concentrated was Belfast. Other industries such as milling, brewing, iron-founding, shipbuilding, rope-making, paper and glass-making expanded in Ireland during the first half of the century, though the growing importance of large-scale production and centralisation was apparent as the number of firms declined, with the larger town-based producers expanding at the expense of others. As transport costs declined further over the next half-century, however, many of these latter sectors also fell prey to British-based rivals.[2]

Krugman (1991a,b) has recently modelled this process by which free-trading regions become differentiated into an industrialised core and an agricultural periphery. He notes that in early nineteenth-century America, as in the UK (which comprised both Britain and Ireland at the time), the combination of weak economies of scale and high transport costs would have induced suppliers of goods and services to the agricultural sector to locate close to their markets; thus there would have been a fairly even spread of industrial activity. The tie of production to the distribution of land was broken, however, as the factory system introduced economies of scale and as the transport system developed. This favoured the centralisation of production in regions with relatively large non-rural populations because of both the large local market and the availability of other goods and services produced there. This initial advantage is then reinforced through time and the process feeds upon itself until the whole of the non-rural population is concentrated in a few core regions, while the rest of the economy de-industrialises to become the rural hinterland.

Models with similar agglomeration implications, though emphasising the importance of technological externalities rather than those associated with demand, have been proposed by Brian Arthur (1989) and Paul David (1990). These models may explain why the Belfast region industrialised as industry elsewhere in Ireland went into decline. This is consistent with O'Malley's (1981) explanation that Belfast was well-suited to become one of the successful textile centres because of well-established export markets and a large population of skilled weavers, existing mills and factory hands. Technological externalities and the importance of learning-by-doing surface more explicitly elsewhere in O'Malley (1981) in his discussion of the origins of Belfast shipbuilding. The region became a centre of steam engine production servicing the local textile industries when steam engines were still essentially non-tradeable. As they became tradeable their production became concentrated in the regions which had been producing them intensively. From steam engine production came boilermaking, out of which in turn came shipbuilding.[3]

Outside the North-east though, Ireland was transformed through the playing-out of agglomeration economies into a rural hinterland of the UK.[4] Irish policy-makers since Independence in 1922 have struggled to overcome that legacy.

Some economists in recent times, though, have questioned whether there is a need for policy intervention in this situation (see for example Walsh, 1990; and Ruane, 1990). There are two problems with this *laissez faire* view, however; one to do with the presence of learning-by-doing effects, and the other with the definition of social welfare in a regional economy.

To take the learning-by-doing issue first, many would argue that the potential for learning-by-doing is greater in industry than in agriculture; this is certainly consistent with Ó Grada and O'Rourke's (1996) finding that the expected growth rate of GDP per head is reduced substantially when agriculture comprises a large share of GDP. Matsuyama (1992) shows that under these circumstances specialising in agriculture in line with static comparative advantage may entail long-run welfare losses. There is clearly scope then for welfare-enhancing intervention to promote industrialisation (though the type of intervention must be determined pragmatically, as discussed below).

The second problem with the *laissez-faire* view is that it ignores the fact that in a regional economy, by which I mean an economy with very elastic supplies of labour through the migration option, policy-makers tend to be concerned not just with incomes per head but also with the size of the economy. We can use total employment as a proxy for the latter. Consider in this light an economy that consists of one internationally-traded sector, agriculture, and a non-traded sector, services. What are the effects in this economy of capital accumulation, which is the mechanism that conventional growth theory suggests will bring about real convergence?[5] Capital accumulation in agriculture will generally displace farming jobs; higher agricultural productivity will increase the demand for services, though, and increase employment opportunities there. Whether there are net job gains or losses depends on the share of spending that goes on services, and on labour-demand elasticities in the two sectors. It is possible then that capital accumulation in agriculture will lead to emigration, which policy-makers regard as undesirable.

Capital accumulation in services is even more likely to have this effect. Productivity growth in non-tradeables displaces labour, and if agriculture cannot employ these workers they have no option but to emigrate.[6] O'Rourke's (1994a) recent criticism of Irish policy-makers' emphasis on the tradeable sectors at the expense of non-tradeables is open to challenge, then, in that it is set in a national rather than regional-economy context.[7] This failure to take account of the specific social-welfare function of policy-makers in a regional economy is evident also in the distinction that Williamson (1994) draws, amongst students of Irish economic history, between 'optimists' such as himself, who focus on Ireland's strong convergence to British wage levels over the last 150 years, and 'pessimists' such as Kennedy, Giblin and McHugh (1988), Lee (1989) and Ó Grada and O'Rourke (1996), who focus on the lack of convergence

Figure 2.1 Irish real wages and GDP per head relative to the UK, 1830–1997:
UK = 100

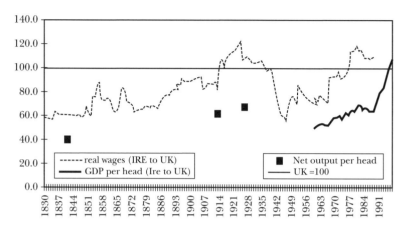

Source: Kennedy, Giblin and McHugh (1988), Ó Grada (1994), O'Rourke
(1994b), Williamson (1995).

between Irish and UK or western European levels of GDP per head
over most of this period (Figure 2.1).[8]

The optimistic perspective appears to us to be misleading if the wage
convergence results from migration while social welfare is cast in terms
of the size of the economy. On the other hand, however, we will be ques-
tioning whether Ireland can really be thought to have underperformed,
as the pessimists argue. From our perspective the lack of convergence in
GDP levels per capita for an agriculturally-based regional economy
appears natural; what appears unnatural and even breathtaking is that
Ireland should have achieved such dramatic successes in terms of both
intensive and extensive growth in recent times; that is, that it should
have converged to core European living standards *and* that this should
have been associated with record levels of employment expansion.

WAGE CONVERGENCE VERSUS CONVERGENCE IN
LIVING STANDARDS

Walsh (1994) raises, but does not answer, the question of why the convergence in wages seen in Figure 2.1 above did not give rise to greater
convergence in living standards. This is the question we now wish to
address.

As in Chapter 1 we will define living standards in terms of GNP rather than GDP per head, though this distinction has only become important over the last couple of decades. Again, as above, we will consider it in terms of its four component parts. GNP per head is the product of GNP per worker (which is productivity), the proportion of the labour force that is working (this is the rate of employment), the proportion of those of active age who are in the labour force (that is, the participation rate), and the proportion of the population who are of active age (which is the inverse of the age-dependency ratio).

We now want to ask which of these components are influenced by the fact that Ireland, as seen in Figures 2.1 and 2.2, has an extremely open labour market. To reduce the dimensionality of the issue, let us assume that the participation rate is dependent on the employment rate, through the discouraged worker effect and through married women entering the labour force when the demand for labour is buoyant. Furthermore, assume that the employment rate is a function of macroeconomic circumstances. From a long-term perspective, then, the openness of the labour market impacts on per capita GNP primarily through its impact on productivity growth and on the age-dependency ratio. Clearly if emigration is concentrated amongst single people of working age this will raise the age-dependency ratio and reduce GNP per capita.

More difficult to analyse, and more interesting, is the impact of labour-market openness on productivity growth. Capital accumulation will

Figure 2.2   Net emigration from Ireland, by decades (except for last period, which runs from 1990–96)

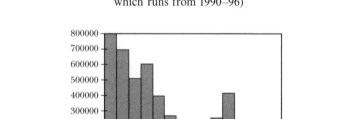

Source: Sweeney (1998).

undoubtedly generate productivity growth. The role of human capital accumulation, however, which is the other mechanism focused upon in conventional growth theory, is more questionable. In a closed labour market an exogenous increase in the stock of human capital will lower the price of skilled labour; this will open up employment opportunities for skilled workers, so raising labour productivity. In an open labour market, however, an increased supply of human capital does not automatically create the conditions for its employment, because there is less room for wages to diverge from levels available elsewhere. The result may then be emigration rather than productivity convergence.[9]

Reference was made earlier to the fact that the low-wage strategy of climbing onto the ladder of comparative advantage would also not be available to regions with open labour markets; migration takes the place of low-wage industrialisation. It is difficult for a manufacturing base to be developed under these conditions which would allow room for learning-by-doing and associated productivity growth. Furthermore, the demand-driven external economies focused upon by Krugman (1991a) and by Murphy, Shleifer and Vishny (1989) will clearly be difficult to achieve for regions which continuously lose population. And finally we can note that in the Krugman and Venables (1990) model of the dynamics of the core–periphery relationship, the periphery can ultimately capture the high-productivity increasing-returns sectors when the gap between core and periphery wages reaches a level sufficient to overcome the benefits of industrial agglomeration in the core; this option is also not available under open labour-market conditions.

For all of these reasons then, we might expect labour-market openness to inhibit productivity growth, making it more difficult to achieve convergence in GNP per head.[10] This is why, from our perspective, the recent convergence of the Irish economy is so impressive.

THE PROTECTIONIST ERA

According to the Census of Industrial Production of 1926, only about 5 per cent of the labour force of the newly-independent Irish Free State was engaged in manufacturing. The government largely pursued a free-trade policy, and the very modest increase in industrial employment over the 1920s arose for the most part in the small number of sectors that were granted tariff protection (Girvin, 1989). A decade after independence, however, in 1932, a much more protectionist policy was introduced which was to last until the early 1960s.

The theoretical arguments we advanced earlier suggest that industrialisation and strong employment growth are unlikely to occur in a peripheral region that is geographically proximate to, and in a free-trade and open labour market relationship with, an already advanced industrial region. It behoves us then to consider some modern versions of the 'infant industry argument' which justifies state intervention to promote industrialisation.

The infant-industry argument relies on the potential for dynamic scale economies, which play an important role in current 'endogenous growth' models.[11] These dynamic economies can arise through: (a) learning-by-doing in the production process, as in Young (1991), (b) human capital accumulation, as in Stokey (1991), or (c) R&D-driven technological progress, as in Grossman and Helpman (1991). The general conclusion of these models is that

> If the industries in which the less developed country has a static comparative advantage are industries in which there are limited opportunities for learning, then the effect of free trade is to speed up learning in the more developed country and to slow it down in the less developed one.   (Stokey, 1991, p. 608)

These models suggest, then, that free trade between core and periphery may slow down learning-by-doing, skills acquisition, R&D and productivity growth in the periphery; and, conversely, that some forms of trade intervention may have the opposite effects. We want to ask now, with the benefit of hindsight, whether Irish import-substituting protectionism had any of these beneficial effects, and if not, why not.

Industrial protectionism did indeed in its initial phase raise the rate of employment growth in manufacturing, from 1.6 per cent per annum in the early years of independence to a growth rate of 3.1 per cent per annum in the period 1932–60 (Kennedy, Giblin and McHugh, 1988). The industries that arose under protectionism proved, however, to be almost exclusively home-market oriented so that the protectionist policy had run out of steam by the 1950s.[12] The inward orientation of the economy insulated it from the European postwar economic boom; exports increased, of course, though not nearly as rapidly as imports. As suggested earlier in discussing the two-sector regional model with traded and non-traded goods, an expansion of the non-traded sector will cause the economy to run into a balance of payments constraint, and the economy will contract. Manufacturing employment growth slowed to

0.8 per cent per annum over the course of the 1950s, and over 400 000 people out of a population of less than 3 million emigrated.

Ó Grada and O'Rourke (1996) point out that, overall, Irish economic growth was very low in that decade, whether measured against the standard of the UK or of western Europe, whether measured intensively or extensively, and whether the Heston–Summers or Maddison data sets are used (Table 2.1).

Barry (1996) addresses the question of why protectionism failed to generate the dynamic scale economies that the endogenous-growth theories suggested may be possible. There are a number of reasons. First, unlike the nineteenth century situation analysed by O'Malley (1981), technology was now so complex and transport costs so low that engineering and capital goods industries would no longer arise naturally to meet local needs. Second, there is the exclusively home-market orientation of the infant industries that developed;[13] the small size of the home market meant that the benefits of economies of scale could not be reaped, while insulation from international competition appears to have given rise to X-inefficiencies. These X-inefficiencies and rent-seeking behaviour dominated the Schumpeterian processes that the Grossman and Helpman (1991) model focuses upon, and so virtually no R&D took place under protectionism.[14] The general impression of the inefficiency of Irish industry at the time is confirmed by the reports of the Committee on Industrial Organisation, a body comprised of the trade unions, government and business, which, in the words of Ó Grada and O'Rourke

Table 2.1   Irish economic growth, 1950–60

	Heston–Summers			Maddison		
	Ireland	*UK*	*W. Eur.*	*Ireland*	*UK*	*W. Eur.*
Annual average growth rate of GDP per capita, 1950–60	2.15	2.51	4.73	2.19	2.46	4.75
Annual average growth rate of GDP, 1950–60	1.67	2.89	5.64	1.71	2.87	5.64

Note: The rows in the table differ because of differences in population growth rates.
Source: Ó Grada and O'Rourke (1996).

(1996) 'painted a bleak picture of an industrial sector beset by shoddy design, poor marketing and short production runs'. These adverse factors associated with protectionism in a small economy dominated the possible beneficial effects to which the endogenous growth literature draws attention.[15]

OUTWARD ORIENTATION

With the very visible failure of the protectionist strategy in the 1950s, Ireland moved towards outward-orientation at the end of the decade; tariffs were progressively reduced, the Anglo-Irish Free Trade Agreement was signed in 1966, and the country in 1973 acceded to what would become the European Union. The new strategy was not just a return to *laissez faire*, however; rather it is more correctly defined as an outward-oriented interventionist strategy, as FDI inflows were aggressively pursued through the offer of capital grants alongside a zero corporate profits tax rate on manufactured exports (replaced in the 1980s by a flat 10 per cent rate on all manufacturing).

While the economic situation improved almost immediately, GNP per head did not begin to converge on UK or EU standards until the late 1980s. We therefore need to explain why there was no convergence until then, in contrast to the predictions of standard growth theory, and, following on from this, what happened over the last decade to change this trend. Again to reduce the dimensionality of the issue, we note that GNP per head is GNP per worker times the proportion of the population that is working. This allows us focus solely on productivity and employment.

Figure 2.3 below reveals that Irish productivity growth, whether measured in terms of GDP or GNP per worker, has been substantially higher than the EU average since the late 1960s.[16] The fact that little real convergence was achieved between the 1960s and the late 1980s alongside this higher productivity growth comes down then to Ireland's poor record in job creation over the period. This is clear also from Figure 2.4 (also appearing as Figure 1.7 in this volume), which indicates the stability of productivity growth alongside the instability of employment growth. Had employment growth in Ireland remained at the EU average since the late 1960s, then, convergence in real income per head would have taken place much sooner. We analyse the productivity growth first and then ask why employment performance has been so much better in recent times.

Figure 2.3   Irish and EU productivity growth (5-year moving average)

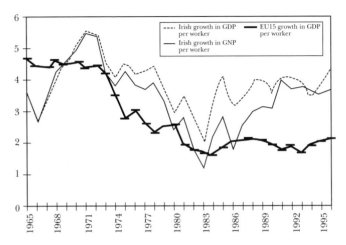

Source: *European Economy* (1997).

Figure 2.4   Decomposition of GNP per capita growth

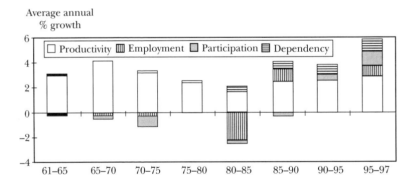

Source: Bradley *et al*. (1997).

Rapid productivity growth can arise from two sources: first, as Irish productivity within individual sectors catches up to average European levels; and, second, as traditional low-productivity sectors are replaced by newer higher-productivity ones. Both processes have been occurring in Ireland.

Table 2.2   Irish net output per worker as a percentage
of UK levels

	1968	1985	1990
Agriculture	55	77	80
Construction	66	91	96
Manufacturing	82	128	151

Source: Birnie (1994).

Let us look at catch-up within sectors first. Table 2.2 taken from
Birnie (1994), shows Irish net output per head as a percentage of UK
levels. We see that considerable catch-up was achieved in some fairly
large sectors, such as agriculture (with 10 per cent of total employment
in 1997) and construction (with 7 per cent of employment). His data
indicate that Ireland remains well behind in some other sectors, however, such as utilities, transport and communications (which together
comprise 7 per cent of employment).

The most impressive achievement according to Birnie's data, however, is for manufacturing. Here Irish productivity appears to grow
from 82 per cent of the UK level in 1968, to 151 per cent by 1990. These
data are untrustworthy, though, because the transfer pricing behaviour
of the large foreign-owned sector in Ireland artificially inflates GDP
(and export) figures.[17] However, even correcting for these effects reveals
that Irish manufacturing-sector productivity has overtaken UK levels.
A rough correction would proceed as follows. Assume that all the profit repatriation identified in the balance of payments arises as a consequence of transfer pricing in the foreign-owned manufacturing sector;[18]
this comes to around 12 per cent of GDP. Manufacturing's reported
share of GDP is around 33 per cent, of which £3747 million is assumed
to come from indigenous manufacturing and £12490 million from
foreign-owned manufacturing.[19] Manufacturing's true share of genuine
value-added then (which corrects for the transfer-pricing distortion)
comes to $(33-12)/(100-12)$, or about 25 per cent; this reduces manufacturing value-added by roughly one-quarter, bringing Irish manufacturing-sector productivity down from 150 per cent of UK levels to
about 110 per cent. So these rough calculations still indicate that Irish
productivity is higher, albeit by a much slimmer margin.

This overtaking of the UK in manufacturing-sector productivity
reflects a sectoral shift within manufacturing, from lower-productivity
indigenous industry to higher productivity foreign industry. This assertion

requires us to verify that productivity in the foreign sector, corrected for transfer pricing, is indeed higher than in indigenous industry. According to our calculations above, value added in indigenous manufacturing remains equal to £3747 million (implying a productivity level per worker of £32100); value added in the foreign-owned sector, however, has been brought down from £12490 million to £8431; productivity per worker in this sector, even overaccounting for transfer pricing as we have done, comes out at £81171 (rather than the £120300 level implied by the official statistics). It nevertheless remains substantially higher than in indigenous industry. Thus we can conclude that Ireland's rapid productivity growth is caused not just by productivity convergence (or 'catch up') within sectors, but also because of an intersectoral shift from low productivity to high productivity sectors in manufacturing (and arguably in market services as well).

We alluded above to the fact that Irish real convergence would have come much sooner had Irish employment growth tracked the European average alongside this rapid productivity growth. During the 1960s, 70s and 80s, however, the rate of job creation in the newer high-productivity sectors was barely sufficient to offset the numbers of jobs disappearing from low-productivity sectors. This is what has changed in the 1990s. The final part of our story then is to ask why this has been so.

It is easiest to consider this sector by sector. We need not consider non-market services or agriculture in great detail; employment in agriculture is in irreversible decline, while employment in non-market services is essentially a derived demand; it cannot be an engine of growth, as the failed fiscal experiment of the late 1970s, discussed in Chapter 4, shows.

Employment in non-tradeables, comprising most of services plus building and construction, is largely dependent on domestic demand, though as we will see it can also be influenced by competitiveness considerations. Why is demand booming so strongly in the 1990s compared to other periods since the 1960s? Clearly the oil-price shocks of the 1970s meant that this was a difficult decade for most of the non-OPEC world, while the 1980s were particularly difficult for Ireland as it struggled to cope with the consequences of the fiscal overexpansion of the 1970s. Demand is booming in the 1990s because of the long-term beneficial effects of the fiscal stabilisation of the late 1980s (discussed in Chapter 4), the current strength of the internationally-tradeable sectors, and the current fiscal stance. Supply-side factors also play a role, however. The moderate wage agreements signed since 1987, and discussed in Chapter 7, had beneficial effects on employment in all sectors. These effects could be particularly strong for services, given the high elasticities of labour demand in this sector reported by Bradley, Fitz Gerald and Kearney (1991).

The weakness of competition policy would also have stymied the development of services (Barry and O'Toole, 1998). This weakness was reflected in the high relative charges that Irish businesses paid for items such as postal services, telephone calls and industrial use of electricity, as pointed out by McCarthy (1986); this image of an inefficient services sector hampered by excessive regulation and the monopoly power of state enterprises is supported by Birnie's (1994) productivity data. Ireland's position in the European league tables in terms of these charges has improved substantially over the last decade. By 1995 Irish electricity prices were almost 7 per cent below the average for the rest of the EU for small industrial users, 13 per cent below for medium users and 12 per cent below for large users. In terms of telecommunications, Ireland went from second most expensive in the EU in 1990 to seventh in 1994 for local call charges; from the most expensive to fifth most expensive in terms of trunk calls; and from third to ninth for European calls. The relative cost of postal services also improved; between 1988 and 1995 Ireland went from fifth to eighth most expensive for external letters, and from fourth to sixth for internal letters (Forfás, 1995).

These reductions in costs would have had beneficial knock-on effects for both industry and services; Ireland's growing importance as a tele-marketing centre provides an obvious example of the latter. A further example of beneficial deregulation is provided by the reduction in air-line costs that emerged from the introduction of competition in that market, and the strong impact this has had on tourism numbers.

This brings us to the tradeable segments of market services. As pointed out in Chapter 1 there has been a strong expansion in inter-nationally-traded services and in tourism. The growth in international financial services is primarily due to the extension to this sector of the low rate of corporate profits tax initially applied to manufacturing. Deegan and Dineen (1997) ascribe the growth in tourism-related employment primarily to the factors we have already described; that is, improvements in cost-competitiveness and the deregulation of the transport sector, alongside a sense of Ireland coming 'into fashion'. They note, in particular, that much of the growth in this sector preceded the Structural Funds allocations to tourism.

Finally, then, we come to manufacturing. Here the indigenous and foreign-owned sectors should be considered separately. Employment in foreign-owned manufacturing largely depends on the major strategic decisions taken by government and bureaucracy over the years. Thus

FDI started to pour into the economy as a consequence of the low corporate profits tax regime and the decision to join the European Common Market in 1973. Inflows expanded very dramatically from the early 1990s, as shown in Chapter 3, as a consequence of the European Single Market programme and as agglomeration economics took hold. Furthermore, Irish-economy expenditures (per job) for these firms increased by over 50 per cent in real terms between 1983 and 1995. In part this reflects a process that occurs naturally over time, though it would undoubtedly be aided by improvements in the cost and quality of indigenous inputs. There was, in consequence, a magnification of the sector's employment-creation effects alongside the strong increase in direct employment that it provided.

This same magnification effect occurred for indigenous industry, and while neither employment not output grew as strongly as in foreign-owned industry it reversed the static or declining employment trend that prevailed in the sector since the mid-1960s. This trend arose because Irish firms lost home-market share while failing to make compensating gains in export markets. The loss in home-market share was stopped around 1988 while the export-orientation of indigenous industry began to rise after 1986 (O'Malley, 1998). The simultaneous occurrence of these events points to a strong gain in international competitiveness around this time.

From Chapters 3 and 5 we can ascribe this gain to the following combination of factors:

1. the improvement in cost-competitiveness achieved from 1986 in terms of wage and non-wage costs as discussed above, and through the use of exchange-rate policy;
2. the fact that the most efficient and more export-oriented firms would have been over-represented in the pool of indigenous firms that remained at that time;
3. the fact that for these firms the development of international-trade-facilitating infrastructures would have been beneficial, whereas it may not have been for the weaker indigenous firms that dominated in the earlier period;
4. the fact that indigenous industry was more heavily concentrated in sectors in which Ireland was predicted to gain from the Single Market than in sectors in which it was predicted to lose;[20] and
5. the changes in industrial policy enacted since the mid-1980s which saw the development agencies focus more directly on the problems encountered by indigenous firms in the international marketplace.

CONCLUSIONS

Ireland's economic problem since the nineteenth century we defined at the outset as the need to become competitive in internationally-tradeable sectors other than agriculture. The *laissez faire* policies followed for over a hundred years prior to protectionism achieved no success in this regard. While the import-substitution strategy that followed created a manufacturing sector, the sector was not internationally competitive and so the economy ran into a balance of payments constraint that limited its size. The high levels of emigration of the 1950s followed.

Industrial policy from the 1960s to the mid-1980s concentrated almost exclusively on encouraging high-productivity foreign manufacturing companies to use Ireland as an export base. This raised productivity substantially, but Ireland failed to converge on European living standards because its rate of job creation lagged behind. In terms of the balance of payments constraint, while foreign-owned industry raised exports, indigenous industry lost market share to competing imports. What then is different in the 1990s? Foreign export-oriented industry has expanded considerably and a much more competitive indigenous manufacturing sector has stopped the loss in home-market share while raising its export orientation. The internationally-tradeable market services sectors are booming. All of these developments raise demand for the non-traded sectors, which have been stimulated on the supply side by deregulation and by improved wage and non-wage competitiveness.

Notes

1. This echoes Ó Grada (1997), who writes that because of easy access to the British labour market 'cheaper labour could do little to compensate for Ireland's relative backwardness and isolation, or to generate the investment necessary for faster economic growth' (p. 217).
2. On Irish industry in the nineteenth century see O'Malley (1981) and Ó Grada (1994, chapter 12).
3. He notes that the first iron vessel launched in Belfast was constructed not in one of the existing shipyards but in an engineering and boilermaking firm.
4. This is the hypothesis most favoured by Ó Grada (1994, chapter 13) also.
5. In the conventional (Solow) growth model, poorer economies have lower levels of capital per head. Thus the productivity of capital is very high. As capital is accumulated, then, poorer economies grow more rapidly than richer economies, and thus they converge in terms of income per head.

6. Formally, the economy runs into a balance of payments constraint since demand for tradeables increases more rapidly than supply, requiring a reduction in the size of the economy.

7. His argument has more force, though, when services are an input into the production of tradeables, and when employment in tradeables is responsive to real product wages, since for a constant relative purchasing power of wages in Ireland and the UK, cost improvements in non-tradeables will lower the cost of labour to the export sectors.

8. Irish income per head rose from 40 to 61 percent of the British level between 1841 and 1913, during which time the purchasing power of the wages of unskilled urban labour rose from over one-half to almost 100 per cent. Irish income per head then remained at a little over 60 per cent up to 1985, while Irish and UK wages also grew at the same rate over this whole period. The story is rather more complicated than presented here, of course, since the wage relationship fluctuated quite dramatically at times, with Irish real wages falling sharply below the UK's in the early 1940s and catching up again only in the late 1970s. The data on income per head come from Kennedy *et al.* (1988) and Ó Grada (1994, p. 242). On the wage relationship see O'Rourke (1994) and Williamson (1994, 1995).

9. The implications of this are even more disheartening if there are positive externalities associated with the stock of human capital employed in the economy, as Lucas (1990) argues.

10. Consider the following formal example. In Harris–Todaro fashion let labour-market openness imply $WL/P = $ constant, where W is the domestic real wage, L/P is the proportion of the domestic population employed, and the constant refers to the exogeneity of foreign wages and the foreign employment rate. If technology and the organisation of the economy are such that domestic capital accumulation raises labour's share of output, WL/Y, then regional divergence, implying a falling level of Y/P, results.

11. These are models in which income growth perpetuates itself through innovation rather than reaching a stable equilibrium which can only be disturbed by exogenous technological change.

12. By 1960, towards the end of the protectionist period, some 30% of exports consisted of live animals, another 30% were of 'Other Foods', and only 19% were of manufactured goods. Furthermore, trade was almost exclusively with the UK.

13. This is not surprising since policy instruments such as tariffs and quotas will do little to encourage export orientation.

14. Thus productivity growth improved, not just in overall manufacturing but in 'traditional' manufacturing as well, when Ireland moved to free trade.

15. A similar conclusion is reached by Sachs (1997).

16. The international datasets used by Ó Grada and O'Rourke (1996) – Heston/Summers and Maddison – give conflicting accounts of productivity growth over the 1964 to 1988 period. Maddison shows Irish productivity growth well above the European average while Heston and Summers shows it as about average.

17. Transfer pricing arises because, with low rates of corporation tax in Ireland, it is in the interests of foreign companies to exaggerate the level of value-added created there. Most of the consequences of transfer pricing show up

in repatriated profits however, and so while GDP figures are distorted GNP figures are reasonably reliable.

18. This is an overestimate, for several reasons: (i) because there will be some level of profits anyway, regardless of the existence of transfer pricing, (ii) because part of the capital outflow will consist of royalties paid by subsidiaries for marketing and R&D carried out by the parent company, and (iii) because not all of the profit outflow originates in manufacturing.

19. These are net output figures from the 1995 Census of Industrial Production.

20. It is significant that the Single Market appears to have benefited indigenous industry as well as raised FDI inflows. Far from making Ireland more peripheral, as Cuddy and Keane (1990), for example, predicted, it appears to have aided in Ireland's transformation from periphery to EU core.

References

Arthur, B. (1989) 'Competing Technologies, Increasing Returns, and Lock-in by Historical Events', *Economic Journal*, 99, pp. 116–31.

Barry, F. (1996) 'Peripherality in Economic Geography and Modern Growth Theory: Evidence from Ireland's Adjustment to Free Trade', *World Economy*, 19(3), pp. 345–65.

Barry, F. and O'Toole, F. (1998) 'Irish Competition Policy and the Macro-economy', in Stephen Martin (ed.), *Competition Policies in Europe* (Amsterdam: North Holland).

Birnie, E. (1994) 'British-Irish Productivity Differences 1930s–1990s', Queen's University Belfast Working Papers in Economics no. 47.

Bradley, J., Fitz Gerald, J. and Kearney, I. (1991) 'The Irish Market Services Sector: An Econometric Investigation', *Economic and Social Review*, 22(4), pp. 287–309.

Bradley, J., Fitz Gerald, J., Honohan, P. and Kearney, I. (1997) 'Interpreting the Recent Irish Growth Experience', in *Economic and Social Research Institute Medium-Term Review: 1997–2003* (Dublin: ESRI).

Cuddy, M. and Keane, M. (1990) 'Ireland: A Peripheral Region', in A. Foley and M. Mulreany (eds), *The Single European Market and the Irish Economy* (Dublin: Institute of Public Administration).

David, P. (1990) 'Factor Market Externalities and the Dynamics of Industrial Location', *Journal of Urban Economics*, 28(3), pp. 349–70.

Deegan, J. and Dineen, D. (1997) 'The Tourism Dimension to Irish Economic Development', in F. Ó Muircheartaigh (ed.), *Ireland in the Coming Times: Essays to Celebrate T.K. Whitaker's 80 Years* (Dublin: Institute of Public Administration).

European Economy (1997) 'Broad Economic Policy Guidelines', 64, Statistical Annex.

Fitz Gerald, J. and Honohan, P. (1994) 'Where Did All the Growth Go?', in *Economic and Social Research Institute Medium-Term Review: 1994–2000* (Dublin: ESRI).

Forfás (1995) *Ireland's Cost and Competitiveness Environment* (Dublin: Forfás).

Girvin, B. (1989) *Between Two Worlds: Politics and Economy in Independent Ireland* (Dublin: Gill & Macmillan).

Grossman, G. and Helpman, E. (1991) *Innovation and Growth in the Global Economy* (Cambridge, Mass.: MIT Press).

Kennedy, K., Giblin, T. and McHugh, D. (1988) *The Economic Development of Ireland in the Twentieth Century* (London: Routledge).

Krugman, P. (1991a) 'Increasing Returns and Economic Geography', *Journal of Political Economy*, 99(3), 483–99.

Krugman, P. (1991b) *Geography and Trade* (Cambridge: MIT Press).

Krugman, P. (1997) 'Good News from Ireland: A Geographical Perspective', in Alan Gray (ed.), *International Perspectives on the Irish Economy* (Dublin: Indecon).

Krugman, P. and Venables, A. (1990) 'Integration and the Competitiveness of Peripheral Industry', in G. de Macedo and C. Bliss (eds), *Unity with Diversity within the European Economy: The Community's Southern Frontier* (Cambridge: Cambridge University Press).

Lucas, R. (1990) 'Why Doesn't Capital Flow from Rich to Poor Countries?', *American Economic Review Papers and Proceedings*, 80(2), pp. 92–6.

Lee, J. (1989) *Ireland 1912–1985: Politics and Society* (Cambridge: Cambridge University Press).

Matsuyama, K. (1992) 'Agricultural Productivity, Comparative Advantage and Economic Growth', *Journal of Economic Theory*, 58, pp. 317–34.

McCarthy, C. (1986) 'Industrial Costs and Industrial Policy', paper presented to Dublin Economics Workshop.

Murphy, K., Shleifer, A. and Vishny, R. (1989) 'Industrialization and the Big Push', *Journal of Political Economy*, 97(5), pp. 1003–26.

Ó Grada, C. (1994) *Ireland: A New Economic History 1780–1939* (Oxford: Clarendon Press).

Ó Grada, C. (1997) *A Rocky Road: The Irish Economy since the 1920s* (Manchester: Manchester University Press).

Ó Grada, C. and O'Rourke, K. (1996) 'Irish Economic Growth, 1945–88', in N. F. R. Crafts and G. Toniolo (eds), *European Economic Growth* (Cambridge: Cambridge University Press).

O'Malley, E. (1981) 'The Decline of Irish Industry in the Nineteenth Century', *Economic and Social Review*, 13(1), pp. 21–42.

O'Malley, E. (1998) 'The Revival of Irish Indigenous Industry 1987–1997', *Quarterly Economic Commentary*, April (Dublin: The Economic and Social Research Institute).

O'Rourke, K. (1994a) 'Industrial Policy, Employment Policy and the Non-Traded Sector', *Journal of the Statistical and Social Inquiry Society of Ireland*, 27ii, pp. 61–80.

O'Rourke, K. (1994b) 'Did Labour Flow Uphill? International Migration and Wage Rates in Twentieth Century Ireland', in G. Grantham and M. MacKinnon (eds), *Labour Market Evolution: The Economic History of Market Integration, Wage Flexibility and the Employment Relation* (London and New York: Routledge).

Pollard, S. (1985) 'Industrialization and the European Economy', in J. Mokyr (ed.), *The Economics of the Industrial Revolution* (London: George Allen & Unwin).

Ruane, F. (1990) Review of O'Malley (1989), *Economic and Social Review*, 21(2), pp. 241–4.

Sachs, J. (1997) 'Ireland's Growth Strategy: Lessons for Economic Development', in Alan Gray (ed.), *International Perspectives on the Irish Economy* (Dublin: Indecon).

Stokey, N. (1991) 'Human Capital, Product Quality and Growth', *Quarterly Journal of Economics*, pp. 587–616.

Sweeney, P. (1998) *The Celtic Tiger: Ireland's Economic Miracle Explained* (Dublin: Oaktree Press).

Walsh, B. (1990) Review of O'Malley (1989), *Studies*, pp. 71–3.

Walsh, B. (1994) 'Wage Convergence and Integrated Labour Markets: Ireland and Britain 1841–1991', unpublished manuscript.

Williamson, J. G. (1994) 'Economic Convergence: Placing Post-Famine Ireland in Comparative Perspective', *Irish Economic and Social History*, XXI, pp. 1–27.

Williamson, J. G. (1995) 'The Evolution of Global Labor Markets since 1830: Background Evidence and Hypotheses', *Explorations in Economic History*, 32, pp. 141–96.

Young, A. (1991) 'Learning by Doing and the Dynamic Effects of International Trade', *Quarterly Journal of Economics*, pp. 369–405.

3 Indigenous and Foreign Industry: Characteristics and Performance

Frank Barry, John Bradley and
Eoin O'Malley[1]

INTRODUCTION

From the early 1930s to the late 1950s high tariff barriers and a broad prohibition on foreign ownership of firms operating in Ireland were the cornerstone of policies designed to promote growth of indigenous manufacturing from the very low base inherited at independence in 1922. By the late 1950s it was clear that protectionism had long outlived its usefulness and that few of the so-called infant industries had matured and become sufficiently competitive to generate much in the way of exports (Ó Grada, 1997).

The changes forced on Irish policy-makers by economic collapse in the late 1950s were fundamental and far-reaching. The Control of Manufactures Act, which prohibited foreign ownership, was abolished and replaced by a policy that systematically cultivated FDI through a zero corporate profits tax on manufactured exports (replaced over the course of the 1980s by a flat rate of 10 per cent on all manufacturing), attractive investment grants and a dismantling of most tariff barriers within less than a decade.

Much of the history of the Irish economy during the following three decades can be explained in terms of the quite phenomenal growth of export-oriented FDI in manufacturing, from a zero base in the late 1950s to a situation where almost 65 per cent of gross output and over 45 per cent of employment in manufacturing is in foreign-owned export-oriented firms. Only over the last decade, on the other hand, has the decline in indigenous manufacturing employment been halted and strong growth in indigenous exports achieved. Table 3.1 illustrates Ireland's success in attracting foreign direct investment in 'greenfield' manufacturing sites; the table refers to US FDI alone, for which the best data is available. The most striking consequence of the FDI inflow

45

Table 3.1   US direct investment (historical cost basis) per manufacturing worker in US$

	1983	1992	1996
Ireland	14 417	19 846	29 948
UK	2 306	3 763	6 423
France	823	3 137	4 042
Germany	1 195	1 939	2 381
Spain	619	2 040	3 042
EU15	1 273	2 627	4 189

Source: US Department of Commerce, Survey of Current Business; OECD Labour Force Statistics.

Figure 3.1   Destination of Irish exports

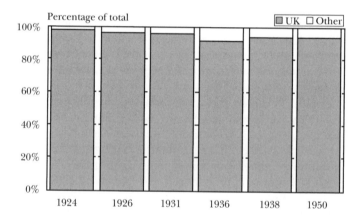

was that it facilitated the decoupling of the Irish economy from an almost total dependence on the United Kingdom as an export destination. The systematic reduction of exposure to the UK market as a destination for Irish exports is illustrated in Figures 3.1, 3.2 and 3.3.

Agricultural products dominated Irish exports prior to the 1960s. Subsequently the importance of manufactured exports increased and by 1969 they surpassed agricultural exports in value. The shift away from the United Kingdom as an export destination (from about 75 per cent in 1960 to under 30 per cent today) was not repeated as strongly for imports, where the traditional cultural links with the United Kingdom

Figure 3.2   Source of Irish imports

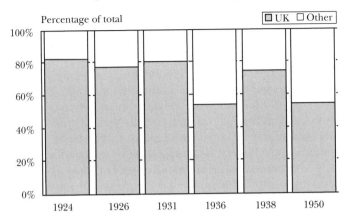

Figure 3.3   UK share of exports and imports, 1960–1995

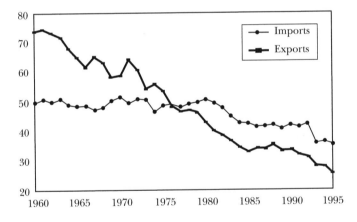

were an important factor in protecting its share of the Irish market. Thus, in Ireland's 'world' the United Kingdom now has a much smaller export weight than in the 1960s, with the rest of the EU having a correspondingly higher weight.

Geographical factors tend to cause 'webs of dependency', where small economies become locked into the growth performance of their encompassing region, which is often dominated by a single large economy (Wijkman, 1990). It is not simply the shift in export destinations, though, that has caused Irish growth to be linked more closely to that of the EU core economies. The growth linkage is a *supply-side* rather than a *demand-side* phenomenon, since it was Irish supply-side conditions that allowed it attract the kind of firms that produced products that were in high demand, and that sold them into high-growth markets in Europe.[2]

O'Donnell (1997), in a shift-share analysis of the causes of Irish export growth, provides strong support for this supply-side explanation. She points out that the EU (minus the UK) has overtaken the UK as an export destination for Ireland over recent decades, and that EU import demand has grown more rapidly than that of the UK; thus the geographical shift favoured Irish exports. Furthermore, these exports have become quite heavily specialised in SITC groups 5 and 7 (chemicals and machinery and transport equipment) for which demand growth is high; thus the commodity composition effect is also positive. Nevertheless, she finds that the vast bulk of Ireland's above-trend export growth, which has seen Ireland's share of OECD exports double from the 0.5 per cent level attained in the early 1970s, cannot be ascribed either to commodity structure or market destination. Irish export success is primarily determined by the general competitiveness of the economy, and particularly by its ability to attract FDI inflows.

This chapter analyses the reasons for Ireland's success in attracting these inflows, and also seeks to understand the factors behind the recent revival of indigenous manufacturing industry. We begin by comparing the sectoral and structural characteristics of the two sectors, which allows us ask whether the expansion of foreign industry over the course of the free-trade era may have contributed to the decline in indigenous manufacturing over most of this period. Whether the sectors are substitutes or complements becomes an increasingly important question as the buoyant labour market begins to exhibit skill shortages. We then analyse recent developments in the two sectors, and a final section presents our conclusions.

CHARACTERISTICS OF FOREIGN AND INDIGENOUS INDUSTRY

Sectoral Destination of FDI Inflows

FDI inflows into Ireland have not gone primarily into sectors in which the economy had a traditional comparative advantage. In fact, traditional measures of revealed comparative advantage are a very poor predictor of subsequent sectoral developments.

There are two reasons for this: firstly, a number of manufacturing sectors remain largely non-tradeable, and developments in these sectors would not therefore be expected to depend on comparative advantage; secondly, and crucially, the substantial FDI inflows that Ireland experienced did not go into the tradeable sectors in which the economy had a revealed comparative advantage. In terms of the 10 sectors for which the 1960s data are available, the sectors into which FDI flows were substantial but in which Ireland had a revealed comparative *dis*advantage were chemicals and metals and engineering (Barry and Hannan, 1996b).

If comparative advantage then had little influence on the sectors into which export-oriented FDI flowed, how do we explain the sectoral destinations of such inflows? It appears from the Irish experience that FDI manufacturing inflows go primarily into sectors in which there are increasing returns-to-scale (IRS) at the level of the firm. Based largely on Pratten's (1988) work, O'Malley (1992) identifies a group of NACE-coded manufacturing sectors as characterised by increasing returns of this type.[3] These sectors, along with the proportions of indigenous and multinational employment located in them, are shown in Table 3.2. The table shows that multinational companies have become much more heavily concentrated in the increasing-returns sectors in Ireland. Indigenous industry, on the other hand, while its proportion is increasing somewhat, is still strongly underrepresented[4] (the proportion of EU-9 employment in these sectors in 1984/5 was 57 per cent).

This suggests that MNCs have a competitive advantage in IRS sectors. The reasons why this might be so are not hard to identify. There are strong advantages to incumbency in IRS sectors, in terms both of low unit costs of production due to having already attained scale economies, and in terms of having established distribution networks. Since the move to multinational operations takes place some significant period of time after the start-up of a firm, multinationals will have already attained some of these benefits of incumbency.

These sectors are deemed to be of importance in the literature on economic geography and endogenous growth. In the model of Krugman and Venables (1990), for example, peripheral economies converge to the living standards of the core as their representation in these sectors rises, because real wages are driven up. In Grossman and Helpman (1991), the increasing-returns sectors are the technologically dynamic ones, and so the same result emerges. Most of O'Malley's subsectors fulfil the characteristics of the subgroups focused upon in this theoretical work; we will see below that sectors in which foreign industry in Ireland is located are indeed both high-wage and R&D-intensive.

Table 3.2 Employment in increasing-returns sectors

NACE code	Industry	Per cent of total indigenous manufacturing employment		Per cent of total foreign-owned manufacturing employment	
		1973	1996	1973	1996
35 (352*)	Vehicles	1.02	1.15	8.59	5.35
36	Other transport	1.18	2.20	2.32	0.75
25 (255*)	Chemicals	2.91	3.03	6.49	13.71
26	Man-made fibres	0.01	0.00	1.06	1.52
22 (223*)	Metals	0.21	0.34	1.81	0.36
33	Office machinery	0.10	1.57	0.83	11.23
32	Mechanical engineering	2.09	4.33	2.47	3.59
34	Electrical engineering	4.01	5.06	5.75	19.78
37	Instrument engineering	0.29	1.34	4.09	10.23
471	Pulp, paper	0.82	0.59	0.97	0.10
241	Clay products	1.30	0.46	0.50	0.12
242	Cement etc.	0.57	0.32	0.00	0.00
247	Glass and glassware	2.37	2.40	0.38	0.04
481	Rubber products	0.43	0.24	1.99	0.85
427	Brewing	0.15	0.15	5.21	1.60
429	Tobacco	0.43	0.13	1.99	0.68
421	Cocoa, chocolate	0.36	0.44	3.09	2.45
423	Other foods	0.97	2.82	2.06	2.18
Total (%)		19.22	26.58	49.60	74.54
Total jobs		29040	31358	37198	73605

Note: * beside a subsector indicates that it is excluded.
Source: O'Malley (1992).

Capital-Intensity, Profitability and Export-Orientation of Indigenous and Foreign Industry

The most recent data for manufacturing classified by nationality of ownership is for the year 1995, and is shown in Table 3.3. Although only 16 per cent of local plants are foreign-owned, they produce 65 per cent of gross output and engage 47 per cent of manufacturing

Table 3.3   Total manufacturing (NACE 15–37)

Nationality of ownership	No. of plants	Total persons engaged	Gross output (£m)	Materials purchased, per cent imported	Percent of gross output exported
Irish	3 879	116 714	11 686	22.5	35.9
Other EU, of which:	346	36 043	4 242	62.9	69
UK	117	11 765	1 726	46.2	50.9
Germany	99	11 483	890	81.8	94.6
Non-EU, of which:	379	67 821	17 654	68.3	93.7
US	289	54 624	14 620	64.7	94.9
Total foreign	725	103 864	21 896	67.1	89
Total	4 604	220 578	33 583	46.6	70.5

Source: Census of Industrial Production, 1995.

employment. About 40 per cent of foreign plants are US-owned, with 16 per cent British and 14 per cent German-owned. Foreign plants are much more likely to import their raw and semi-processed material inputs than are indigenous plants. Irish plants export on average around 36 per cent of output while foreign plants export 89 per cent, rising to 95 per cent for US-owned plants. Thus, the domestic market is of little significance to the foreign plants; they locate in Ireland to produce for export.

Three further differences between foreign and indigenous plants appear in Tables 3.3 and 3.4. Foreign plants tend to be larger (measured in terms of gross output, or in numbers employed, per plant); they are more productive (measured in terms of net output per person engaged);[5] and they are much more profitable (measured in terms of profits per person engaged, where profit is proxied by deducting the wage bill and material inputs from gross output, that is as the remainder of net output). Thus, in terms of these proxy measures US plants are very much larger than Irish plants, are five times as productive, and eight times as profitable.[6]

A final characteristic difference between Irish and foreign plants concerns export destinations. Within the foreign plants there are interesting differences; UK-owned plants (which export 51 per cent of output) send over 70 per cent of their exports to the UK market, and

Table 3.4 Manufacturing plants: characteristics by ownership

	Net output per person engaged (£K)	Profit per person engaged (£K)	Destination of exports			
			UK	OEU	USA	ROW
Irish	32.1	18.6	42.1	32.2	7.3	18.4
Other EU, of which:	62.8	45.9	32.9	50.6	6.5	10
UK	84.3	64.7	71.1	14.7	5.6	8.7
Germany	39.5	25	11.5	74.6	6.6	7.3
Non-EU, of which:	150.8	133.9	20.7	51	11.6	16.7
US	157.7	141.1	20.9	52.4	10.4	16.2
Total foreign	120.3	103.3	22.5	50.9	10.8	15.7
Total	73.6	58.5	26	47.6	10.2	16.2

Source and notes: Census of Industrial Production, 1995; £K denotes thousands of Irish pounds; OEU denotes EU countries other than the UK; ROW excludes USA as well as EU.

only 15 per cent to the rest of the EU. US-owned plants (which export 95 per cent of output) send only 21 per cent to the United Kingdom and over 52 per cent to the rest of the EU.

In summary, then, the foreign plants in Ireland are predominately of US, UK and German ownership. They have a much higher propensity to import their material inputs, are more export oriented (with only the UK plants having any significant reliance on the domestic market), and are larger, more productive and (with the exception of German MNCs) more profitable than the indigenous plants.

Since the foreign-owned manufacturing sector is so large, it has economy-wide as well as sectoral implications. Thus, the overall health of the economy is dependent on the performance of the foreign-owned sub-sector of manufacturing. However, the mainly tax-based FDI incentive system, and the fact that Ireland features as a production platform rather than as a market, means that opportunities exist for transfer pricing. This is reflected in the extent of profit repatriation, as seen in the balance of payments on current account. Ireland runs a large deficit on net factor income, the main element of which arises from the distribution of branch profits to their foreign owners. This introduces a wedge of some 10–12 per cent between GDP and GNP.

Skills and Wages in Foreign and Indigenous Industry

A considerable proportion of employment in the foreign sector of Irish manufacturing is located in relatively high-technology sectors – for example chemicals (14 per cent), office machinery (11.2 per cent), and electrical engineering (19.8 per cent). It comes as no surprise, then, that skill levels in foreign industry are higher than in indigenous industry. It has become conventional to measure skill levels in a sector as the proportion of administrative and technical staff in total employment. Although the relevant Irish data are not disaggregated into foreign and indigenous components, it is possible to identify a number of sectors which are dominated by foreign firms (that is, in which over 70 per cent of employment is in foreign firms), and these four sectors account for over 70 per cent of employment in foreign industry in Ireland.

Table 3.5 reveals that the foreign-dominated sectors employ substantially higher proportions of skilled labour than does manufacturing industry on average. The proportion of technical and administrative staff to total employment in these sectors is 19 per cent, compared to 14 per cent for total manufacturing. Furthermore, Barry and Hannan (1996a) have replicated on Irish data the finding of Sachs and Shatz (1994, pp. 32–3) for the United States that skills upgrading in recent decades has been greater in the most highly skilled sectors so that the gap between indigenous and foreign industry has been increasing.

Table 3.5   Skill levels by sector

Foreign-dominated sectors	Administrative and technical staff as % of total
Beverages, tobacco	17
Segments of textiles	10
Chemicals	25
Electrical and optical	18
of which: computers	23
Total foreign-dominated sectors	19
Total manufacturing	14

Source: Census of Industrial Production, 1993.

In line with these findings, the average wage in foreign industry (£17 000 in 1995) is approximately 25 per cent higher than in indigenous industry. Furthermore, focusing specifically on *unskilled* workers, the average wage in foreign-dominated sectors is several thousand pounds higher than for the rest of manufacturing.

R&D Expenditures in Foreign and Indigenous Industry

Business expenditures on in-house performed R&D (henceforth simply called R&D) in Ireland, expressed as a percentage of GDP, increased from 38 per cent of the EU average in 1986 to 87 per cent in 1995 (Forfás, 1997b). Given the rapid rate of GDP growth in Ireland over this period, this means that the growth rate of R&D spending has been more dramatic still. Furthermore, as Forfás notes, it may be more appropriate to compare Irish R&D spending to that in other smaller European economies, given that the EU average will be driven by the very large R&D spenders. Thus, Ireland caught up to the level of spending taking place in economies such as the Netherlands and Denmark (see Table 3.6).

In 1995, foreign firms operating in Ireland accounted for 64 per cent of R&D spending in Irish manufacturing, down marginally from the 66 per cent it accounted for in 1986. Thus R&D spending in both indigenous and foreign manufacturing increased substantially over the period. Forfás (1997b) shows that the reasons foreign subsidiaries spend more than indigenous firms on R&D boil down to differences in the average size of plants (with foreign firms substantially larger) and to the sectors in which production takes place (with foreign firms more likely to be represented in the high-tech sectors).

Table 3.6   Business expenditures
on R&D, as a percentage of GDP

	1986	1995
Total EU	1.25	1.17
Netherlands	1.3	1.06
Denmark	0.73	1.05
Ireland	0.48	1.02

Source: Forfás (1997b).

The Size Distribution of Indigenous and Foreign Manufacturing

NESC (1989) shows that foreign firms across all sectors tend to be substantially larger than indigenous firms. Furthermore, from the 1960s to the late 1980s when indigenous manufacturing was declining (in employment terms, and in terms of market share), indigenous industry decreased in scale in virtually all tradeable sectors, including chemicals, clothing and footwear, textiles, wood and furniture, other manufacturing, and metals and engineering; this arguably reflected a retreat into non-traded segments where customised service is important.[7] The story is brought up to date in Figures 3.4 and 3.5. Sectors such as non-metallic minerals and drink and tobacco, with low export-to-output ratios (of 14 and 23 per cent respectively for 1995), show a continuing decline in the largest size categories and a continuing increase in the smallest size categories. This would appear to reflect a retreat into niche markets that are under continuing pressure from imports. For highly export-oriented indigenous sectors, on the other hand, such as food and textiles (with equivalent proportions of 53 and 67 per cent), we see a decline in the most recent period in both the smallest and the largest size categories. Since indigenous industry has been performing well in this latter period, this appears to reflect a more successful move into niche markets, with the expansion in the proportion of employment in middle-size establishments reflecting both an expansion of the home market and niche marketing in the face of continuing pressure from large foreign competitors. Figures 3.4 and 3.5 present examples of these changes, for indigenous non-metallic minerals and food.

Figure 3.4   Employment distribution of indigenous plants in the non-metallic minerals sector by plant size

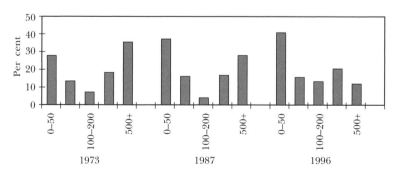

Source: Forfás, unpublished data.

Figure 3.5   Employment distribution of indigenous plants in the food sector by plant size

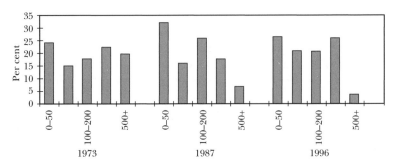

Source: Forfás, unpublished data.

Figure 3.6   Employment distribution of foreign plants in the food sector by plant size

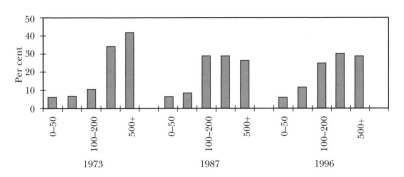

Source: Forfás, unpublished data.

Progressive trade liberalisation had much less effect on the size structure of multinational establishments in Ireland, on the other hand, suggesting an ability on their part to surmount the entry barriers that appeared until recently to inhibit indigenous industry. In Figures 3.6 and 3.7 we depict the changing size structure of two fairly representative foreign sectors, food and metals and engineering. We see that the proportion of employment in the largest size categories cycles rather than showing trend-decline.

Figure 3.7   Employment distribution (%) of foreign plants in the metals and engineering sector

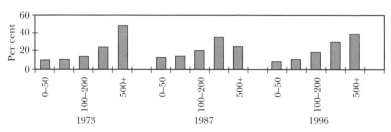

Source: Forfás, unpublished data.

Figure 3.8   Indigenous and foreign manufacturing employment in Ireland, 1973–97

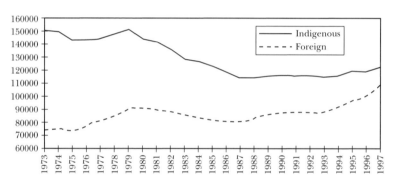

Source: Forfás, unpublished data.

FOREIGN AND INDIGENOUS INDUSTRY: SUBSTITUTES OR COMPLEMENTS?

Before going on to discuss recent developments in indigenous and foreign-owned industry we need at this stage to discuss the relationship between the two sectors. This is likely to comprise both positive and negative aspects. The symbiotic elements, whereby the growth of the foreign sector expands the potential for indigenous manufacturing, through backward and forward linkages for example, are discussed in the next section. Figure 3.8 indicates, though, that for most of the outward-oriented era employment growth in the foreign-owned sector occurred alongside employment decline in indigenous industry, a particularly disappointing development since unemployment remained high throughout most of this period. Our task in this section, then, is to consider whether growth in the foreign sector may have inhibited expansion in the indigenous sector.

A number of circumstances in which FDI inflows can have negative employment consequences for indigenous industry, or even adverse consequences for overall economic welfare, have been identified in the literature. We now explore whether these circumstances may have arisen in the Irish case.

Decline in the Market Share of Indigenous Firms

The international-trade literature suggests that national welfare can be reduced by FDI inflows if MNCs capture market share from indigenous firms and reduce the latter's excess profits (see for example Krugman and Venables, 1990). This argument is illustrated in Figure 3.9.

Let p_0 be the pre-FDI price of the good in question, p_1 the post-FDI price, and c the (constant) marginal cost. Q_0 is the initial quantity sold (all by the domestic firm), Q_1 is the post-FDI quantity, which consists of q_1 sold by the domestic firm and $Q_1 - q_1$ by the foreign firm. In this event the rectangle marked ' $-$ ' is the net rent loss to domestic producers, and the triangle market ' $+$ ' is the net gain to consumer surplus. It is clear that if price effects are very modest, then the economy can suffer a net loss. The more competition that ensues, however, the more profit levels are driven towards zero, and the greater the likelihood of net gains. Thus there are net losses associated with weak competition

Figure 3.9   The capture of market share by foreign firms

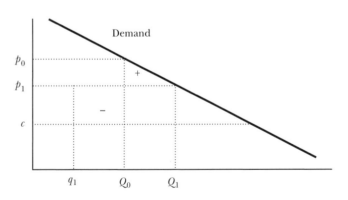

from the new (foreign) firms while, beyond some threshold level, net gains expand with further competition.

There are a number of reasons why this argument does not appear particularly strong in the Irish case. Firstly, there is the fact that the argument was originally presented in the context of *foreign-based* firms capturing market share from domestic firms. In a full-employment context, the location of the foreign firm is largely irrelevant. If labour-markets are distorted, however, so that the economy is initially in an underemployment equilibrium, it appears preferable that the goods-market crowding-out results from FDI rather than imports, because of the employment-generating effects associated with FDI.

Theoretical considerations aside, these events are in any case highly unlikely to characterise the Irish experience, given that Irish-based foreign MNCs, as seen above (p. 51), largely use Ireland as an export platform, and that domestic industry pre-free-trade had a comparative disadvantage in precisely those sectors in which foreign industry grew (as seen above). A further empirical consideration that reduces the relevance of the theory under discussion is the fact that potential profits in domestic sectors that are insulated from foreign competition are frequently dissipated in X-inefficiencies (Caves and Krepps, 1993; Barry, 1996).

Employment and the Dutch Disease

The question has been raised as to whether 'Dutch-disease' type factors could cause total employment to decline as a consequence of FDI inflows. Barry and Hannan (1995) explore this issue under the assumptions, arguably appropriate to the Irish case over the last few decades at least, that neither labour nor capital can be regarded as scarce factors of production; in fact the Irish labour market is the most open in the EU, with large actual and potential migration flows, mainly with the United Kingdom. This removes the 'resource-movement' effect found in the Dutch-disease literature, though the 'spending effect' remains (Corden and Neary, 1982). Barry and Hannan conclude that total employment would not decline under the sterling-link exchange rate regime that prevailed in Ireland up to 1979, because the induced service-sector employment expansion resulting from GDP growth (that is, the 'spending effect') would dominate the contraction in indigenous manufacturing employment that occurs as the price of non-tradeables is bid up.

They argued that a more pessimistic scenario could have applied under the more flexible post-1979 exchange rate regime (when the link with sterling was broken), as FDI-inflows strengthen the exchange rate. If nominal wages were downwardly rigid, this strengthening of the exchange rate would magnify the adverse employment effects on indigenous sectors. The authors conclude however that even these latter effects are unlikely to have been strong enough in practice, because even though the strength of the exchange rate may have put downward pressure on prices, inflation remained positive. Downward nominal wage adjustment in response to FDI was therefore never required for employment levels to be maintained.

Disequilibrating Wage Developments

An arguably more plausible hypothesis is that the strong FDI inflows led to excessive wage demands, through the impact on wages of the high productivity growth of the foreign sector. This could have led to an *excessively rapid* decline of the traditional manufacturing sectors (which display slower productivity growth), and an increase in unemployment.

Barry (1996) presents evidence suggestive of this. In 1980, net output per head in the modern sector (comprising pharmaceuticals, office and data processing machinery, electrical and instrument engineering and cola concentrates)[8] was more than double that in the traditional sector, notwithstanding which it grew far more rapidly than productivity in traditional industry. Average weekly earnings, however, grew almost identically in the two sectors. In the whole 1980 to 1992 period, employment in the modern sector, where productivity growth far outstripped wage growth, grew by 54 per cent; employment in the far larger traditional sector, where wage growth outstripped productivity growth, declined by 27 per cent; while total manufacturing employment fell 15 per cent.

The plausibility of the hypothesis that FDI inflows have generated disequilibrating wage developments is disputed by some commentators who argue that employment in the high-technology foreign sectors is too small to drive wage developments in this way. However, this argument runs counter to the widely-held view that wage developments in the manufacturing sector frequently drive wage increases in the larger services sector ('the Scandinavian model'): Bradley *et al.* (1993). Disequilibrating effects of the type posited by Barry (1996) have also been noted by Nankani (1979) in a number of developing economies experiencing resource booms. High real wage levels in the booming sectors occasionally spread to the rest of the economy, Nankani argued.

This was in spite of the fact that employment levels in these sectors were relatively low, and that some wage dualism existed. The result was a worsening of overall unemployment. From this perspective the recent growth in employment in indigenous industry would have been strengthened by the wage moderation discussed in Chapter 7 of the present book.

Neglect of Indigenous Firms

There seems little doubt that the importance of efficiency and competition in the Irish non-traded sectors was lost sight of due to the heavy emphasis traditionally laid on the promotion of manufacturing (O'Rourke, 1994). A more controversial hypothesis is that the attention of policy-makers may have been distracted from the requirements of indigenous manufacturing by the high profile attached to the attraction of multinationals. It could be argued that there was little potential for the bulk of indigenous industry which had grown up under the protectionist policies in place until the early 1960s, and that the authorities could have done little to assist its reorientation towards the international marketplace. Another view, however, which surfaced in a number of reports on the conduct of Irish industrial policy commissioned over the course of the 1980s, held that a more energetic attempt should have been made to assist indigenous industry.

The specific needs of indigenous industry were addressed by a number of policy initiatives taken in the mid-1980s, and there has been a noticeable improvement in the performance of the indigenous sector since then. These issues will be addressed further below.

DEVELOPMENTS IN INDIGENOUS AND FOREIGN INDUSTRY OVER TIME

Over the entire free-trade period, until 1988, employment in indigenous industry had been static or declining. This poor performance has been ascribed to cost-competition in easily entered low-wage sectors alongside an inability, until recently, to surmount the entry barriers on world markets that face indigenous firms from late-industrialising regions (O'Malley, 1989; National Economic and Social Council, 1989). Certainly the sectors that performed worst over the whole free trade era were highly exposed indigenous sectors such as chemicals, clothing and footwear, and textiles, whilst in a number of other tradeable sectors, as mentioned above, there appeared to be a retreat into non-traded segments of the market.

While indigenous industry was in decline, however, Ireland was experiencing substantial success in attracting FDI inflows. The reasons for this, in the initial stages at least, are clear:

1. Ireland was one of the first countries to adopt the strategy of targeting multinational firms, so that its industrial development agency developed skills and experience in this area which placed it ahead of its competitors;
2. the country had a very low rate of corporation profits tax and a generous grant system;
3. Ireland represented an English-language environment; and
4. Ireland had relatively low labour costs compared to more advanced industrial countries, and favourable access to large export markets compared to less-developed countries with lower labour costs.

It is of particular interest now to ask whether agglomeration economies have begun to come into play, so that the economy's success in attracting FDI has begun to feed on itself.

The growth in foreign manufacturing employment in Ireland since the late 1980s is apparent from Figure 3.8 above. In fact, again focusing on US FDI data, not only did US FDI flows into Europe increase substantially at this time, but Ireland's share of these flows increased even more dramatically as shown in Figure 3.10.

Figure 3.10   US FDI inflows (in constant dollar terms) into EU15, and Irish and UK shares of these inflows

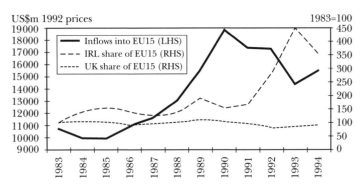

Source: US Department of Commerce, *Survey of Current Business*, various issues.

Is there any evidence that a critical mass of FDI may have been in place at this time, allowing agglomeration economies to come into play and generating a self-sustaining process? We can identify the development of a labour pool with specific skills, the possibility of information spillovers across firms and input–output linkages as factors that could be important in generating agglomeration. We shall consider these alongside others such as entrepreneurial spillovers, and the reduction in information costs spent in searching out suitable locations by firms considering new overseas operations.

Consider input–output linkages first. That these have developed over time is clear from Table 3.7, which shows that Irish economy expenditures per employee have risen by over 50 per cent in real terms between 1983 and 1995 for foreign firms, and by a little under 50 per cent for indigenous firms.[9] The table also shows the high proportion of Irish-economy expenditures by foreign firms that goes on services, in contrast to indigenous firms for whom the bulk of spending goes on materials. A recent study by O'Malley (1995) shows that, primarily for this reason, there is more employment created per manufacturing-sector job by the backward linkages of foreign firms than of indigenous firms.

O'Malley (1995) shows that there are increasing numbers of both service sector and indigenous manufacturing jobs associated with every

Table 3.7   Irish-economy expenditures (IEE) of indigenous and foreign manufacturing firms, 1995 pounds

	1983		1994		1995	
	Irish	*Foreign*	*Irish*	*Foreign*	*Irish*	*Foreign*
IEE per employee, of which (%):	65 624	41 785	88 133	59 983	90 376	65 517
wages per employee	23.6	35.4	19.4	33.6	18.7	31.1
Irish materials per employee	57.4	35.8	57.2	30.2	58.3	30.8
Irish services per employee	17.7	25.3	16.4	30.5	15.0	32.6
profits (tax) per employee	1.3	3.5	7.0	5.7	7.9	5.4

Note: The final row shows all profits for indigenous firms, and corporation tax paid by foreign-owned firms.
Source: Unpublished IDA data, Forfás (1997a).

100 jobs in foreign manufacturing. The ratio of secondary employment in services to direct manufacturing employment for overseas industry increased from 93 secondary jobs in services per 100 direct manufacturing jobs in 1983, to 105 per 100 in 1992 (p. 3). He approximates that the number of jobs in indigenous manufacturing producing industrial products for overseas industry rose from 10 to 13 per 100 overseas manufacturing jobs over the same period (p. 4). For indigenous industry the trend is less monotonic; nevertheless, after falling between 1983 and 1990 the number of secondary service jobs per 100 indigenous manufacturing jobs rose each year thereafter up to the end of his sample period, 1992 (p. 2). O'Malley's calculation of the *first-round* backward linkages is reported in Table 3.8.

Recalling Hirschman's (1958) argument that economic development is accelerated by investment in industrial projects with strong backward or forward linkage effects, the demonstration that these have developed over time provides part of the explanation for why recent Irish industrialisation has promoted real economic convergence.

As suggested above, spin-off benefits of FDI might also include a role as 'incubators' for new entrepreneurs. What little evidence there is on the backgrounds of entrepreneurs involved in new firm start-ups does point to this. Within electronics, for example, the ratio of spin-off Irish-owned companies to existing companies in the early 1980s was 1:15 for foreign companies and 1:35 for Irish-owned companies, though the bias towards spin-offs from MNCs was substantially less when the relative employment levels of the two categories were taken into account (Cogan and Onyemadum, 1981). More recently, a study on clustering in indigenous manufacturing finds that in the indigenous software sector one-third of entrepreneurs had worked in foreign firms

Table 3.8   First-round backward linkages of manufacturing sectors

	Services jobs	Manufacturing jobs
Induced by:		
Indigenous industry	34 (36)	17 (19)
Foreign industry	46 (40)	16 (12)

Note: Table displays number of jobs in input-producing sectors per 100 direct manufacturing jobs in indigenous and overseas sectors for the years 1991 (1983).
Source: O'Malley (1995).

immediately before the start up of the new firm, while two-thirds of entrepreneurs had worked in foreign firms at some stage in their careers (Clancy *et al.*, 1997). The study also found that foreign firms located in Ireland were an important source of demand, with a requirement for high standards, in the early stages of new company start-ups. Thus, the foreign firms in Ireland play a role somewhat similar to that of the domestic market in wealthier economies, facilitating the transition to export activity (Porter, 1990).

Arguably the most important externality effect in the Irish case, however, is one very often overlooked, though it has been emphasised by Barry and Bradley (1997) and Krugman (1997). It is possible that multi-national companies, when searching for a new overseas location, focus particularly on areas which their rivals have already explored and found to be satisfactory. Hence the possibility that the development process exhibits self-sustaining characteristics once a critical mass of firms has been achieved. In the Irish case, surveys of executives of newly arriving foreign companies in the computer, instrument engineering, pharmaceutical and chemical sectors indicate that their location decision has been strongly influenced by the fact that other key market players are already located in Ireland.

It is difficult to prove conclusively the importance of agglomeration economies. Krugman (1991) tends to interpret data on industrial concentration as evidence in this regard, though this is controversial.[10] For what it is worth, the Irish evidence does indeed suggest increasing concentration within foreign industry, with the share of foreign employment in the ten largest foreign-employment 3-digit NACE-code sectors rising from 42 per cent in 1973 to 55 per cent in 1996 (see Table 3.9).[11] There has been no such increase in concentration within indigenous industry, suggesting that agglomeration economies are less important to its success.

Agglomeration economies therefore seem to have a role to play in explaining Ireland's strong success in recent times in capturing foot-loose foreign direct investment. They do not help explain recent success in indigenous manufacturing, however. We now turn to look at recent developments in this sector.

Since 1988, indigenous industry has reversed the trend of employment-decline apparent since the 1960s. By 1997, employment in the sector was up 9 per cent on its 1988 figure, which contrasts with the decline in manufacturing employment in the EU and OECD over the same period.[12] Nor has this been due simply to the buoyancy of the domestic economy. Instead, we see that the proportion of indigenous industrial

Table 3.9   Proportion of foreign and indigenous manufacturing
employment in top 10 industries

	1973	1987	1996
Foreign			
% of foreign employment	42	46	55
no. of jobs	31 300	37 000	53 900
Indigenous			
% of indigenous employment	48	48	44
no. of jobs	72 500	54 800	51 700

Source: Forfás, unpublished data.

output that was exported rose from 26.6 per cent in 1986 (unchanged
from the 1973 and 1976 levels), to 33.4 per cent in 1990 and 35.9 per
cent by 1995. Furthermore, the growth in exports of Irish indigenous
industry was substantially faster than the growth of industrial exports
from the EU or the OECD,[13] and the growth in export ratios occured
across a wide range of manufacturing sectors (Forfás, 1997a; O'Malley,
1998). Profit rates in indigenous manufacturing are also up very considerably, from the 1 per cent of sales level prevailing in the mid-1980s
(for firms with more than 30 employees) to almost 4 per cent (for all
firms) in 1989, rising to over 6 per cent by 1995.[14]

We suggested above that this recent success was unlikely to be due
to agglomeration. This is supported by some findings in a recent study
by Clancy *et al*. (1997) that looked at the issue of clustering in indigenous manufacturing. Their starting point was Porter's (1990) argument
that 'the phenomenon of industry clustering is so pervasive that it
appears to be a central feature of advanced national economies'. The
study identified a short-list of 11 relatively successful indigenous industries (out of a group of 46). In six of the sectors, – glass and glassware,
basic industrial chemicals (including fertilisers), the indigenous parts
of pharmaceuticals and electrical appliances, aerospace equipment
(including manufacturing and repairing), and 'other food products' –
the successful performance depended largely on just one large company (or two in the case of other foods). Two of the other 11 sectors,
meat processing and dairy products, operate largely in a regulated
environment and so it would be difficult to deem them strongly successful on a competitive basis. The final three sectors were agricultural
machinery and tractors, animal and poultry foods, and printing
and allied industries. These sectors, however, appeared to be only

moderately successful rather than outstanding. Hence the finding that 'it is difficult to identify unequivocal examples of strong and competitive indigenous manufacturing sectors'.

This conclusion is reinforced by our findings above on the lack of concentration within indigenous industry, and by its underrepresentation in increasing-returns sectors. While we saw that both indigenous and foreign firms expanded their linkages with the rest of the economy substantially, these symbiotic elements in the relationship between industry and the rest of the economy also appear insufficient to explain current success. This raises the question as to what caused the recent improvement in competitive performance. O'Malley (1998) presents evidence that changes in industrial policy instituted since the mid-1980s, which shifted the focus towards a more hands-on approach by the development agencies towards the problems encountered by indigenous firms in the marketplace, have begun to pay dividends.[15]

Besides this, the poor state of the Irish economy during most of the 1980s would have left exporting firms overrepresented in the pool remaining at the end of the period; these firms could not but gain by the development of the transportation infrastructure, while home-market oriented firms, based on historical experience, could well have lost out (Krugman and Venables, 1990). Furthermore, only the most resilient firms would have been left in place by the time conditions improved in the late 1980s. These firms would have been well-positioned to gain export market share because of the competitiveness improvements achieved after 1987 by the reduction in the tax burden and the slowing down of wage growth relative to the economy's trading partners (see Figure 3.11). Thus these conventional factors must provide a large part

Figure 3.11   Wage competitiveness: relative hourly earnings in common currency

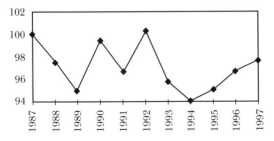

Source: Irish Central Bank Reports, Table E2, Winter 1990 and Spring 1997.

Table 3.10   Percentage of job creation due to firm entry and expansion, and of job destruction due to firm exit and contraction

| | Indigenous | | | | Foreign | | | |
| | job creation | | job destruction | | job creation | | job destruction | |
	entry	expansion	exit	contract	entry	expansion	exit	contract
1976–79	28.7	71.3	35	65	22.1	77.9	33.3	66.7
1980–87	34.1	65.9	36.4	63.6	21.2	78.8	35.1	64.9
1988–94	26.5	73.5	37.7	62.3	17.3	82.7	30.1	69.9
1995–96	21.3	78.7	42.9	57.1	7.4	92.6	26.9	73.1

Source: Forfás, unpublished data.

of the explanation for the successful performance of indigenous industry post-1987.

Further evidence suggesting that the recessionary period of 1980–87 left the economy with a high proportion of efficient indigenous firms is provided by the data on gross job flows. Table 3.10 shows that a historically very high proportion of new jobs created in the indigenous sector since that time are created by the expansion of existing establishments rather than by the coming on stream of new firms. That the same is true of foreign firms in Ireland is a reflection of the benign economic climate.

CONCLUDING COMMENTS

Since the adoption of outward-oriented policies at the beginning of the 1960s, Ireland has proved an attractive location for foreign-owned manufacturing sector firms. FDI inflows into Ireland increased substantially in the 1990s; this reflected not just increased inflows into the EU, but also a substantial increase in Ireland's share of these inflows. There is a qualitative as well as a quantitative change in the impact these inflows have on the economy, however; this can be seen in terms of foreign-sector linkages, industrial concentration, R&D expenditures, and the growth in skill requirements of the foreign sector.

To take linkages first: foreign-sector expenditures within the economy per employee have increased 50 per cent since 1983. Because a high proportion of this spending is on labour-intensive services, backward employment linkages per job in the foreign sector are now higher than for indigenous industry. We have seen that foreign-owned industry has also become more concentrated in a narrow range of sectors; this may or may not signify the presence of agglomeration economies, but is likely to generate such economies in the future. The foreign sector in Ireland is also relatively heavily engaged in R&D. Its R&D expenditures as a proportion of GDP have doubled since 1986, so that Irish manufacturing now spends the same proportion as Denmark and the Netherlands on research and development. Not only are the foreign-owned manufacturing sectors amongst the most highly skilled sectors in the economy (and, concomitant with this, amongst the most highly paid, for both skilled and unskilled labour), but the growth in skill levels has exceeded that in indigenous industry. On all these grounds it is reasonable to believe that Irish industry is rapidly growing in complexity, which promotes real convergence towards the income levels of the country's trading partners.

Irish indigenous industry has also been performing successfully in recent times. Its 1997 employment level is up 9 per cent on the 1988 figure, which goes against EU and OECD trends, its profit levels as a proportion of sales are six times higher than they were in the mid-1980s, and its export growth has been above the trend for OECD countries. We ascribe this to the benign economic environment of the 1990s, to the fact that only the most resilient and outward-oriented of indigenous firms would have survived the traumatic decade of the 1980s, and to the increased focus of industrial policy on the development of a strong indigenous sector. Amongst the beneficial environmental factors one would include the strong domestic-demand conditions that came in the wake of the stabilisation of the public finances, the improvement in cost competitiveness seen in Figure 3.11 above, the improved physical infrastructure associated with the EU Structural Funds, and the fall in costs of formerly heavily state-regulated utilities such as electricity, post and telecommunications services.

Finally, we should say something about the worry frequently expressed that the health of the economy may now be over-reliant on footloose foreign multinationals. To some extent this fear may be justified by our characterisation above of indigenous success being based on 'comparative advantage' while success in attracting FDI is based on 'absolute advantage' (Jones, 1980). An economy can lose its absolute advantage overnight while comparative advantage may change but can never be annihilated. A relevant analogy is between the specialisation recommended by international trade theory and the portfolio diversification advocated by financial theory. Has the economy earned a sufficiently high return from its specialisation (in multinational-dominated sectors) to pay for the increased risks of instability it is thought to bear?

We feel that the answer is 'yes', for two reasons. First, if the foreign sector, through the provision of opportunities for learning-by-doing and through tax revenues generated, has helped the economy to 'climb the ladder of comparative advantage' by developing its physical and human-capital infrastructure, then its very presence will have reduced the adjustment costs associated with a collapse in the availability of FDI. The economy would remain a relatively attractive base for whatever forms of FDI remained available, and indigenous industry would be stronger than it would otherwise have been.

The second point is that the risk of a catastrophic collapse may itself be overstated, if strong linkages with the indigenous economy have been developed and if the agglomeration economies discussed above are truly important. In this way, absolute advantage may over time mutate into comparative advantage. In this regard it is worth pointing out that the rates of both job creation and job destruction in domestic industry were substantially higher than in foreign industry, indicating substantially more job turnover in that sector (Strobl, Walsh and Barry, 1996). Thus, the average duration of a manufacturing sector job in Ireland, although lower than the roughly 18 years prevailing in the United States and the United Kingdom, is higher at 13 years in the foreign sector than in the indigenous sector of the economy, where it is 10 years. Net employment growth in the foreign sector is also more dependent on continuing establishments than is the case with indigenous industry. These findings support the conclusions of an earlier study by McAleese and Counahan (1979) that characterised foreign firms operating in Ireland as 'stickers' (concerned primarily with building up a long-run business) rather than 'snatchers' (concerned mainly with seizing a quick profit).

This evidence, then, alongside the increasing linkages and increasing R&D expenditures of foreign firms in Ireland suggests that the dangers of instability due to having such a large foreign-owned sector may be overstated. Certainly it is rarely suggested that the economy of Singapore is balanced on a knife-edge, even though multinational companies form an even greater share of employment there than in Ireland (O'Malley, 1989). Nevertheless, as skill shortages develop in some branches of industry in Ireland, the foreign and indigenous sectors may begin to crowd each other out in more dramatic fashion than appears to have been the case up to now. This may well represent a dilemma for policy-makers in the future.

Notes

1. This chapter is based in part on Barry and Bradley (1997). We thank Aoife Hannan and Eric Strobl for assistance with the data.
2. Coe and Helpman's (1995) results notwithstanding, the fact that Ireland's import links with the United Kingdom were largely preserved appears to us of much less consequence for Irish growth than the changes in the geographical destination of its exports, which largely reflected the changing sectoral production structure of the economy.
3. O'Malley's classification of the increasing-returns sectors is also used by Barry (1996). Ireland does not appear to attract FDI into sectors in which there are strong IRS at the plant level (e.g., in the automobile industry), arguably because of the small size of the country.
4. In 1987 around 23 per cent of indigenous employment and 63 per cent of multinational employment operated in these sectors.
5. Total factor productivity would be preferable, but data on capital stock employed are not easily available.
6. These comparisons are, of course, heavily distorted by transfer pricing.
7. This general decline in the size structure of indigenous industry as trade was liberalised runs counter to the experiences of Canadian and German industry; Horstmann and Markusen (1986) report that average Canadian plant size increased by 33 per cent over the 1970–79 period of trade liberalisation, while Muller and Owen (1989) report the same qualitative effect of trade on German plant size between 1963 and 1978. Note, though, that average plant size declined in many core countries over the period that the Irish data reports on; Van Ark and Monnikhof (1996).
8. Over 40 per cent of foreign employment in Irish manufacturing is now in these sectors, compared to a little over 10 per cent of indigenous employment.
9. Backward linkages *per unit of output* are low for the foreign sector. Rodriguez-Clare (1996) argues, however, that backward linkages should be measured *per job* as is done here.
10. It could alternatively be interpreted as evidence of comparative advantage. In the Irish case yet another alternative springs to mind; increasing concentration in foreign industry could be taken as evidence that the industrial development authorities targeted foreign firms in these particular sectors.
11. Alternatively, though, this could also reflect targeting of these sectors by the industrial development authorities.
12. The volume of indigenous manufacturing output by 1995 was up 37 per cent on its 1987 level, compared to 17 per cent for the OECD and 15 per cent for the EU (O'Malley, 1998).
13. Measured in US dollars, indigenous exports increased by 156 per cent in the period 1986–95 compared to the 139 per cent increase for EU manufactured exports, and the 145 per cent increase for the OECD over the same period (O'Malley, 1998).
14. Unpublished IDA data from 1985, Forfás (1997a).

15. Other changes included the establishment of the Company Development Programme to build up selected companies regarded as relatively promising, and the National Linkage Programme to develop further the indigenous sub-supply of components to the foreign sector.

References

Baker, T. (1988) 'Industrial Output and Wage Costs, 1980–87', *Quarterly Economic Commentary*, October, pp. 33–43 (Dublin: The Economic and Social Research Institute).

Barry, F. (1996) 'Peripherality in Economic Geography and Modern Growth Theory: Evidence from Ireland's Adjustment to Free Trade', *World Economy*, 19(3), pp. 345–65.

Barry, F. and Bradley, J. (1997) 'FDI and Trade: The Irish Host-Country Experience', *Economic Journal*, 107(445), pp. 1798–1811.

Barry, F. and Hannan, A. (1995) 'Multinationals and Indigenous Employment: An Irish Disease?', *Economic and Social Review*, 27(1), pp. 21–32.

Barry, F. and Hannan, A. (1996a) 'Education, Industrial Change and Unemployment in Ireland', Centre for Economic Research, working paper WP96/18, University College, Dublin.

Barry, F. and Hannan, A. (1996b) 'On Comparative and Absolute Advantage: FDI and the Sectoral and Spatial Effects of Market Integration', Centre for Economic Research, working paper WP96/19, University College, Dublin.

Bradley, J., Whelan, K. and Wright, J. (1993) *Stabilization and Growth in the EC Periphery: A Study of the Irish Economy* (Aldershot: Avebury).

Caves, R. and Krepps, M. (1993) 'Fat: The Displacement of Nonproduction Workers from US Manufacturing Industries', *Brookings Papers on Economic Activity*, 2, pp. 227–88.

Clancy, P., O'Malley, E., O'Connell, L. and van Egeraat, C. (1997) 'Culliton's Clusters: Still the Way to Go?', paper presented to National Economic and Social Council seminar, November.

Coe, D. and Helpman, E. (1995) 'International R&D Spillovers', *European Economic Review*, 39(5), pp. 859–87.

Cogan, D. and Onyemadum, E. (1981) 'Spin-off Companies in the Irish Electronics Industry', *Irish Journal of Business and Administrative Research*, 3(2), pp. 3–15.

Corden, M. and Neary, J. (1982) 'Booming Sector and Deindustrialization in a Small Open Economy', *Economic Journal*, 92, pp. 825–48.

Forfás (1997a) *Annual Survey of Irish Economy Expenditures: Results for 1995* (Dublin: Forfás).

Forfás (1997b) *Survey of Product and Process Innovation in Irish Industry 1993–1995* (Dublin: Forfás).

Grossman, G. and Helpman, E. (1991) *Innovation and Growth in the Global Economy* (Cambridge, Mass.: MIT Press).

Hirschman, A. O. (1958) *The Strategy of Economic Development* (New Haven: Yale University Press).

Horstmann, I. and Markusen, J. (1986) 'Up the Average Cost Curve: Inefficient Entry and the New Protectionism', *Journal of International Economics*, 20, pp. 225–47.

Jones, R. (1980) 'Comparative and Absolute Advantage', *Schweizerische Zeitschrift fur Volkswirtschaft und Statistik*, 3, pp. 235–60; also available as Reprint Series no. 153, Institute for International Economic Studies, University of Stockholm.

Krugman, P. (1991) *Geography and Trade* (Cambridge, Mass.: MIT Press).

Krugman, P. (1997) 'Good News from Ireland: A Geographical Perspective', in Alan Gray (ed.), *International Perspectives on the Irish Economy* (Dublin: Indecon).

Krugman, P. and Venables, A. (1990) 'Integration and the Competitiveness of Peripheral Industry', in de Macedo and Bliss (eds), *Unity with Diversity within the European Economy: The Community's Southern Frontier* (Cambridge: Cambridge University Press), pp. 56–77.

McAleese, D. and Counahan, M. (1979) 'Stickers or Snatchers? Employment in Multinational Corporations during the Recession', *Oxford Bulletin of Economics and Statistics*, 41(4), pp. 345–58.

Muller, J. and Owen, N. (1989) 'The Effect of Trade on Plant Size', in A. Jacquemin and A. Sapir (eds) *The European Internal Market: Trade and Competition* (Oxford: Oxford University Press).

Nankani, G. (1979) 'Development Problems of Mineral-Exporting Countries', World Bank, Staff Working Paper, no. 354, Washington.

National Economic and Social Council (1989) *Ireland in the European Community: Performance, Prospects and Strategy*, Report no. 88 (Dublin: NESC).

O'Donnell, M. (1997) 'The Changing Commodity Structure and Destination of Irish Exports 1972–90', Working Paper, Trinity College, Dublin.

Ó Grada, C. (1997) *A Rocky Road: The Irish Economy since the 1920s* (Manchester: Manchester University Press).

O'Malley, E. (1989) *Industry and Economic Development: The Challenge for the Latecomer* (Dublin: Gill and Macmillan).

O'Malley, E. (1992) 'Industrial Structure and Economies of Scale in the Context of 1992', in *The Role of the Structural Funds: Analysis of Consequences for Ireland in the Context of 1992*, Policy Research Series Paper no. 13 (Dublin: The Economic and Social Research Institute), pp. 203–49.

O'Malley, E. (1995) *An Analysis of Secondary Employment Associated with Manufacturing Industry*, General Research Series Paper no. 167 (Dublin: The Economic and Social Research Institute).

O'Malley, E. (1998) 'The Revival of Irish Indigenous Industry 1987–1997', *Quarterly Economic Commentary*, April, pp. 35–62 (Dublin: The Economic and Social Research Institute).

O'Rourke, K. (1994) 'Industrial Policy, Employment Policy and the Non-Traded Sector', *Journal of the Statistical and Social Inquiry Society of Ireland*, XXVII(ii), pp. 61–80.

Porter, M. (1990) *The Competitive Advantage of Nations* (London: Macmillan).

Pratten, C. (1988) 'A Survey of Economies of Scale', Economic Paper no. 67, Directorate-General for Economic and Financial Affairs (Brussels: Commission of the European Communities).

Rodriguez-Clare, A. (1996) 'Multinationals, Linkages, and Economic Development', *American Economic Review*, 86(4), pp. 852–73.

Sachs, J. and Shatz, H. (1994) 'Trade and Jobs in US Manufacturing', *Brookings Papers on Economic Activity*, 1, pp. 1–84.

Strobl, E., Walsh, P. and Barry, F. (1996) 'Aggregate Employment Flows in Irish Manufacturing', paper presented to annual conference of the Irish Economic Association, TCD working paper 96/3.

Van Ark, B. and Monnikhof, E. (1996) 'Size Distribution of Output and Employment: A Data Set for Manufacturing Industries in Five OECD countries, 1960's–1990', *OECD Working Paper*, 166.

Walsh, B. (1994) 'Wage Convergence and Integrated Labour Markets: Ireland and Britain 1841–1991', unpublished manuscript.

Wijkman, P. (1990) 'Patterns of Production and Trade', in W. Wallace (ed.), *The Dynamics of European Integration* (London: Pinter).

4 Fiscal Adjustment and Disinflation in Ireland: Setting the Macro Basis of Economic Recovery and Expansion

Patrick Honohan

THE FISCAL CRISIS AND ITS RESOLUTION

In a few short years in the latter half of the 1980s Ireland moved from a position of near-bankruptcy in the fiscal accounts to near balance. The improvement was sustained: having jumped to over 120 per cent in 1987, a decade later the debt-to-GDP ratio had fallen by almost one-half, and promised to slip below the demanding Maastricht target of 60 per cent by the start of EMU in 1999.

The decisive turning point in this story was the decision of the incoming government in 1987 to abandon their opposition to fiscal restraint and instead to pursue with vigour policies advocated but weakly implemented since 1981. By 1989, the major adjustment had been accomplished, and the public finances resumed a more normal pattern of growth in spending and taxation broadly in line with real economic growth, and with little borrowing.

The recent evolution of Irish public finances thus falls into four phases:

A   Unsustainable expansion, 1977–81
B   Good intentions, 1981–86
C   Decisive action, 1987–89
D   Finally a new equilibrium from 1989 on.

Table 4.1 shows the main aggregate features of the adjustment process. It reveals how discretionary spending began to be cut considerably in phase B, but that this was more than offset by the growth in elements of spending dominated by automatic or exogenous factors. In particular,

Table 4.1   Main elements of the public finances 1977–96

Change in % share of GNP	Phase A 1977–81	Phase B 1981–86	Phase C 1986–89	Phase D 1989–96
Primary deficit	4.5	−5.4	−9.6	−0.9
Borrowing	6.8	−2.7	−11.1	−4.1
Dissaving (current deficit)	4.8	0.9	−7.4	−2.1
Total tax	3.0	4.8	−0.9	0.3
Cycle-related and predetermined spending:				
interest	2.2	2.6	−1.4	−3.3
transfers	2.2	5.5	−3.0	0.6
Discretionary spending:				
wages	3.4	−0.8	−3.4	0.4
capital	2.5	−3.7	−3.6	1.3

the primary deficit was already falling sharply from 1982 on, but debt-servicing costs continued to grow.

Phase A: Unsustainable Expansion, 1977–81

Governments had run substantial deficits before 1977, though mostly for the purpose of financing capital accumulation. A ballooning current deficit in the mid-1970s, associated with the first oil crisis, had been brought partly under control by 1977 when a new government introduced what was immediately recognized by economists as an unsustainable fiscal expansion. Public sector borrowing surged from 10 to 17 per cent of GNP despite growing taxation (see Figure 4.1).[1]

In order to understand the dynamics behind the evolution of public spending in this and subsequent periods, it is instructive to examine some of the major components separately (Figures 4.2 and 4.3). In the late 1970s all categories of spending showed an expansion. Wages and salaries increased sharply as lavish national pay agreements resulted in increased wage rates, and as public bodies took on more staff in response to the government's desire to use an expansion of public sector employment as a tool to beat unemployment. Interest payments increased in response to a growing debt burden and to higher domestic and world interest rates. Transfers increased, partly in line with more generous income support payments, but also (after 1979) in response to a rapid increase in unemployment associated with the UK recession.

Figure 4.1   Deficit as percentage of GNP

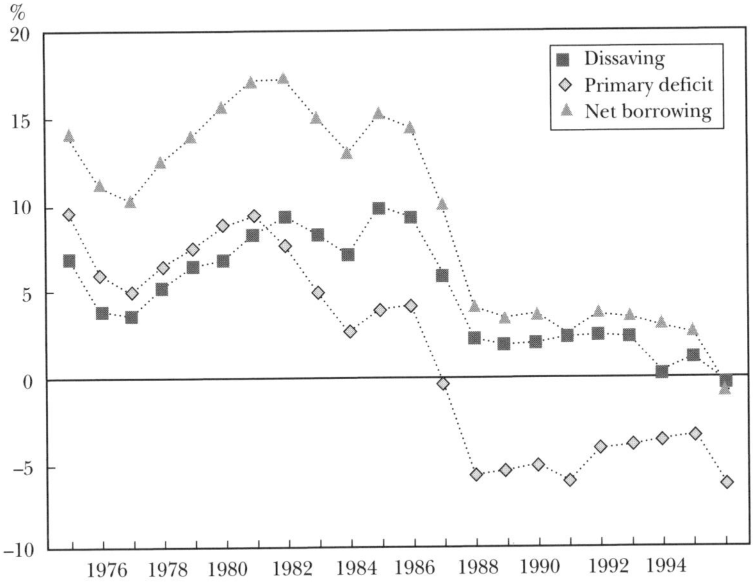

Source: Public authorities (national accounts adjusted for timing of EU payments).

Finally, an ambitious programme of public infrastructure expansion saw capital spending increase also.

There was also a loss of fiscal control. Expenditure began to outrun budgeted quantities by a very wide margin – over 7 per cent in 1981. By the change of government in June of that year it had become evident that the borrowing and its determinants had a momentum which would be hard to stop. Ireland was beginning to attract adverse international attention for its high fiscal deficit (and the associated current account balance of payments deficit).

Phase B: Good Intentions, 1981–86

The incoming government in 1981, a minority coalition, made an initial response in a mid-year mini-budget, but it also made its own task harder by responding to the growing unemployment levels by increasing the real value of social welfare benefits. The commitment to decisive

Figure 4.2   Transfers and interest as percentage of GNP

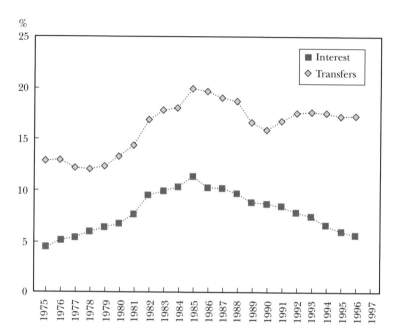

Source: Public authorities (national accounts adjusted for timing of EU payments).

fiscal action received a fatal blow, however, when the budget proposal of January 1982, which would have imposed a larger negative fiscal impulse than any before or since, was defeated in the Dáil due to the government's failure to secure the votes of two, hitherto supportive, independents.

Though there was no return to the expansionism of the late 1970s, the consequence of the budgetary defeat was not only a change of government, but also a more tentative and limited containment of the fiscal position over the next five years than originally envisaged by that budget proposal. Nevertheless, budgetary control was recovered in this period, and the budgets of 1982–84, especially 1983, were all sharply deflationary as shown by measures of their fiscal impulse (see Figure 4.4).[2] The primary deficit fell sharply from over 9 per cent in 1981 to less than 3 per cent in 1984 (Figure 4.1).

These were years of recession, partly imported from the UK but also exacerbated by the fiscal cutbacks.[3] Most discretionary spending was held or reduced as shown in Figure 4.3, especially capital spending,[4]

Figure 4.3   Wages and capital spending as percentage of GNP

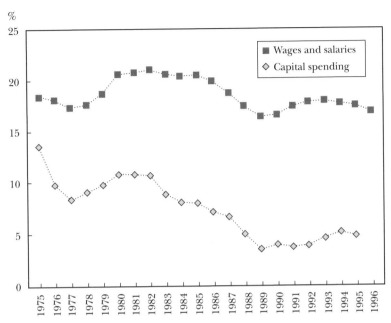

Source: Public authorities (national accounts adjusted for timing of EU payments).

and tax rates were increased sharply resulting in a growing tax-to-GNP ratio (Figure 4.5). But this did not reduce the need for borrowing by enough in the face of a still-growing interest burden, and of an increasing cost of transfers now aggravated by ever-increasing unemployment (Figure 4.2).[5]

Imposed on a narrow base, which excluded food and clothing as well as much of agricultural and corporate income and residential property, the growing tax take entailed some very high marginal rates. By 1984 it was accepted that the tax burden had become unsustainable, and that no further reliance could be placed on it for redressing the fiscal imbalance. Although the ratio of public-sector borrowing to GNP had been reduced by 5 percentage points, the debt-to-GNP ratio continued to grow as shown in Figure 4.6, and there was little or no reduction in the psychologically important current budget deficit. The fiscal achievements were not enough to secure political support for further action, and the fiscal situation showed little improvement between

Figure 4.4   Fiscal impulse: change in cyclically adjusted primary deficit

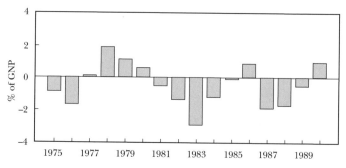

Source: Bradley *et al.* (1997).

Figure 4.5   Tax and non-interest spending as percentage of GNP

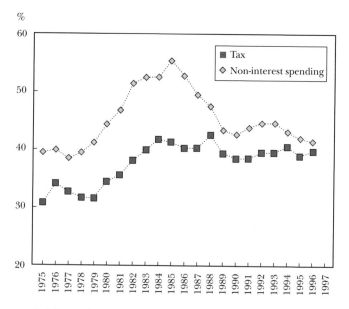

Source: Public authorities (national accounts adjusted for timing of EU payments).

1984–86. Interest rates increased sharply in late 1986 as it became evident that there would be a change of government, and that the opposition were promising a solution that did not involve cut-backs. Irish governments of the 1980s are listed in Table 4.2.

Figure 4.6　National debt 1975–96, percentage of GNP, year-end

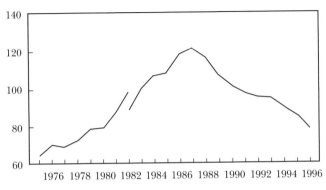

Note:　From 1981, data are consolidated to remove double-counting.

Table 4.2　Irish Governments of the 1980s

Taoiseach	Parties	Date of election
Lynch, Haughey	Fianna Fáil	June 1977
Fitz Gerald	Fine Gael, Labour	June 1981
Haughey	Fianna Fáil	February 1982
Fitz Gerald	Fine Gael, Labour	November 1982
Haughey	Fianna Fáil	February 1987
Haughey	Fianna Fáil, Progressive Democrats	June 1989

Note:　All but the first were minority governments during at least part of their administration.

Phase C: Decisive Action, 1987–89

In the event, the incoming government in 1987 reversed its stated views and unexpectedly espoused an aggressive policy of retrenchment.[6] A freeze on recruitment, an early retirement scheme[7] and a deferral of special pay awards brought substantial reductions in the public pay bill. Extensive cutbacks and postponements of public infrastructure (including public housing) were implemented (Figure 4.3).

This renewed assault on the public finances bore fruit. Suddenly the fiscal crisis was over. The primary deficit was eliminated in 1987 and moved into strong surplus from 1988; the debt-to-GNP ratio started falling sharply from its 1986 peak. It was not only the domestic action: the external environment improved dramatically also. As a result, the less discretionary elements of the budget improved (Figure 4.2); interest rates fell at home and abroad. Numbers at work stopped falling and the UK boom sucked in migrants from Ireland, lowering the unemployment rate at home. The appreciation of sterling helped Irish wage competitiveness, and this was copperfastened by a moderate national wage agreement reflecting not only the weakened position of trade unions, but also a new awareness on their part of the nature of the economic crisis and the appropriate response to it. Though taxation was not increased, an effective tax amnesty (combined with credible threats for those who did not comply) brought in a huge revenue windfall, especially in 1988, and also helped secure improved collection in subsequent years.

Finally, the doubling of EU structural funds offered a new source of revenue, especially for infrastructural investment, and allowed an early resumption of deferred projects from 1989 on.[8]

Phase D: A New Equilibrium, 1989-97

The painful experience of fiscal adjustment ensured that, once the restoration of balance in the public finances had been achieved, there would be no early slippage back into heavy borrowing. Adoption of the Maastricht criteria from 1992 cemented the commitment to low borrowing and debt reduction. The primary surplus has remained in the region of 5 per cent of GNP since 1988 (Figure 4.1).

But government spending resumed its upward trend in real terms, financed by buoyant tax receipts associated with the economic boom which took hold from 1988 and has continued since then with only a modest slowing during 1991-93. Even as a percentage of GNP, public non-interest spending (after declining in the late 1980s) has remained above the figures recorded at the end of the 1970s, and taxation has declined only modestly from its peak share of GNP in 1984.[9] Interest spending has continued to decline along with the debt ratio.

Disentangling the winners and losers from the process of fiscal consolidation is not easy, particularly since the question goes well beyond measurement of who benefits directly from public spending and who pays the taxes (Callan and Nolan, 1992). The impact on unemployment is likely to have been the dominant channel of effect on income distribution, far larger than the effect of reduced food subsidies and health spending cut-backs, for example. The lower rates of social welfare benefits were more than insulated from the contractionary process and advanced steadily in real terms, and eventually by comparison with average earnings in the economy (Callan, Nolan and Whelan, 1996). The range of weekly benefit payments was compressed, so that higher rates of benefit fared less well.

A revealing feature of the budgetary process in these years has been systematic overshooting in both tax receipts and spending relative to each year's budget. This suggests both conservative budgeting and a relatively high marginal propensity to spend unanticipated tax receipts in the year that they arise.

The small reduction in the overall share of taxation masks some considerable shifts and a moderate degree of structural reform in taxation. Corporation tax receipts have greatly increased following the widening of the base through the elimination of export sales relief, restrictions on depreciation allowances and a number of other tax-based investment incentives, and helped also by revenue from the (largely tax-driven) off-shore financial services centre. Top tax rates have also come down, in line with global trends, though the income tax burden at low and middle incomes is still high, especially for unmarried persons.[10] Asset markets are no longer seriously distorted by tax privileges, partly because taxation of deposit interest has been rationalized and because insurance premiums are no longer allowed as a deduction from taxable income, and mortgage interest only partly allowed, but especially because lower inflation reduces the distorting effect of remaining privileges. Clothing is now in the VAT net, and other indirect taxes are no longer pitched at levels so high as to induce widespread cross-border smuggling at household level.

There has not, however, been anything like a wholesale tax reform, along rationalizing lines that would include integration of tax and social welfare, systematic taxation of fringe benefits, full imputation of corporation tax, an easing of stamp duties (especially those payable on property transactions), and a worthwhile and viable tax on residential property. Indeed, much of tax-policy thinking has been inspired by the idea that a well-targeted tax break can generate worthwhile employment-creating economic activity. This thinking has been behind reliefs for hotels construction, urban renewal and film-financing among others, and the low (10 per cent) rate of corporation tax for manufacturing and internationally-traded services has been the cornerstone of industrial development policy throughout the period under review.

Likewise, the relatively modest reforms that have been introduced to alleviate the unemployment and poverty traps are piecemeal in nature and fall short of what might have been achieved.

WHY WAS REFORM DELAYED?

The prolonged delay before effective stabilization was accomplished, and the speed with which the eventual turnaround occurred, raise questions of political economy. Why did the successive governments of the 1980s, despite recognizing the problem, fail to deliver the adjustment they promised?[11]

Ireland is not the only country in which stabilizations have been delayed, and the international literature distinguishes a number of explanations of which the institutional deficiency hypothesis and the war of attrition are worth examining to see to what extent they are congruent with the Irish experience.

Institutional Deficiency Hypothesis

This hypothesis proposes that it is the institutional procedures for government decision-making that are to blame. These institutions are not well-adapted to combat the common pool problem of public spending whereby interest groups press for more spending on their preferred projects in the expectation that the cost will be spread across society at large. This free-rider aspect tends to generate a higher level of overall spending than is socially optimal (cf. Hallerberg and von Hagen, 1997). As a result adjustment is delayed beyond what is socially optimal.

This hypothesis has been employed especially in critiques of US Congressional procedures. The old US procedures used a 'bottom-up' approach to determination of total spending, and as such the analysis does not immediately transpose to the Irish system in which (as in the UK) it is the government that makes (top-down) spending proposals to parliament.

Nevertheless, elements of the common pool problem certainly beset the policy process. This was exacerbated during the 1980s by a widespread perception that relatively painless solutions should be available through the elimination of 'waste', tightening up on tax avoidance and the like. Having satisfied themselves that there was no waste in the particular spending programmes he or she was promoting, each government minister struggled to maintain the budget of their individual departments while still acknowledging the need for greater spending restraint overall. The fact that substantial broad-based tax increases were agreed in the early years, when specific spending cuts could not be, is also surely a reflection of common pool aspects.

Inasmuch as a single-party government can internalise some common pool externalities, the fact that resolution had to await the election of a single-party government in 1987 also provides some support for the idea that institutional structures contributed to the delay. Although it was a minority government, game theoretic considerations show that the 1987 administration was not at all as vulnerable to parliamentary threat as its predecessor had been (Seidman, 1987). In addition, within-party discipline was much higher in the Fianna Fáil party than in the Labour party that had formed part of the weak 1982–86 coalition.

But this is not the whole story. For one thing, the government's commitment from 1987 was bolstered by the main opposition party's promise not to precipitate an election providing the fiscal adjustment was maintained. Perhaps the most problematic aspect for the institutional deficiency hypothesis is that the crisis was ultimately resolved without any material change in institutional procedures. To be sure, the annual 'estimates campaign', in which the government departments' initial spending proposals to the Minister for Finance are scrutinised and pared down through bilateral negotiations, was conducted with enhanced vigour and effectiveness in the late 1980s; but it remained a procedure that in essence had not been substantially changed.

War of Attrition Hypothesis

This hypothesis (Alesina and Drazen, 1991) also involves divergent interest groups but now the delay arises because of information gaps: each interest group knows that spending will have to be cut, but delays conceding on its preferred spending in the hope that others will do so first. In the absence of perfect information about the willingness of each group to accept cuts, there will be a time-consuming learning process with the effect of delaying the adjustment.

It is less easy to find evidence of this kind of behaviour in the Irish experience. True, there is the case of healthcare, a specific spending area which was cut back quite sharply in the early phase in line with the model's prediction that certain interest groups will cave in along the way. And the fact that resolution came with a change in government could be thought of as reflecting the consequences of an alteration of the balance of power between interest groups.

But it is important to recognise how little ideological polarisation was involved throughout. The rhetoric of fiscal retrenchment in Ireland was largely free of Thatcherism, despite being contemporaneous with it. The real fear was of a financial meltdown with foreign and domestic financial market refusal to rollover debt. Parliamentary opposition to the cutbacks was opportunistic rather than ideological, for example the adoption by the 1987 government of the programme of retrenchment repeatedly announced but imperfectly implemented by their predecessors. Above all, the war of attrition idea seems to lose much of its applicability when it is recognised that delay was not at first the main feature of the Irish situation. It was rather the failure to maintain the momentum of 1982–84 that delayed the ultimate resolution.

External Conditions and Changing Sacrifice Ratio

Other theories rely on shifting external factors to explain the timing of adjustment. Thus, external conditions were very hostile to fiscal contraction in the early 1980s (Table 4.3). The UK recession both reduced demand for Irish exports and effectively closed off the usual safety valve of emigration. World interest rate conditions were also much more hostile in the early 1980s than later. In short, fiscal retrenchment was procyclical in the early unsuccessful phase, and anticyclical in the later successful phase. Inasmuch as the cost of adjustment was dramatically increased by these external conditions, it is easy to understand the political reluctance to take more aggressive action early on.

An important contributory factor to the faltering of the adjustment process in 1985–86 is largely ignored in the literature, namely the fact that policy-makers became sceptical about the effectiveness of the adjustment measures they had been pursuing and increasingly alarmed at their cost. Real GNP had fallen by a cumulative 3 per cent in 1982 and 1983, and a further decline in 1986 left it below its 1981 level. Unemployment had increased by a factor of $2\frac{1}{2}$. Considering the fact that the debt-to-GNP ratio was still growing, this suggested a much higher sacrifice ratio than had been anticipated. Indeed, as late as 1989 Dornbusch was arguing that the costs of fiscal adjustment were too high and that continued servicing of the existing debt might prove impossible.

Table 4.3   External conditions

	UK GDP growth % per annum	UK change in % unemployment average per annum	US$ short interest rate %
1981–84	1.8	1.4	12.0
1986–89	4.1	−1.2	7.6

It was against this background that a minimalist strategy became politically acceptable in 1985–86.[12] The 1984 National Plan was essentially constructed on the basis of such a minimalist strategy designed to achieve correction over a prolonged period in order not to deepen the recession, while at the same time protecting the state's access to capital markets. Thus it was proposed merely to stabilize the debt ratio by 1987, and there was slippage from even this limited objective as the elections approached.

CONSEQUENCES OF THE FISCAL CRISIS

A number of recent studies have taken the Irish experience as a central case study in exploring the general question of how a fiscal contraction affects the real economy.[13] The traditional debate here contrasts the Keynesian presumption that spending cuts or tax increases will be contractionary, against the neo-Ricardian view that intertemporal shifts in the financing of government spending may have no effect on aggregate demand, inasmuch as far-sighted individuals will use the financial markets to smooth any cash-flow impact. The newer literature examines possible positive short-run effects of fiscal contraction. The mechanisms that could give such an 'anti-Keynesian' result include financial crowding-in, wealth, confidence and credibility effects, and labour market effects (Barry and Devereux, 1995; Lane and Perotti, 1995; Alesina and Perotti, 1997).

Alesina and Perotti (1997) have assembled persuasive evidence that fiscal consolidation is likely to be more successful in terms of its impact on economic growth if it relies little on increased taxation. Tax increases adversely affect competitiveness and profitability. They fail to signal any intention to bring public spending under control and thus leave the door open to further rounds of spending and tax increases in a way that increases uncertainty, discourages investment and generally damages the credibility of the policy programme. Certainly, this story rings true in terms of the contrast between the 1982–84 and 1987–89 phases of the Irish fiscal contraction. The cumulative negative fiscal impulse of the two phases is approximately the same, but the first relied heavily on tax increases. The damaging and unsustainable nature of the upward trend in taxation was recognized and permanently ended in 1984.

The 1987–89 cuts included important reductions in public consumption, even including some reductions in public sector employment.[14] This is the sort of less-reversible measure that is seen by Alesina and Perotti as contributing to a successful adjustment.

On the other hand, cutting public infrastructure spending, which was a central feature of the 1987–88 cuts, is seen as a less-effective way of tackling over-spending. Although capital cuts can often be quite easily effected with modest political disruption and technical waste, they convey little credibility because they are easily reversed, and can also be damaging to long-term growth prospects (Rogoff, 1990).

An additional factor relevant in the Irish context is the so-called 'opportunity cost' theory of the response to recessions, according to which the lower opportunity costs during recessions of effort devoted to reorganisation encourage businesses to restructure their activities in a way that yields substantial long-term benefits and may enhance growth following the end of the recession (Aghion and Saint-Paul, 1991; Saint-Paul, 1997). In the Irish context, the lengthy recession, exacerbated by the prolonged and faltering fiscal contraction of the early 1980s, resulted in the closure of many old-established enterprises, and forced as well as facilitated others to rationalize. Soaring unemployment and falling union membership induced a change in the attitudes of union leadership and their perception of the optimal role for organised labour in promoting good job opportunities and job security.

It is evident that a crude application of the 'expansionary fiscal contraction' hypothesis to suggest that the dramatic fiscal recovery of 1988–90 is substantially attributable to fiscal action cannot stand up to criticism. For one thing the sequence of events is in the wrong order; for the recovery was export-led, followed by a recovery of consumption with investment spending becoming important only late on (see Table 4.4). The UK and world economic boom created the demand, to which an increasingly cost-competitive industrial sector responded. This competitiveness in turn was underpinned by wage restraint and by favourable exchange rate movements. Into this upturn in foreign demand, the new wave of fiscal contraction could be more easily absorbed, and the adjustment accomplished through a virtuous circle in which each new success reinforced credibility and enhanced confidence.

Table 4.4   Percentage real growth in demand aggregates

	1987	1988	1989	1990
Exports	13.7	8.9	10.3	8.9
Consumption	3.1	4.8	6.4	2.0
Investment	− 5.5	− 4.0	21.9	24.1

EXCHANGE RATE AND INTEREST RATE POLICY

Although the fiscal contraction was centre-stage in the policy debate of the 1980s, exchange rate and interest rate policy were also influential, albeit in a more passive sense. The fiscal crisis did interact with the monetary sphere, notably contributing to higher domestic interest rates, but it did not trigger a severe exchange rate or financial crisis. Neither the precise choice of exchange rate regime (the EMS) nor the precise conduct of monetary policy was helpful in keeping interest rates as low as they might have, but it is wrong to suggest that rigid adherence to a policy of disinflation was at the root of the recession.

The ERM: A Zone of Stability or a Dragging Anchor?

Ireland's experience in the EMS has been the subject of intense debate and widely divergent views. Some authors see membership as a hard currency option which imparted a deflationary bias and contributed to recession and unemployment. In fact, the EMS was subject to realignments and represented at best an anchor that could drag. Despite lip service to a strong option, credibility for such a policy was never fully achieved.

That the debate has been hard to resolve reflects the wide movements of relative exchange rates of Ireland's trading partners during the 1980s, as well as the fact that the UK recession and Irish fiscal crisis coincide in time with the early years of the EMS. But a few simple, essential facts throw much light on this issue, and help demolish some of the myths which have emerged in the literature.

Ireland joined the exchange rate mechanism of the EMS from the outset in March 1979, and this entailed a break in the long-standing one-for-one link with sterling by the end of that month. The sharp appreciation of sterling against all EMS currencies during 1979–81 brought the Irish pound as low as £stg 0.74 – a nominal bilateral depreciation of over a quarter in just two years. This was also a substantial real bilateral depreciation against the UK whether measured in terms of wages or prices, as inflation was running almost as high in the UK as in Ireland. On the other hand, the higher rate of wage and price inflation in Ireland as compared with most of the other ERM member states meant that the early years of the EMS saw real appreciation against those countries.

Competitiveness

The best general purpose measures of overall cost competitiveness are those which average over the major trading partners and which use wage rates, rather than consumer prices or unit labour costs.[15] Figure 4.7 provides such a measure and shows that a trend in annual real appreciation of about 1 per cent per annum has persisted from the early 1970s with no change in trend in the EMS period, at least until the late 1980s. Such an appreciation is fully consistent with the theory of Balassa and Samuelson that countries with rapidly growing productivity in the production of traded goods will tend to experience a real appreciation. Indeed, the data of Figure 4.7 make it well nigh impossible to sustain an argument that the change in exchange rate regime had the effect of imparting a new deflationary bias to the economy. That is not to deny that a slower rate of real appreciation might have helped employment and output – the upward trend evident in Figure 4.7 ends in the late 1980s as a result of domestic wage restraint.

Inflation and Realignment Policy

Reflecting UK inflation to 1980 and the nominal depreciation against that currency, Irish inflation rose during 1979–81 but fell back subsequently,

Figure 4.7   Wage competitiveness: Ireland vs Germany, UK and US

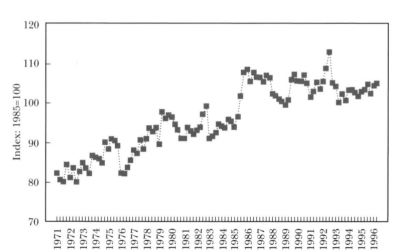

Note: In constructing the index, the weights allocated to Germany, the UK and the US are 0.3, 0.5 and 0.2 respectively.

with consumer price inflation dipping below 5 per cent per annum in 1985 and remaining in low single digits permanently thereafter. The taming of Irish inflation has often been attributed to ERM membership, but this is very hard to justify.[16] For one thing it must be borne in mind that UK inflation fell even more sharply. Furthermore, an exchange-rate based price stabilisation would normally be accompanied by a surge in the real exchange rate, and often by other macroeconomic developments not evident in the Irish data.[17] Above all, the parity of the Irish pound in the ERM was subject to change.

There were 17 realignments in the ERM, of which 11 came before 1990. On seven of the 11 early realignments the Irish pound was devalued against the DM. With such flexibility in the peg, it is not clear what the nominal anchor in the system was. In fact, with two exceptions, Ireland always pursued the modal realignment.[18] The two exceptions represented the opening of a safety valve: they were triggered by the two sharp real appreciations that occurred.[19] Thus the policy is consistent with a simple rule: be at the mode unless there has been a sharp real appreciation. The two exceptions imparted an additional cumulative 9 per cent depreciation to the Irish pound in the 1980s, making it weaker than all but the French franc and the lira in that period.

So, was it exchange rate policy or the weakness of the labour market that ensured the decline in inflation in 1981–87? The indications from actual realignment policy, as summarised above, are that an excessive real appreciation would have been accommodated by further depreciation.[20] If so, then it must surely have been the weakness of the labour market, itself exacerbated by the fiscal tightening, that ensured that this kind of pressure did not emerge. By 1988–89, with inflation low and the 'new EMS' spirit abroad, it appears that there was some tightening of policy in that the old rule would probably have triggered a devaluation towards the end of 1989; and that of January 1993 was rather late in coming.

Interest Rate Policy

Although the 1983 and 1986 realignments were important in avoiding overvaluation, it has sometimes been argued that they might have weakened credibility, thereby increasing both the general level of interest rates and the sensitivity of those rates to sterling movements. Indeed, Irish interest rates have been very high during the EMS period, though part of this reflects the depreciation of the Irish pound against the DM during this period (Figure 4.8). But depreciation does not explain all of the differential: short-term rates have consistently displayed excess returns against the DM (Figure 4.9), with only occasional partial reversals.

Figure 4.8   Irish pound against DM and sterling, March 1979 to September 1997

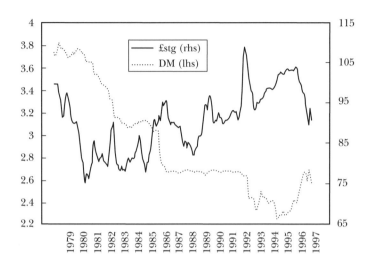

Figure 4.9   Cumulative excess returns on short-term Irish assets against DM, March 1979 to September 1997

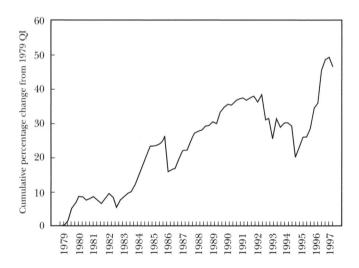

The excess returns have been higher during periods of sterling weakness (including the winter of 1989–90). This points to excessively pessimistic market expectations about the Irish pound and about the degree to which sterling weakness was a predictor of Irish pound realignments. However, these characteristics persisted throughout the ERM period and were not worsened by the realignment of August 1986 (Honohan, 1993; Honohan and Conroy, 1994).

Domestic policy has also contributed adversely to risk premia and excess returns on Irish pound interest rates. For one thing, high government borrowing drove up yields at both the long and the short end (Honohan, 1993; Lynch, 1997). In addition, it can be argued that the monetary authorities did not do enough to smooth the impact of liquidity shocks on interest rates, at least before 1988 when a more accommodating policy was put in place (Honohan, 1993). Both aspects are illustrated by the interest rate hike of October 1986, which immediately followed the announcement of very unfavourable government borrowing data and reflected a sudden market reassessment of the risk that the debt would ultimately be monetized through a weak currency policy. This jump in interest rates marked the low point of the fiscal adjustment. Rates eased considerably following the adoption of a tight budgetary stance by the new government early in the following year.[21]

The Wide Bands and towards EMU

The Irish pound has taken full advantage of the wider ERM bands introduced in August 1993, as the impact of sterling movements has been dampened. Sterling weakness in 1995–96 brought the Irish pound on the one hand quite close to the bottom of the ERM band, and on the other as high as £stg 1.04; whereas sterling's strength during 1997 has brought the Irish pound to the top of the ERM band, and as low as £stg 0.87. No explicit policy has been announced, but this loose tracking of an average of sterling and DM rates has evidently been to the authorities' satisfaction. Meanwhile, exhibiting some concern about asset market over-heating, they have maintained relatively high short-term interest rates through liquidity policy, with long yields reflecting the market's rising degree of confidence that rates will converge after 1999.

As compared with the flexibility of the ERM, both before and after 1993, EMU will represent a much more rigid nominal policy. No safety valve such as those exercised in 1983, 1986 and 1993 will be available, and the burden of adjustment to maintain competitiveness will fall much more heavily on the mechanism of wage bargaining. Interest rates, although they may be lower on average than in the past, will no longer be available to damp down overheating. Even fiscal policy will be constrained by the rules of the stability pact, at least in principle. In short, most domestic macroeconomic policy instruments will, for good or ill, be removed.

CONCLUSION

The story of fiscal and supportive monetary policy in Ireland over the past quarter century has been a chequered one. Excessive fiscal expansion brought the state close to the point where partial default might have been considered. Instead, a protracted and costly fiscal adjustment was undertaken in adverse external circumstances triggering an unexpectedly deep and lengthy recession. After an interval of adjustment fatigue in the mid-1980s, retrenchment resumed in more favourable circumstances from 1987 and the economy turned around more quickly than most had come to expect.

Many lessons were learnt along the way. For example, the limitations of tax increases as a means of correcting a deep fiscal imbalance became evident, as did the desirability of social consensus on the direction for fiscal policy. But the rapid growth of the economy in the 1990s has masked the need for further structural reforms in the design of taxation and spending policy, including welfare payments. This has been a period of missed opportunities, as the needed reforms will be harder to accomplish in bad times.

Nor has the 20-year history of the Irish pound as an independent currency been an unqualified success. It has been associated with very high and volatile interest rates and a fairly volatile exchange rate against all of the major trading partners. Nevertheless, it has to be acknowledged that the fiscal crisis was not allowed to spill over into monetary excesses and accelerating inflation, such as have been experienced in many other countries in fiscal crisis, and the financial system has proved sounder than most.

The economic recovery of the late 1980s owed much to external factors, but the successful fiscal correction, supported by a political and social consensus, injected a crucial element of long-term confidence about the direction of policy. That the recovery was sustained through the mid and later 1990s may also owe much to the legacy of the fiscal adjustment: to a succession of realistic and restrained national pay agreements, and to a sense of the need for self-reliance borne in on the new generation of labour force entrants by the recent history of adversity.

Notes

1. The figures are based on the public authorities' tables in the national accounts.
2. The fiscal impulse shown is from Bradley *et al.* (1997) and is based on the ESRI macroeconometric model. Note the procyclical pattern of fiscal impulse, also documented by Lane (1998). The simpler approach to measuring annual fiscal impulse suggested by Blanchard (1990) gives a broadly similar picture, but is not very precise for Ireland because the relationships between tax and transfer spending (on the one hand) and unemployment rates (on the other) is not sufficiently stable.
3. Both through reduction in aggregate demand and through knock-on effects of tax increases on wage rates (cf. Barry and Bradley, 1991).
4. On reasonable estimates, real cyclically-adjusted non-interest spending fell during this period.
5. Other major shocks with potential and actual fiscal consequences included the collapse of a state-owned shipping company and two large private insurance companies. All three resulted from imprudent risk-taking and poor financial planning.
6. The striking electoral success of a new party, the Progressive Democrats, committed to spending cuts and achieving 16 per cent of first preference votes in the election, may have contributed to the policy switch.
7. A squeeze on recruitment had already begun in 1981, with the result that Exchequer-financed employment had fallen by 2 per cent in 1982–85, compared with an increase of 15 per cent in the previous four years. The tighter policy from 1987 brought numbers back close to their 1978 level by 1991, yielding a gross saving in pay costs of the order of 2 per cent of GNP. Since 1991, the decline in numbers has only partly been reversed.
8. Structural fund receipts from the EU averaged 1.5 per cent of GNP in the 1980s, and 2.6 per cent in the 1990s. Payment timing of the other main source of EU funds, namely those associated with the Common Agricultural Policy, mean that published data can be misleading on the sequencing of fiscal policy changes in the late 1980s; the present discussion adjusts for this by treating the EU agricultural intervention agency as being off-shore. It is worth mentioning two other elements of non-tax receipts which can cause confusion. One is the consolidation of different accounts in the public sector which led to reduced gross figures for non-tax receipts and for the national debt (cf. Figure 4.6). The other is the exceptional recourse to central bank financing in 1985 and again in 1987–89. In order to help fund the cost of the 1985 ICI insurance company failure (cf. Honohan and Kelly, 1997), the bank advanced an amount equivalent to 0.6 per cent of GNP (to be repaid by 2000). In 1987–89, the bank brought forward dividend payments to the government to help finance the public service early retirement scheme: the amounts peaked at a cumulative 0.4 per cent of GNP by 1989, falling back substantially thereafter.
9. Ignoring the amnesty-bloated figure for 1988.
10. As of 1998 and compared with 1985, the top rate of income tax has come down from 65 per cent to 46 per cent; of corporation tax from 50 per cent to 32 per cent; of capital gains tax from 60 per cent to 20 per cent and of capital acquisitions tax from 55 per cent to 40 per cent.

11. It is interesting to note that as early as 1979, when he came into office, Taoiseach C. J. Haughey took the unusual step of making a television address to the nation in which he emphasised that there would have to be fiscal restraint. But action in line with these sentiments was not taken until much later.

12. The National Planning Board, an independent body of experts reporting in 1984, recommended only modest fiscal tightening at that juncture. Their proposals would not even have stabilized the debt-to-GNP ratio by 1987 (Honohan, 1988).

13. Cf. Alesina and Perotti (1997), Dornbusch (1989), Giavazzi and Pagano (1990). The historical material presented by these authors is not always totally accurate, and there is a risk of some very misleading mistakes becoming embedded in the literature. Thus, to take the most recent paper Alesina and Perotti (1997), for example:

    (i) It is not true to state that unemployment followed a rising trend for 25 years before 1988: in fact, Irish unemployment is quite closely correlated with UK unemployment and as such exhibited several cycles in the 1960s and 1970s. The rate in 1960 was 5.6 per cent, in 1979 it was 7.1 per cent having been as high as 9.9 per cent in 1976. The sharp increase in unemployment that began in 1979 mirrored the rise in UK unemployment at that time, as did the downturns in 1988–90 and 1994–97.

    (ii) The important devaluation improving the competitiveness of the Irish economy in 1987–89 occurred in August 1986, not 1987, and as such was not a deliberate part of the successful adjustment package embarked upon by the new government of 1987.

    (iii) The cuts in social spending after 1986 were not 'mainly in health' (cf. Honohan, 1992); it was before 1986 that health spending was cut.

14. A partial employment embargo had been in effect since 1981, but was tightened considerably in 1987. In addition an early retirement scheme was brought into play. Public sector employment fell, yielding savings of about 2 per cent of GNP per annum.

15. Consumer price inflation in this period included the effects of substantial increases in indirect taxes which did not directly affect international competitiveness; unit labour cost trends were severely distorted by composition changes as an increasing share of manufacturing was devoted to low labour-share sectors associated with tax-driven transfer pricing behaviour.

16. Regression results that imply a shift in the relative importance of UK and continental inflation during the early or mid-1980s do not prove it (Callan and Fitz Gerald, 1989; Kremers, 1990).

17. For instance, Rebelo (1997), summarising the experience of many countries which have used an exchange-rate based stabilisation, states that they

    tend to experience an increase in GDP, a large expansion of production in the non-tradable sector, a contraction in tradables production, a current account deterioration, an increase in the real wage, a reduction in unemployment, a sharp appreciation in the relative price of non-tradables and a boom in the real estate market.

This description has few points of contact with the Irish economy of the 1980s.

18. In April 1986 the Irish pound was at the lowest of the three modes.
19. About 5 per cent in the six months before the realignment of March 1983 – in which Ireland depreciated by 9 per cent against the DM, more than any other country; and about 15 per cent in the year before the 8 per cent unilateral realignment of August 1986 (cf. Figure 4.7).
20. Though it might be argued that this would not have happened if the real appreciation had emerged sufficiently slowly.
21. Improved debt management tactics also helped at that point, notably through a quiet pre-funding of 1987 needs on the international market in 1986.

References

Aghion, P. and Saint-Paul, G. (1991) 'On the Virtue of Bad Times: An Analysis of the Interaction between Economic Fluctuations and Productivity Growth', CEPR Discussion Paper, no. 578.

Alesina, A. and Drazen, A. (1991) 'Why are Stabilizations Delayed?', *American Economic Review*, 81, pp. 1170–88.

Alesina, A. *et al.* (1992) 'Default Risk on Government Debt in OECD Countries', *Economic Policy*, 7, pp. 427–63.

Alesina, A. and Perotti, R. (1995) 'Fiscal Expansions and Adjustments in OECD Countries', *Economic Policy*, 21, pp. 205–40.

Alesina, A. and Perotti, R. (1997) 'Fiscal Adjustments in OECD Countries: Composition and Macroeconomic Effects', *IMF Staff Papers*, 44, pp. 210–49.

Barry, F. G. and Bradley, J. (1991) 'On the Causes of Ireland's Unemployment', *Economic and Social Review*, 22, pp. 256–86.

Barry, F. G. and Devereux, M. B. (1992) 'Crowding-out Effects of Government Spending', *Economic and Social Review*, 23, pp. 199–221.

Barry, F. G. and Devereux, M. B. (1995) 'The "Expansionary Fiscal Contraction" Hypothesis: A Neo-Keynesian Analysis', *Oxford Economic Papers*, 47, pp. 249–64.

Bertola, G. and Drazen, A. (1993) 'Trigger Points and Budget Cuts: Explaining the Effects of Fiscal Austerity', *American Economic Review*, 83, pp. 11–26.

Blanchard, O. J. (1990) 'Suggestions for a New Set of Fiscal Indicators', OECD Economics and Statistics Department, working paper no. 79 (Paris: OECD).

Bradley, J., Fitz Gerald, J., Honohan, P. and Kearney, I. (1997) 'Interpreting the Recent Irish Growth Experience', in D. Duffy *et al.* (eds), *Medium-Term Review 1997–2003* (Dublin: ESRI).

Callan, T. and Fitz Gerald, J. (1989) 'Price Determination in Ireland: Effects of Changes in Exchange Rates and Exchange Rate Regimes', *Economic and Social Review*, 20, pp. 165–88.

Callan, T. and Nolan, B. (1992) 'Distributional Aspects of Ireland's Fiscal Adjustment', *Economic and Social Review*, 23, pp. 319–342.

Callan, T., Nolan, B. and Whelan, C. T. (1996) *A Review of the Commission on Social Welfare's Minimum Adequate Income* (Dublin: Economic and Social Research Institute).

Detragiache, E. and Hamann, A. J. (1997) 'Exchange-Rate Based Stabilization in Western Europe: Greece, Ireland, Italy and Portugal', IMF working paper WP/97/75.

Dornbusch, R. (1989) 'Credibility, Debt and Unemployment: Ireland's failed stabilization', *Economic Policy*, 8, pp. 173–209.

Geary, P.T. (1992) 'Ireland's Economy in the 1980s: Stagnation and Recovery, a Preliminary Review of the Evidence', *Economic and Social Review*, 23, pp. 253–81.

Giavazzi, F. and Pagano, M. (1990) 'Can Severe Fiscal Adjustments be Expansionary?', in O. J. Blanchard and S. Fischer (eds), *NBER Macroeconomics Annual 1990* (Cambridge, Mass.: MIT Press), pp. 75–111.

Giavazzi, F. and Pagano, M. (1996) 'Non-Keynesian Effects of Fiscal Policy Changes: International Evidence and the Swedish Experience', *Swedish Economic Policy Review*, 3, pp. 135–65.

Hallerberg, M. and von Hagen, J. (1997) 'Sequencing and the Size of the Budget: A Reconsideration', CEPR Discussion Paper, no. 1589.

Honohan, P. (1987) 'Macroeconomic and Fiscal Deviations from Plan 1985–87' in C. Ó Grada and R. Thom (eds), *Perspectives on Economic Policy* (Dublin: UCD Centre for Economic Research), 1, pp. 121–37.

Honohan, P. (1989) 'Comment on Dornbusch: "Credibility, Debt and Unemployment"', *Economic Policy*, 8, pp. 202–5.

Honohan, P. (1992) 'Fiscal Adjustment in Ireland in the 1980s', *Economic and Social Review*, 23, pp. 285–314.

Honohan, P. (1993) *An Examination of Irish Currency Policy* (Dublin: Economic and Social Research Institute).

Honohan, P. and Conroy, C. (1994a) *Irish Interest Rate Fluctuations in the European Monetary System* (Dublin: Economic and Social Research Institute).

Honohan, P. and Conroy, C. (1994b) 'Sterling Movements and Irish Pound Interest Rates', *Economic and Social Review*, 25, pp. 201–20.

Honohan, P. and Kelly, J. (1997) 'The Insurance Corporation Collapse: Resolving Ireland's Worst Financial Crash', *Administration*, 45, pp. 67–77.

Kremers, J. J. M. (1990) 'Gaining Policy Credibility for a Disinflation: Ireland's Experience in the EMS', *IMF Staff Papers*, 37, pp. 116–45.

Lane, P. R. (1998) 'On the Cyclicality of Irish Fiscal Policy', *Economic and Social Review*, 29(1), pp. 1–16.

Lane, P. R. and Perotti, R. (1995) 'Profitability, Fiscal Policy and Exchange Rate Regimes' mimeo, MIT.

Lynch, T. (1997) 'Ireland and the European Monetary System', M.Litt. thesis, Trinity College, Dublin.

Rebelo, S. (1997) 'What Happens When Countries Peg Their Exchange Rates? (The Real Side of Monetary Reforms)', CEPR Discussion Paper, no. 1692.

Rogoff, K. (1990) 'Equilibrium Political Business Cycles', *American Economic Review*, 80, pp. 21–36.

Saint-Paul, G. (1997) 'Business Cycles and Long-run Growth', CEPR Discussion Paper, no. 1642.

Seidman, D. (1987) 'The Strength of Parties in Dáil Éireann', *Economic and Social Review*, 19, pp. 61–8.

Tanzi, V. and Zee, H. H. (1997) 'Fiscal Policy and Long-run Growth', *IMF Staff Papers*, 44, pp. 179–209.

Walsh, B. M. (1993) 'Credibility, Interest Rates and the ERM: The Irish Experience, 1986–92', *Oxford Bulletin of Economics and Statistics*, 55, pp. 439–52.

5 The European Dimension: The Single Market and the Structural Funds

Frank Barry, John Bradley and Aoife Hannan

INTRODUCTION

Membership of the European Union has impacted on Ireland and the Irish economy in many ways. The primary focus of this chapter is on the impact of the Single Market process and the Structural Funds expenditure programmes. To many readers is might appear strange that we have little to say on the impact of the Common Agricultural Policy (CAP). There are two reasons for this. The first is that, as is clear from Chapter 1, agricultural output has not contributed to Ireland's dramatically improved output performance over the course of the 1990s, while employment in agriculture has continued to fall. Since the present study is concerned with identifying the causes of the strong performance of the economy, we need not therefore linger too long on agriculture. (This is not to suggest of course that agriculture is unimportant, merely that it is tangential to the present study.) The second reason why we ignore the consequences of the CAP is that is it difficult to determine the alternative or baseline scenario against which these consequences are to be measured. Is it, for example, a situation where an equivalent degree of protection has to be funded by domestic taxpayers and consumers, or is it instead a free world market in agricultural products? Fortunately we do not have to consider this difficult question here.

THE SINGLE MARKET

The Single European Market (SEM) programme was directed at the integration of the individual segmented national markets of the EU member states over an eight-year period up to 1992. Measures adopted included the relaxation of border controls, the harmonisation of technical standards, the opening up of public procurement, and the liberalisation of financial and other service sectors. These measures were predicted to facilitate efficiency-enhancing industrial restructuring and, by promoting competition, to reduce price discrimination across national markets. Most of the economic gains would come through standard supply-side effects of liberalisation such as lower production costs and increased productivity. The Cecchini Report, details of which are provided in Emerson *et al.* (1988), presented the results of detailed micro and macroeconomic studies that on balance predicted, over the medium term, a level of EU GNP about 4.5 per cent higher than it would otherwise have been, an extra 1 840 000 EU jobs, and some improvement in the overall external and budgetary balances of the member states.

A recent European Commission publication, Monti (1996), charts the progress that has been achieved so far towards reaching these goals. It reports that the Single Market programme has knocked more than 5 billion Ecus a year off the costs of European traders and road hauliers because they no longer have to stop at internal EU borders for routine customs and fiscal checks; that it has almost doubled the share of public sector purchases from other member states from 6 per cent in 1987 to 10 per cent in 1994; and that it has reduced the variance of EU prices for identical consumer goods from 26 per cent in 1980 to 19.5 per cent in 1993, and from 18 per cent to 14.5 per cent for identical equipment goods.

In overall macroeconomic terms, however, achievement of the Cecchini goals remains some distance away in the future. Monti (1996) reports that the most recent estimates of the consequences of the Single Market suggest that it has increased output in the EU by a little more than 1 per cent, and has raised the level of employment by between 300 000 and 900 000 jobs.[1] It is also noted that progress towards completion of the Single Market remains disappointing in at least two respects: that small and medium-sized companies have benefited less than larger companies, which had the structures to exploit new opportunities more dramatically, and that the whole programme has taken longer to implement than was originally anticipated. The report argues, however, that the process has allowed the poorer member states (including Ireland) to grow faster than the richer ones. The purpose of this section is to analyse this proposition with respect to Ireland, and to ask what contribution the Single Market has made to Ireland's recent growth performance.

Comprehensive analyses of the likely impact of the Single Market on the Irish economy were carried out by Bradley, Fitz Gerald and

Kearney (1992) and Barry *et al.* (1997). The first of these studies predicted that the impact on Irish GNP would be very close to that predicted by Cecchini for the overall EU, that is 4.5 per cent. That study largely followed the Cecchini methodology in analysing separately the effects of the four '1992' shocks – border controls, public procurement, financial services and the 'supply effects'. Thus, it is perhaps not so surprising that the results closely matched Cecchini's. The second study, however, which analysed the likely response of the other 'Objective 1' economies – Greece, Spain and Portugal – as well as Ireland, started from the position that the processes underlying the development of the small open economies of the EU periphery might be quite different from those underlying the development of the 'core' EU economies, upon which the Cecchini analysis had been based.

For example, the recent economic-geography and endogenous-growth literatures discussed in Chapter 2 above emphasise that peripheral and core economies can be affected by trade liberalisation in quite different ways. This led the authors to attempt to model the process by which non-tradeables become tradeable, and to pay attention to the determinants of whether the country's industries would be successful or not in these newly tradeable sectors. A further difference between the core and periphery is that foreign direct investment inflows from the core are one of the crucial factors determining periphery development.

The study by Barry *et al.* (1997) analysed the consequences for the EU periphery of a series of 1992-related shocks; the total factor productivity improvements alluded to by Cecchini; the gains and losses for individual sectors as trade liberalisation proceeds; the effects of structural change in the manufacturing sector as goods shift from the non-tradeable to the tradeable categories; and the effect on the structurally-changed small open economies of the increase in European demand for tradeables as the overall EU expands. Of these the second and the last shocks generally turned out to be the most important ones; the response of peripheral economies to both of these shocks turned out, in turn, to depend on the extent to which they were deemed able to attract FDI inflows.

Ireland's attractiveness as a base for MNCs and the contribution of FDI inflows to the recent growth performance have already been discussed in Chapter 3. We saw that US FDI inflows into Europe expanded quite dramatically in the late 1980s, and the US Department of Commerce Survey of Current Business (March 1991) attributes much of this to the Single Market initiative. We saw there also that Ireland's share of these inflows jumped dramatically in the early 1990s. In terms of FDI inflows alone, then, the Single Market programme proved highly beneficial for the Irish economy.[2]

Barry *et al.* (1997) supplemented their macroeconomic analysis with an attempt to model likely sectoral gains and losses. In modelling these, the authors were influenced by Krugman and Venables (1990) who argued, in contrast to the traditional view of international-trade theorists, that the net effect of the sectoral gains and losses resulting from trade liberalisation could be negative. This view was held because of the historically poor employment performance of indigenous manufacturing under free trade. In forming a view on which sectors would gain and which would lose, the authors made full use of the sectoral analysis reported in *European Economy* (1990). That analysis identified 40 out of about 120 NACE 3-digit manufacturing sectors as being likely to be affected by the Single Market. These sectors, characterised by high price dispersion across states, were ones in which restrictive public procurement policies operated or in which differences in national standards were found to hinder trade.

On the basis of the individual country study of Ireland presented in the *European Economy* (1990), and on subsequent work by its author, O'Malley (1992), sectors were classified into those that were predicted to do well, given Irish conditions (the S or 'successful' sectors), and those that were predicted to do badly in Ireland (the D or 'declining' sectors). The characteristics that determined whether a sector was in the S or D category were largely based on measures of revealed comparative advantage.[3] Both S and D sectors were then further subclassified by digits 1 and 2: a value of 1 indicating that these sectors right across the EU were deemed likely to be strongly affected, whether positively or negatively, by the SEM (as would be the case for sectors in which strongly restrictive public procurement policies applied pre-SEM), and a value of 2 indicating that these sectors were likely to be less strongly affected (for example when only quite low non-tariff barriers applied). The four-way classification of sectors into S1, S2, D1 and D2 is shown in Table 5.1.

We see that by 1987 Ireland was much more strongly represented in sectors in which it could be expected to be successful (62 000 jobs in S sectors in 1987), than it was in sectors in which it could be expected to do poorly (23 000 jobs in the D sectors at that date). In fact Ireland was the only one of the four EU periphery countries studied for which this finding emerged. Perhaps even more surprisingly, this finding was true for indigenous industry (with an employment level of over

Table 5.1   Sectors deemed likely to be affected by the Single Market (Job numbers)

	NACE	Sector	Indigenous 1987	Foreign 1987	Indigenous 1996 less 1987	Foreign 1996 less 1987
S1	330	Office and DP machinery	1 269	5 559	587	5 530
	344	Telecommunications equipment	696	3 246	679	5 508
	341	Insulated wires and cables	1 287	1 157	-540	284
	421	Cocoa, chocolate	445	2 211	74	209
	372	Medical and surgical equipment	417	4 436	380	2 578
S2	251	Basic industrial chemicals	1 186	1 247	-118	-294
	257	Pharmaceuticals	730	4 728	571	4 519
	345	Radios, TVs etc.	295	770	3	1 329
	346	Domestic electrical appliances	797	2 085	438	-512
	351	Motor vehicles	704	28	-119	-28
	428	Soft drinks	1 200	1 100	77	-145
	325	Plant for mines, steel	380	705	10	194
	364	Aerospace equipment	2 040	104	235	396
	413	Dairy products	9 591	421	-1 851	-171
	427	Brewing, malting	161	2 977	15	-1 400
	247	Glass and glassware	3 468	52	-637	-13
	322	Machine tools	517	336	377	-9
	323	Textile machinery	18	0	-17	0
	324	Food, chemical machinery	300	209	197	-130

Table 5.1 (Continued)

NACE	Sector	Indigenous 1987	Foreign 1987	Indigenous 1996 less 1987	Foreign 1996 less 1987	
326	Transmission equipment	57	48	1	17	
327	Other machinery	85	39	96	-32	
432	Cotton industry	48	1 572	-42	-693	
481	Rubber products	222	990	66	-155	
491	Jewellery	1 066	265	-293	115	
494	Toys and sports goods	252	336	-23	326	
						All S sectors
Total employment in S		27 231	34 621			61 852
Total employment change in S, of which:						
S1				166	17 423	17 589
S2				1 180	14 109	
				-1014	331	

						All D sectors
						23 306
D1	342	Electrical machinery	364	1 825	213	1 344	
	361	Shipbuilding	421	124	−104	7	
	417	Spaghetti, macaroni	41	0	−21	0	
D2	256	Other chemical products	255	1 087	122	226	
	321	Agricultural machinery	1 257	47	327	5	
	493	Photographic labs	271	0	100	0	
	431	Wool industry	1 001	767	−51	−670	
	453	Clothing	9 023	4 835	−3 261	−2 342	
	455	Household textiles	756	302	−107	−120	
	248	Ceramic goods	523	277	322	−84	
	347	Electric lamps	93	37	−66	−37	
	438	Carpets, floor coverings	0	0	16	0	
	451	Footwear	0	0	0	0	
Total employment in D			14 005	9 301			
Total employment change in D of which:					−2 510	−1 671	−4 181
D1					88	1 351	
D2					−2 598	−3 022	

Source: Barry *et al.* (1997).

27 000 in S sectors compared to a level of 14 000 in D sectors) as well as for the foreign manufacturing sector (with a ratio of almost 35 000 jobs in S to 9000 jobs in D).

On the basis of assumptions made about the increased import penetration of the D sectors and the increased export market share of the S sectors, Barry *et al.* (1997) predicted that this industrial restructuring effect would be of about the same magnitude as the effect on the economy of the European SEM-driven expansion. In terms of the latter, the study generally found an almost one-for-one response by Ireland to more rapid EU growth, because of the openness of the economy.[4] Hence its conclusion that Ireland would do substantially better out of the Single Market than would the richer countries of the EU. We can see from the outcomes in the table that our sectoral predictions have been largely borne out: employment growth in the S sectors totalled almost 18 000 in the period 1987–96 (with the vast bulk of this occurring in the S1 sectors), while employment in the D sectors declined by 4000. Furthermore, both indigenous and foreign industry expanded in the S sectors and declined in the D sectors.[5]

Can it be concluded, then, from Table 5.1 that

1. indigenous industry suffered from the SEM, since its expansion in the S sectors was less than its contraction in the D sectors; and
2. that the SEM accounts for almost all of the increase in foreign manufacturing in Ireland over this period (since the net increase in the table above, at almost 17 000, is close to the actual increase of 19 000 over the 1987–96 period)?

The answer on both counts is no. First, recall that these sectoral effects come on top of the expansionary effects on the whole economy of the increase in EU GDP, which Cecchini predicted to be around 4.5 per cent and which Monti (1996) calculates at a little over 1 per cent; these would have had further beneficial effects, even on home-market-oriented indigenous industry. Secondly, we can see from the table that the biggest declines in both indigenous and foreign employment were in the clothing sector; while this was predicted to do badly on account of the SEM, the decline seen is a continuation of the long-term trend for this sector. Thirdly, Ireland's success in quadrupling its share of US FDI inflows into the EU between 1983 and 1993 can hardly be ascribed solely, if at all, to the development of the Single Market.

One can conclude unequivocally, however, that the Single Market has been of net benefit to the Irish economy. Furthermore, Ireland appeared to benefit more than the EU core countries (since the effects on these countries were the ones computed in the Cecchini Report), and the Single Market would therefore have hastened Irish real convergence. In the light of this finding, it is paradoxical that Ireland should have done so well in terms of its allocation of the increased Structural Funds available from 1989 onwards, since part of the rationale for the increased funding levels was the fear that further market integration would widen regional disparities.[6]

THE STRUCTURAL FUNDS

From the date of Ireland's entry into the then European Economic Community (EEC) in 1973, structural assistance was received from the Regional Development and Social Funds (ERDF and ESF) as well as from the guidance section of the Agricultural Guidance and Guarantee Fund (FEOGA). In 1988, as the move to market completion started in earnest, the range of structural funds programmes was reformed, reorganised and expanded. This entailed the development of the Community Support Frameworks (CSF) as coherent multi-year programmes agreed between the Commission and the national authorities, with the aim of promoting economic and social cohesion throughout the EU.

The first CSF (also referred to as the Delors I package) ran for five years from 1989–93, and the second (referred to as Delors II) spanned the six-year period 1994–99. These programmes are funded by a combination of Community, domestic national authority and domestic private-sector finance. In what follows we are concerned with evaluating the contribution of Community funding only. In addition to the CSF programmes, however, other EU structural funds are disbursed through the Cohesion funds, the EEA financial mechanism and through Community initiatives (Honohan, 1997, p. 4). Since these non-CSF funds cover measures and projects closely related to those financed by the CSF, we will attempt to gross up the estimated impact of EU-funded CSF spending to take them into account.

Following the reforms of 1988, the level of EU structural funding was increased substantially. This is shown in Figure 5.1, where the bar measures the funding level in millions of pounds and the line shows funding as a percentage of GNP. Thus, while funding levels remained largely constant over the course of the 1990s, funding as a proportion of GNP fell because of the strong GNP growth during this period.

Figure 5.1   Structural fund receipts, 1975–79

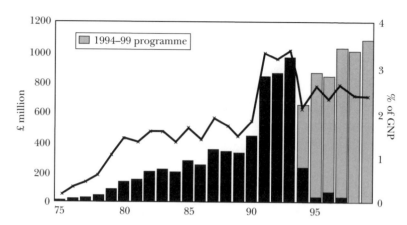

Source: Honohan, 1997, p. 29.

Total EU funding of the first CSF and related programmes amounted to around 3500 million pounds, in 1994 prices (ESRI, 1993, p. 217). Funding of the second CSF amounted to around 4600 million, also in 1994 prices (Honohan, 1997, p. 23), on top of which came another 1500 million in non-CSF structural funds over the second CSF.[7]

The CSF investment funding programmes under discussion serve three main functions:

- to develop the economy's stock of physical infrastructure;
- to assist private sector development in areas such as investment, marketing and innovation; and
- to contribute to the development of the human resources of the economy through professional and technical training and through job retraining.

The allocation of expenditure across the most heavily funded functions, for the two CSF programmes and for total structural funds during the Delors II period, is shown in Table 5.2. The bulk of spending on physical infrastructure goes on roads and, to a lesser extent, on other transport facilities such as ports and airports. This spending is designed to offset the significant adverse effects that high transport

Table 5.2   Allocation of CSF and Structural Funds

	Allocation of CSF funds, 1989–93 (%)	Allocation of CSF funds, 1994–99	Allocation of structural funds, 1994–99
Physical infrastructure	29	19.8	36.3
Human resources	30.3	30.8	28.4
Production/investment aid to the private sector of which:			25.8
industry and services	22.9	26.4	
agriculture, forestry and fisheries	17.7	18.2	
Income support			9.5

Source: ESRI (1993), p. 218; Honohan, pp. 24, 34.

costs have on the competitiveness of Irish business.[8] Smaller initiatives are directed towards sectors such as energy and telecommunications, where ongoing infrastructural spending is carried out by the enterprises directly involved in service provision, such as the ESB (electricity) and Telecom Eireann (telecommunications). The purpose of this structural fund spending is to raise productivity in the rest of the private sector through reducing transport, energy and other business costs.

Spending on the training programmes categorised under human resource development, as well as on infrastructure, is justified through appeal to the 'externalities' associated with such development; this means that not all of the benefits of an increased stock of human capital in the economy, for example, accrue to the individuals who participate in the education or training (Lucas, 1988). Thus, if a more highly educated workforce increases the attractiveness of the economy for foreign direct investment, the FDI inflows will raise the demand for unskilled labour also. The macroeconomic effects of these programmes are felt through a reduction in unit labour costs.

The rationale behind expenditure on productive services is less clear, since these are activities that businesses would normally be expected to undertake for themselves. Some, however, would offer the so-called 'infant-industry' argument as justification; that is, the notion that industry in a late-developing economy will be at a disadvantage in world markets because of the extent of learning-by-doing already achieved by incumbent competitors (O'Malley, 1989). Others would point to the possibility that a certain threshold of economic activity must occur before a take-off into self-sustained growth can be achieved (ESRI, 1993, p. 11). This is related to the 'big push' theory of economic development, rejuvenated recently by Murphy, Shleifer and Vishny (1989). On a practical level, this spending will stimulate business activity through reducing the cost of capital.

The impact of all these spending programmes can be categorised in terms of demand (short-run) and supply (longer-run) effects. All programmes will have demand effects, for example as construction work is undertaken on new infrastructural and private-sector investment projects, and as trainees are taken onto new courses. This expenditure will raise income and labour demand in the short term. The rationale of the expenditure programmes, however, is that even when this initial round of spending is finished, the consequences of the enhanced productivity of workers and the enhanced profitability of businesses will remain; these are the longer-term supply-side effects.

The demand-side consequences are relatively easy to evaluate, as the mechanisms through which economies respond to expenditure shocks have been the traditional subject matter of macroeconomics; the benefits of increased spending fall primarily on non-tradeable services and construction sectors in Ireland; employment rises in these sectors, wages respond (which hurts the tradeable sector and worsen the trade balance), and the employment increase is eventually halted. Recognition of the crucial importance of the supply-side effects is of much more recent origin, however, and the methodology employed in recent studies of the effects of structural fund spending in Ireland – Bradley *et al.* (1992), ESRI (1993), Barry *et al.* (1997) and Honohan (1997) – is still at the exploratory stage.

These studies attempt to capture the externality effects discussed above through assuming that particular rates of return apply to particular forms of expenditure. The rates of return assumed are generally in line with those reported in international studies. Achievement of any given rate of return requires, of course, that the expenditure be carefully targeted and be undertaken with care; it is to ensure this that evaluations such as ESRI (1993) and Honohan (1997) are commissioned by the domestic public authorities and the European Commission. Reports from the European Commission are positive towards these aspects of Irish expenditures, and the most recent evaluation is very upbeat, concluding that

> capacity and capability have been increased in the productive sectors; there has been a quantum leap in the provision of public infrastructure; education and training attainment forges ahead; and experimental institutional arrangements have galvanised local initiatives.
> (Honohan, 1997, p. xv)

Notwithstanding this optimistic assessment of how well the structural funds have been spent, all the studies use conservative estimates of the appropriate externality elasticities.

The rates of return assumed on public infrastructure can be compared to Munnell (1993), who, in a survey of econometric results, reports that the elasticity with respect to public capital ranges from an upper bound of 0.39 for the entire US, through 0.2–0.15 for individual states, to lower bounds of 0.08–0.03 for individual metropolitan areas. All the Irish studies test the sensitivity of results to different values of the elasticities chosen; generally it is varied between 0.0 and 0.1 (Barry *et al.*, 1997; ESRI, 1993, p. 309).

The rate of return on investment in education in Honohan (1997) is 7.5 per cent (that is, 0.075); this is conservative in comparison with Psacharopoulos (1994), who found that even in the richer OECD countries, the social rate of return to higher education (which is the least beneficial case) is over 8 per cent. Taking into account their microeconomic critique of the operation of various training schemes in Ireland, the Honohan study assumes a lower rate of return of about 6 per cent for investment in training (Honohan, 1997, p. 43).

Aid to the private sector is typically assumed not to have externality effects. The impact on private investment of a change in the grant provision can be modelled directly, however (Bradley, Fitz Gerald and Kearney, 1993). The longer-term effects of the increase in supply, resulting in higher exports and employment, can then be tracked through a macroeconometric model; either the ESRI Medium-Term Macromodel used in three of the four Irish studies mentioned above, or the smaller more experimental HERMIN model used in Barry *et al.* (1997). The procedure used in all studies is to define a baseline scenario of how the economy might be expected to develop into the future in the absence of structural funds. The model is then run into the future with the structural funds expenditure taken into account, and the results are then compared with the benchmark case.[9]

The various studies carried out report fairly similar results. Barry *et al.* (1997) report results for the Delors I and II CSF packages combined under the assumption of zero, low and high elasticities; in the low elasticities case, externality elasticities associated with public infrastructure and human capital that operate directly on manufacturing output are set at 0.05 and all other are set at 0.02; in the high elasticities case the first group are set at 0.1 and the others at 0.04. Table 5.3 presents the study's estimates of the impact on real GDP in various years on the assumption that EU CSF funding halts in 1999.

The zero externalities case reported in the bottom row of the table isolates the demand-side effects of the CSF expenditures. Real GDP in 1999 is estimated to be 1.9 per cent higher than it would have been in the absence of this stimulus to domestic demand. Once the funding is stopped (in 1999 by assumption) the demand effects obviously disappear. With high externalities, by contrast, the combination of demand and supply effects serves to almost double the estimated effect on 1999 GDP. After that date the demand-side effects again disappear, though the supply-side effects remain since the economy is left with a greater stock of both physical infrastructure and human capital. Thus GDP in the year 2000 would be 1.4 per cent higher than in the absence of these supply-side effects. Since stocks depreciate over time, however, GDP by the year 2010 is only around 1 per cent higher than it would otherwise have been.

Table 5.4 reports results from Honohan (1997) of the estimated effects on GDP, GNP, employment and a host of other variables *of the Delors II package only.* Care must be taken in comparing the two tables above since the first study includes the effects of both Delors I and II. If there were no externalities, then the 1.7 per cent effect on 1995 GDP seen in the first table would represent the effect of Delors II only (since there would be no lingering supply side effects from Delors I). This number is very close then to the 1.8 per cent increase

Table 5.3 Effects on real GDP of EU-funded Delors I and II CSF programmes

	1995	*1999*	*2000*	*2010*
High externalities	2.7	3.5	1.4	0.9
Low externalities	2.2	2.7	n.a.	n.a.
No externalities	1.7	1.9	0	0

Source: Barry *et al.* (1997).

in 1995 GDP reported in the second table. The 2.7 per cent reported in the top table for 1999 in the low externality case includes a lingering supply-side effect of Delors I that must be well below 1 per cent, and so while the Honohan (1997) study is more optimistic about overall CSF effects, the gap between the 1999 results also may not be too large.

Figures 5.2 and 5.3 (taken from Honohan, 1997, Figures A and B, p. xix) show the overall results of the Honohan study on the combined effects of the CSF I and II packages. The authors of that study conclude that the combined effect in the period 1995 to 1999 is to raise the level of GNP by between 3 and 4 per cent above the level it would have been without EU funding of the CSF. The long-run impact of the two CSF packages after termination in 1999 will be to raise the level of GNP by about 2 per cent above the level it would have been without them, according to Honohan (1997), and by about 1 per cent according to Barry *et al*. (1997).

Table 5.4   Effects of EU-funded CSF II only

	1995	*1999*	*2000*	*2005*
GDP	1.8	2.7	1.2	0.7
GNP	2.3	3.1	1.2	0.9
Employment (000s)	20.4	32.7	6.1	1.3

Source: Honohan (1997).

Figure 5.2   CSF 1989–93 and 1994–99

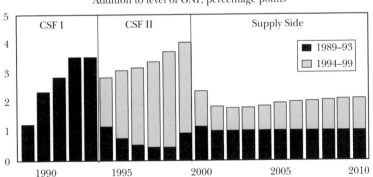

Addition to level of GNP, percentage points

Source: Honohan (1997).

Figure 5.3   Ireland compared to EU

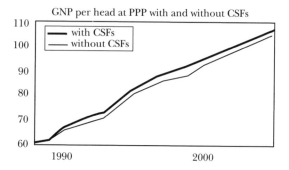

Even multiplying these results by the ratio of the total Structural Funds to CSF funding (that is, by a factor of about 1.3) cannot change the conclusion that the proportion of recent national income growth accounted for by the Structural Funds is very low (contributing perhaps one half of one percentage point per annum to GNP growth over the course of the 1990s, to yield around the 4 per cent increase in 1997 GNP that we intuit from Figure 5.2).[10] There are several (related) reasons, however, why one might not like to push this conclusion too far. One is that the studies cited have all been rather conservative in terms of the externality elasticities adopted. While such conservatism is warranted in the context of studies that seek to advise policy-makers on the likely consequences of large and often dramatic expenditure changes, the conclusions derived from such an approach may well prove overly pessimistic. This is certainly the position of de Melo and Robinson (1992) to whom externalities are so pervasive and of such magnitude that 'if there are externalities to be exploited, policymakers should pursue them aggressively, and not worry overmuch about getting the instruments just right'.

The second reason why these studies may have underestimated the effects of the CSF is that expenditures can have highly non-linear effects, while the models used to study the effects tend to be largely linear. Thus the models suggest that a £15 million expenditure will have three times the effect of a £5 million one, whereas in fact if the first project represents the completion of a major road artery while the second represents simply the development of some minor roads, the relative effects will be very much greater (see, for example, Kelly, 1997).

A third reason is that the interaction between various policy changes may give rise to much more dramatic effects than would emerge were all the changes to take place in isolation. For example, we saw in Chapter 3 above that US FDI inflows into the EU expanded considerably in the lead-in to the Single Market, and that the proportion of these flows that Ireland captured also increased considerably. The latter may not have occurred had not Irish physical infrastructure been improving substantially during this period, and had the fiscal crisis not been successfully overcome. For all of these reasons it may be impossible to isolate the precise contribution of any one of these factors to recent Irish growth and convergence.

CONCLUSIONS

Part of the rationale for the large increase in structural funds allocated from 1989 onwards was the belief that the move towards a Single European market would widen regional disparities within the EU. We have argued that this is unlikely to have been the case for Ireland, and for Portugal and Spain as well. Of the countries of the EU periphery only Greece, it appears, may have benefited less than the economies of the EU core. Though even EU Commission evaluations recognise that the benefits achieved up to now fall far short of those predicted by the Cecchini Report, many measures have been implemented, transnational transport costs and price disparities have fallen, and public procurement policies have been liberalised. To the extent that the EU core has gained from these measures, we find that the direct benefits to Ireland have been at least as large. The indirect benefits, however, may be much more substantial since the 1992 project triggered a dramatic increase in US FDI into the EU, much of which went into sectors that had been predicted to be strongly affected by the Single Market programme, and Ireland, we find, has succeeded in capturing a very much increased share of these inflows.

We went on to consider the effects on the Irish economy of EU-funded CSF expenditures. The studies we surveyed reach broadly similar conclusions; that is, that these expenditures may have raised GNP in the late 1990s by 3 to 4 percentage points above what it would otherwise have been. These effects are probably about evenly divided between short-run demand-side and longer-lasting supply-side effects. Finally, we considered some arguments that suggest that these estimates may err on the pessimistic side. Of these perhaps the strongest is that the interaction between the various changes in the policy environment, such as the simultaneous occurrence of the fiscal stabilisation, the move towards a single market and the rapid development of infrastructure, may have given rise to much more dramatic results than would have emerged had the effects of all these changes been evaluated in isolation from each other.

Notes

1. EU-12 output per capita by 1993 was a little over 1 per cent higher than it would have been if the EU had continued to expand at its pre-1987 rate, while Japanese output was only 0.2 per cent higher and US output was 2 per cent lower; Monti (1996, p. 106). Model simulations of the SEM effects, he reports, show the same result arising by 1994.
2. Indeed Chapter 3 above understates the case by concentrating on US FDI inflows; Monti (1996) points out that 'the smaller Benelux countries in the geographical core of the EU, and Ireland, Spain and Portugal on its periphery, were the main gainers of foreign investment coming from other EU states' (p. 85).
3. This is somewhat problematic since these would have been strongly influenced by the performance of MNCs within the sector, though our results below suggest that this worry may be overstated.
4. In traditional small open economy (SOE) models export-market growth should not exert demand effects on the tradeable sector of the SOE, other than through its influences on world prices. Barry et al. (1997) adopt the MNC-location model of Bradley and Fitz Gerald (1988) to surmount this difficulty.
5. Nor were these predictions made 'after the fact'. When the Barry et al. (1997) study was written the Irish Censuses of Industrial Production were not yet available for the 1990s, and the authors did not at the time have access to the Forfás employment surveys which have been used in the present analysis.
6. In a study of the four EU periphery countries, Barry et al. (1997) found that Ireland and Portugal were likely to do better from the Single Market than would the EU core countries, while Greece and Spain would do worse. If the increased FDI inflows into Spain since the late 1980s were considered a Single Market effect rather than an EU accession effect, however, Spain would also benefit more from the SEM than would the EU core.
7. Exact details of the two Irish CSFs are contained in the CSF treaty documents, EC (1990) and EC (1994).
8. While Krugman and Venables (1990) warn that lower transport costs can harm industry in peripheral regions under certain conditions, we argued above in Chapter 3 that these conditions do not apply to the highly export-oriented foreign sector of Irish manufacturing, and no longer apply to Irish indigenous industry.

9. By expressing the structural funds effect relative to the benchmark case, the importance of the assumptions one makes in defining the benchmark case diminishes significantly.

10. Gaspar and Pereira (1992), using a totally different modeling approach, come to almost exactly this conclusion for the impact of the CSF on Portugal. Rather than the static models discussed above, they work with a growth model that incorporates externalities, and find the impact of the CSF on Portuguese GDP growth to be around 0.4 percentage points.

References

Barry, F., Bradley, J., Hannan, A., McCartan, J. and Sosvilla-Rivero, S. (1997) *The Single Market Review: Aggregate and Regional Impact – The cases of Greece, Spain, Ireland and Portugal*, (London: Kogan Page in association with the Commission of the European Communities).

Bradley, J. and Fitz Gerald, J. (1988) 'Industrial Output and Factor Input Determination in an Econometric Model of a Small Open Economy', *European Economic Review*, 32, pp. 1227–41.

Bradley, J., Fitz Gerald, J. and Kearney, I. (1992) *The Role of the Structural Funds: Analysis of Consequences for Ireland in the Context of 1992*, Policy Research Series no. 13, (Dublin: The Economic and Social Research Institute).

Bradley, J., Fitz Gerald, J. and Kearney, I. (1993) 'Modelling Supply in an Open Economy using a Restricted Cost Function', *Economic Modelling*, January, pp. 11–21.

de Melo, J. and Robinson, S. (1992) 'Productivity and Externalities: Models of Export-led Growth', *Journal of International Trade and Economic Development*, 1(1), pp. 41–69.

Economic and Social Research Institute (ESRI) (1993) *The Community Support Framework 1989–93: Evaluation and Recommendations for the 1994–97 Framework* (Dublin: Economic and Social Research Institute).

Emerson, M., Aujean, M., Catinat, M., Goybet, P. and Jacquemin, A. (1988) *The Economics of 1992: The E.C. Commission's Assessment of the Economic Effects of Completing the Internal Market* (Oxford: Oxford University Press).

European Commission (1990) *Community Support Framework 1989–93: Ireland* (Luxembourg: Office for Official Publications of the European Communities).

European Commission (1992) 'The Impact of the Internal Market by Industrial Sector', *European Economy*, special issue.

European Commission (1994) *Community Support Framework 1994–99: Ireland* (Luxembourg: Office for Official Publications of the European Communities).

Gaspar, V. and Pereira, A. (1992) 'A Dynamic GE Analysis of EC Structural Funds, with an Application to Portugal', working paper, University of California at San Diego.

Honohan, P. (ed.) (1997) *EU Structural Funds in Ireland: A Mid-Term Evaluation of the CSF 1994–99*, Policy Research series no. 31 (Dublin: The Economic and Social Research Institute).

Kelly, M. (1997) 'The Dynamics of Smithian Growth', *Quarterly Journal of Economics*, August, pp. 939–64.

Krugman, P. and Venables, A. (1990) 'Integration and the Competitiveness of Peripheral Industry', in C. Bliss and J. Braga de Macedo (eds), *Unity with Diversity in the European Economy* (Cambridge: Cambridge University Press).

Lucas, R. (1988) 'On the Mechanics of Economic Development', *Journal of Monetary Economics*, 22, pp. 3–42.

Monti, M. (1996) *The Single Market and Tomorrow's Europe: A Progress Report from the European Commission* (London: Kogan Page in association with the Office for Official Publications of the European Communities).

Munnell, A. (1993) 'An Assessment of Trends in and Economic Impacts of Infrastructure Investment', in *Infrastructure Policies for the 1990s* (Paris: OECD).

Murphy, K. M., Shleifer, A. and Vishny, R. W. (1989) 'Industrialisation and the Big Push', *Journal of Political Economy*, 97(5), pp. 1003–26.

O'Malley, E. (1989) *Industry and Economic Development: The Challenge for the Latecomer* (Dublin: Gill & Macmillan).

O'Malley, E. (1992) 'Industrial Structure and Economies of Scale in the Context of 1992', in *The Role of the Structural Funds: Analysis of the Consequences for Ireland in the Context of 1992*, Policy Research series no. 13 (Dublin: The Economic and Social Research Institute).

Psacharopoulos, G. (1994). 'Returns to Investment in Education: A Global Update', *World Development*, 22(9), pp. 1325–43.

6 Education and Growth in the Irish Economy

Joseph Durkan, Doireann Fitz Gerald and Colm Harmon[1]

INTRODUCTION

The link between education and economic growth derives from two areas of research – the first deals with individual returns to education while the second examines the impact of education on human capital as one element in a growth model.

Post-compulsory education in general, and higher education in particular, contribute to wealth creation in the economy in many ways. For example, technology transfer and direct links between education/ research institutions and business/industry, which improve the capacity of the economy to appropriate the benefits of technological advances made elsewhere, serve to enhance both the economic well-being and social cohesion of a region. Some of these benefits, in the form of higher wages, are captured by the individuals who make the investments in their own 'human' capital that generate this wealth creation.

The recent resurgence of interest in the theory of economic growth has stimulated an interest in indices of human capital stocks. This literature describes the behaviour of economies using aggregate production functions – hence the need for aggregate indices of human and physical capital. Empirical work in this literature has concentrated heavily on cross-section regressions in order to explain the determinants of economic growth. Thus, measures of human capital which are amenable to cross-country comparisons are preferred in empirical work. In consequence, some of the measures used are very crude. For instance, Mankiw, Romer and Weil (1992) and Barro (1991) use school enrolment rates as a proxy for human capital stocks. Other studies on developing-country growth such as Romer (1990) have used literacy rates as a proxy for human capital stocks. The crudeness of these measures has been recognised, and several attempts have been made to come up with measures which make theoretical sense, and can be calculated using available data.

Different theories of human capital emphasise different characteristics and formation processes. Education, on-the-job training, work experience and health have all been emphasised as determining labour quality. If these theories are correct, the human capital embodied in the labour force and employed population will depend on the education received by individuals in the past, the age structure, the experience of unemployment, the prevalence of on-the-job training, the state of medical technology and the healthiness of the environment.

This chapter begins with a discussion of the theory of human capital. The next section outlines the methodology from which an indicator of the impact the education sector has has on economic growth may be estimated for Ireland. The third section presents the results obtained, and discusses possible refinements. Concluding sections discuss some international comparisons and the implications of the findings.

THEORY OF HUMAN CAPITAL AND ESTIMATES OF THE ECONOMIC RETURN TO SCHOOLING

Human Capital Theory

Analysis of the demand for education is guided by issues central to the classic human capital approach as pioneered by Gary Becker (1964) and Jacob Mincer (1974), in particular the notion of education as an investment of current time and effort in return for future returns. The benchmark model for the development of empirical issues in schooling returns is the key relationship developed by Mincer (1974). In this framework, assuming a given stock of homogeneous human capital at the point where schooling begins, the model explores the schooling decision denoted by years of schooling.

The earnings equation as pioneered by Mincer (1974) is:

$$y_i = \alpha \mathbf{X}_i + \beta S_i + \delta E_i + \gamma E_i^2 + u_i$$

where y_i is an earnings measure for an individual i such as earnings per hour/week, S_i represents a measure of their schooling, E_i is an experience measure (typically age or age when person left schooling), $\mathbf{X}_i$ is a set of other variables assumed to affect earnings, and u_i is a disturbance term representing other forces which may not be explicitly measured, usually assumed independent of $\mathbf{X}_i$ and S_i. Experience is included as a quadratic term to capture the concavity of the earnings profile.

β can be considered the private return to schooling (see Ashenfelter, Harmon and Oosterbeek (1998) for more details).[2]

The Irish Education System

The Irish educational system has changed substantially since the 1960s. Comprehensive descriptions can be found elsewhere (Tussing, 1978; Sexton and O'Connell, 1997), but a brief overview is provided here. The system is split into primary, secondary and third levels. Primary school typically starts at five years of age, and ends at 12, upon which the individual enters secondary school. At the end of primary school there was an examination known as the Primary Certificate. This was abandoned in the late 1960s as secondary education was developed and state funding at the second level meant the removal of fees. This fee-paying aspect to secondary education was a major hurdle for families, so typically among the older generation those that received secondary/third level education came from a wealthier socio-economic background. For the modern student the secondary school is where the decision to leave first presents itself. The minimum school leaving age was raised from 14 to 15 in 1972, again as part of the general restructuring of the education system.

The first of the state exams are now studied for at second level. The Group Certificate and Intermediate Certificate were usually examined at approximately ages 15 or 16. The Group Certificate was typically taken by those with a more vocational aspect to their talents, with the academically more rigorous Intermediate Certificate usually, but not always, leading the student to study for the final Leaving Certificate examination, which ends their secondary schooling at approximately age 18.[3] Following on from this is third level study to certificate, diploma, degree or postgraduate level. Participation in education at third level has, over the years, been highly skewed, with high levels of participation for the children of those with higher occupational status, and much lower participation for those whose parents were engaged in unskilled or semi-skilled manual occupations. However, the intro-duction of a means-tested third-level grant system in line with the general restructuring already outlined opened up the university system to many who otherwise would not have taken their education to this level. Concurrent with this grant system an expansion of the third-level sector took place with the development of the Regional Technical Colleges, which typically offered sub-degree-level courses in engineer-ing, the sciences and business studies. A summary indication of the changes in the system can be gleaned from the fact that the proportion of the age-cohort taking the Junior cycle examinations rose from about 40 per cent in 1967 to close to 100 per cent in 1994; and the proportion taking Senior cycle examinations rose from about 21 per cent to about 82 per cent. (Whelan, Smyth and Hannan, 1996).

Private Returns to Schooling for Ireland

Many of the earlier studies on economic returns to schooling are discussed in Durkan, Sheehan and Walsh (1993). One publication of a human capital earnings function estimated on Irish data is Walsh and Whelan (1976), using 1972 data from a restricted category of the labour force, but little has been achieved in the interim period owing to the lack of microeconomic data for Ireland over this period. The Walsh and Whelan study showed returns to schooling of around 3 per cent per year, which is modest compared to recent international estimates but in line generally with the findings for the time (see Psacharopoulos, 1973). There is also some evidence of credentialism in the system, with 'spikes' in the returns to schooling at common exit points from the system corresponding to the points where certified state examinations are taken.

Reilly (1987) estimates Mincerian type earnings functions on a sample of employed youth workers aged 15–24. Unlike Walsh and Whelan, this study does not consider years of schooling, but rather controls for education by the inclusion of dummy variables for the different level of attainment. However, annualising the suggested returns would indicate a higher return than the earlier Walsh and Whelan study. A similar sample was used by Sexton et al. (1988) and largely supported the findings of Reilly (1987).

The advent of large-scale micro-level data in the 1987 ESRI survey of Income Distribution, Poverty and Usage of State Services allowed for work comparable to the typical large-sample studies of other countries. Callan and Wren (1994) estimate returns to a year of schooling in the order of 6–7 per cent, with some evidence of a male–female differential in the returns at lower schooling levels. The same dataset was used in Callan and Harmon (1998) where two different specifications are estimated, using four different subsets of the dataset: all suitable male employees, and three different age groups. Given econometric problems involved in estimating wage equations for women, both specifications are estimated for men only. In the first equation, the log of hourly wages is regressed on dummies for various education levels, on years in work and years in work squared (YRSW), on years unemployed and years unemployed squared (YRSNW), and on various other variables. Those with only primary education are the base group. In the second equation, the log of hourly wages is regressed on years of education, years in work and years in work squared, years unemployed and years unemployed squared, and on various other variables. Table 6.1 illustrates the Callan and Harmon findings.

The specific estimates for educational returns as reported in columns (1) and (5) for the complete sample, clearly show a positive and significant return almost 8 per cent per schooling year, while higher educational qualifications are consistently associated with higher wage rates suggesting strong returns to credentials. Returns for each of the three

Table 6.1 Wage equations (least squares estimates): overall and by age cohort

	All		*Age 18–32*		*Age 33–49*		*Age 50–64*	
	Coeff.	*Std. error*	*Coeff.*	*Std. error*	*Coeff.*	*Std. error*	*Coeff.*	*Std. error*
Equation	*(1)*		*(2)*		*(3)*		*(4)*	
YEARED	0.083	0.005	0.092	0.012	0.085	0.009	0.088	0.011
YRSW	0.045	0.004	0.121	0.014	0.054	0.021	0.085	0.050
YRSW^2	−0.001	0.000	−0.004	0.000	−0.008	0.000	−0.001	0.000
YRSNW	−0.021	0.008	−0.099	0.024	−0.015	0.012	−0.035	0.023
YRSNW^2	−0.000	0.000	−0.002	0.003	−0.000	0.001	−0.002	0.000
Equation	*(5)*		*(6)*		*(7)*		*(8)*	
SECOND	0.160	0.040	0.082	0.088	0.120	0.059	0.188	0.078
GROUP	0.162	0.041	0.058	0.082	0.107	0.059	0.221	0.123
INTER	0.195	0.041	0.058	0.081	0.144	0.073	0.151	0.098
LEAVING	0.374	0.038	0.193	0.081	0.385	0.060	0.573	0.088
OTH3RD	0.505	0.053	0.395	0.103	0.450	0.085	0.573	0.108
DEGREE	0.794	0.050	0.847	0.110	0.710	0.076	0.736	0.105
YRSW	0.046	0.004	0.122	0.014	0.043	0.021	−0.018	0.054
YRSW^2	−0.001	0.000	−0.004	0.001	−0.001	0.001	0.000	0.001
YRSNW	−0.034	0.008	−0.030	0.023	−0.037	0.012	−0.039	0.023
YRSNW^2	0.001	0.001	−0.001	0.003	−0.001	0.001	0.001	0.002
N	1 144		464		456		224	

Notes: YEARED = years of schooling; YRSW/YRSNW = years since school finished spent working/not working; SECOND = some second level above Primary Certificate minimum level; GROUP/INTER/LEAVING = educated to Group/Intermediate/Leaving Certificate level; OTH3RD = some (non-degree) third level; DEGREE = educated to degree (including postgraduate) level.
Source: 1987 ESRI Survey. Reprinted from Callan and Harmon (1998)).

lowest levels of qualification (some secondary education, Group or Intermediate Certificate) are not significantly different from each other, but each is significantly higher than the base category of no educational qualification beyond primary level, and significantly below the return to a Leaving Certificate qualification.

It might be argued that the nature and content of courses has changed over time, or that a Leaving Certificate qualification obtained in the 1950s had a 'scarcity value' which does not obtain today. In the results reported in columns (2)–(4) and (6)–(8) we explore this issue somewhat by estimating separate wage equations for three different age groups. Using YEARED the estimates point to a slightly increased return for the younger grouping. However, there is little difference between the pooled sample estimate and the estimated return for the middle and older cohort. The picture presented by the educational qualifications is much more complex. In general we find that the coefficients for the youngest age group lie below those of the other cohorts until the acquisition of degree-level qualifications. For example, the return from completing the Leaving Certificate rises dramatically as we move through the age cohorts from youngest to oldest. Returns to other third-level qualifications also rise (though less dramatically) with age, but for degree-level qualifications we see the opposite, with higher returns for those in the youngest age cohort. The fall in the value of a Leaving Certificate qualification could be seen as evidence of 'qualification inflation'; but the rise in the value of degree-level qualifications tends to contradict this view.

Since 1987 the limited evidence that there is on this subject suggests that there have been some changes in the pattern of relative wages. Barrett, Callan and Nolan (1997) estimate human capital earnings functions using 1987 and 1994 data. Their results show small changes in the returns to different levels of education over that seven-year period.

The 1995 OECD *Economic Survey: Ireland* compared private and social returns in higher education in Ireland and a range of other countries. Private returns were estimated at 16.0 per cent compared with 13.1 per cent for referenced countries, while social returns were 12.0 per cent compared with 10.3 per cent.

GROWTH AND EDUCATION

Overview

Over a very long period what matters is the growth of the supply capacity of the economy and this depends on the growth of the labour force and the capital stock, technological change and the extent to which markets function well. The Solow growth model decomposes growth as follows:

Growth rate $= \alpha$ (growth in labour) $+ (1-\alpha)$ (growth in capital stock)

$+$ (technical change)

where the labour force and the capital stock are weighted by their relative importance in output (α, and $1-\alpha$ respectively). It is possible to measure both the growth in labour input and growth in the capital stock – the balance, referred to as the Solow residual, is the rate of technical change, often referred to in the literature as *total factor productivity* (TFP). The residual has been estimated to account for between one-third and one-half of GDP growth in industrial countries.

The Solow residual (or TFP) is thus relatively large and there must be some concern about such a large unexplained contribution to growth. This is more important when we consider that TFP for many countries has declined over a very long period with the greatest decline occurring since 1973. Accordingly, it is worthwhile to explore the extent to which we can explain the Solow residual. When considering labour and capital we recognise that both embody quality changes – labour through human capital development and capital through technology shifts. We present below a measure of employment embodying changes in the level of educational attainment – an education adjusted employment index – using data from the 1981 and 1991 censuses and extending the results to 1996.

Education-Adjusted Employment

The 1981 census and the 1991 census both provide limited information in relation to the level of education of the population. This information was not sought in either the 1986 or the 1996 censuses so the data needed for analysis are limited. We will first consider the data available from the 1981 and 1991 censuses and use education statistics to update the figures to 1996.

Nothing better illustrates the educational transformation than the data contained in Table 6.2. The table shows the highest level of education attainment using three levels of education – primary, secondary and third level. The table also distinguishes between different categories of person – taking the population as a whole, those who are in the labour force, those who are in employment, those unemployed, and finally all those who are not in the labour force (referred to as the Rest).

Table 6.2 Education attainment, 1981–91 (%): persons
aged 15+ whose education has ceased

| | Highest level of education attained | | |
	Primary	Secondary	Tertiary
All			
1981	45.5	46.8	7.7
1991	36.7	50.2	13.1
Labour force			
1981	34.6	54.5	11.0
1991	25.0	57.0	18.0
Employed			
1981	32.8	55.4	11.9
1991	22.0	57.6	20.4
Unemployed			
1981	49.9	46.9	3.3
1991	39.8	54.3	5.9
Rest >15			
1981	60.6	36.2	3.2
1991	54.2	39.9	5.8

The critical figures relate to those who are in the labour force, and within this grouping between those that are employed and unemployed. The level of educational attainment of those in the labour force is greater than the remainder of those aged 15 and over (who are dominated by those aged 65 and over). Within the labour force the level of education is greatest among those employed. Comparing 1991 and 1981, the level of education of both employed and unemployed increased, as in both cases the proportion with just primary education fell between 1981 and 1991, and the proportions with secondary and third level rose. There are also quite large differences in these proportions by age group, and between 1981 and 1991. Table 6.3 examines the differences for those employed.

Younger age groups by 1991 have much greater levels of educational attainment than in 1981. The importance of this cannot be overstressed. Over time, as those in older age categories leave employment through death and retirement, the general level of education increases and the labour force becomes more educated. These data are, of course, proportions. Table 6.4 summarises the basic raw data. While there was only a slight change in the level of employment between 1981–91 there

Table 6.3   Education attainment, 1981–91 by age grouping
(%): persons 15 and over in employment whose
education has ceased

| | Highest level of education attained | | |
	Primary	*Secondary*	*Tertiary*
15–19			
1981	12.3	86.3	1.4
1991	10.7	84.0	5.1
20–24			
1981	10.1	78.0	11.9
1991	5.9	73.9	20.3
25–44			
1981	28.7	55.0	16.3
1991	14.6	61.1	24.2
45–64			
1981	56.3	34.3	9.4
1991	42.2	39.7	17.1
> 64			
1981	73.1	20.2	6.7
1991	65.7	24.1	10.1

was a very significant change in the education level. The question posed earlier is the extent to which this increase in the level of educational attainment represents an increase in the effective employed labour force, that is, what weights must be attached to education differences to generate an 'education-adjusted employment/labour force' taking 1981 as a base.

The most appropriate weights are differences in earnings by age and education. The basic point is that education, in general, will lead to differences in output per head, as will experience, and earnings are a good measure of these differences. We derived information on earnings by age and education from a 1987 survey of living conditions carried out by the ESRI, and applied the weights to both 1981 and 1991 employment data. (As noted earlier there are very little differences between the 1994 and 1987 survey results in returns from education, thereby suggesting that using fixed weights may not distort the results.) As might be expected there are very big differences by age and education attainment. Taking the earnings of a person aged 15–19 with just primary education as 100, the earnings of a person aged 25–44 with third-level education were estimated from the survey to be 266.5.

Table 6.4 Employment by age and education attainment, 1981–91
(000s) (persons 15 and over whose education has ceased)

	Total	Highest level of education attained		
		Primary	Secondary	Tertiary
15–19				
1981	115.0	14.1	99.3	1.6
1991	60.1	6.5	50.5	3.1
20–24				
1981	196.5	19.9	153.0	23.6
1991	165.8	9.7	122.5	33.6
25–44				
1981	486.4	139.5	267.4	79.5
1991	595.9	87.0	364.6	144.3
45–64				
1981	292.2	164.4	100.3	27.4
1991	290.9	125.7	115.4	49.9
65+				
1981	47.8	35.0	9.7	3.2
1991	36.3	23.9	8.8	3.7
Total				
1981	1137.8	372.8	629.7	135.3
1991	1149.1	252.8	661.7	234.5

Table 6.5 Education-adjusted employment (EAE), 1981–91

	Total employment (000s)	EAE (1981 = 100)
1981	1137.8	100.0
1991	1149.1	114.4
% change	1.0	14.4

Differences in earnings are taken to represent differences in output. The employed labour force is weighted by these earnings to generate a new measure of employment that takes account of differences in output per head. The results of this exercise are given in Table 6.5 which shows that while employment grew by only 1 per cent between 1981 and 1991, when the numbers are adjusted for the increase in the level of educational attainment there was a rise of 14.4 per cent in the education-adjusted employment (EAE) level. This represents an additional 1.2 per cent per annum. In effect, while total employment rose by just 1 per cent over the period there was an increase of 14.4 per cent in effective employment.

Extensions of Analysis

The data above referred to 1981 and 1991. It is now proposed to extend the analysis taking in the two census years, 1986 and 1996, where the census data in relation to education are not complete. It is possible to get a reasonable profile of educational attainment both in 1986 and 1996 from published data on educational participation and from survey work. Table 6.6 sets out our estimates for 1986 and 1996, compared to the 1981 and 1991 census data reported earlier. The 1986 figures are of course affected by the decline in employment that took place in the early 1980s and the difficulty in obtaining work experienced by new entrants to the labour force. In one sense this explains the increased participation in education. These data, suitably broken down by age group, can be used to provide an estimate of an education-adjusted employment (EAE), the results of which are shown in Table 6.7.

Table 6.6   Education attainment, 1981–96 (% of those in employment)

	Primary	*Secondary*	*Tertiary*
1981	32.8	55.4	11.9
1986	22.8	61.2	16.0
1991	22.0	57.6	20.4
1996	17.0	59.6	23.4

Table 6.7   Education-adjusted employment (EAE), 1981–96 (1981 = 100)

	Total employment	*EAE*
1981	100.0	100.0
1986	95.1	102.5
1991	101.0	114.4
1996	113.0	134.1
% change 1986–96	18.8	30.8
% change 1986–96 (p.a)	1.7	2.7

Table 6.8   Growth in output, employment, capital and total factor
productivity (TFP), 1986–96

	Growth			Contribution of		
	GNP	Labour (EAE)	Capital	Labour (EAE)	Capital	TFP
1986–96	5.3	2.7	2.25	1.8	0.8	2.7
1986–91	4.8	2.3	2.25	1.5	0.8	2.5
1991–96	5.8	3.2	2.25	2.1	0.8	2.9

Over the period 1986–96 the improved education level added 1 per cent
per annum to the effective labour force.

Table 6.8 illustrates the impact of these estimates on the distribution
of growth between labour, capital and technical change over the rapid
growth period 1986–96. The capital growth figures were obtained by
grossing up estimates of the capital stock. The first columns show the
growth rates in GNP, capital and our EAE measure. From this we are
able to decompose total GNP growth into the contributions made by
labour (EAE) and capital in terms of the Solow model discussed earlier.
The residual element, our measure of total factor productivity for the
whole period, is high by comparison with those for other countries,
but is quite close to that (2.2) estimated by Brendan Walsh for the
period 1960–85 (Walsh, 1996).

The sub-periods are also interesting. In the second half of the
ten-year period growth was more rapid – by about 1 per cent. What
made this possible was the faster growth in EAE and the rise in total
factor productivity. There is an important point here in that greater
education adjustment may do more than just raise output per head by
a fixed amount – it also generates a continuous learning process so
that total factor productivity will continue to rise. Ideally this should
be captured in a proper measure of human capital but we only have
crude measures of this.

Education-Adjusted Labour Force over the Medium Term

Over the period of rapid growth, 1986–96, the increased level of
educational attainment added 1 per cent to the effective level of employment, and this was important in allowing the growth to continue.

In considering the potential growth in the economy over the next
decade the impact of education on the effective labour force may also

Table 6.9   Education-adjusted labour force (EALF), 1996–2006

	EALF	% change	Labour force	% change
1996	100.0	—	1475.35	—
2001	116.2	16.2	1647.57	11.6
2006	127.2	9.5	1738.92	5.5

be important. The continued rise in participation in education is gradually working its way into the labour force and its impact will be felt for some time: new entrants are better educated than those retiring, and at every age group new entrants on average are also better educated. Thus, in addition to the growth in the labour force there is likely to be a sharper rise in the education-adjusted labour force, as the numbers in the relevant age groups increase. We have taken some estimates of potential labour force growth over the period 1996–2006 and examined the effect of the increased level of education attainment on the potential labour force, using the methodology outlined above. The results are shown in Table 6.9.

Over the period to 2001 the average growth in the EALF is just over 3 per cent per annum, which is slightly faster than in the decade 1986–96, and just marginally below that of 1991–96. The average rate of increase falls to 1.8 per cent in the subsequent five-year period. The impact of education is to add 0.8 per cent per annum to the labour force over the whole decade, somewhat less than in the 1986–96 period.

It is readily apparent that the growth in the education-adjusted labour force (EALF) is very rapid over the next decade, while easing somewhat in the second half of the period. Thus there is unlikely to be a major labour force constraint, though there could be specific shortages. The situation may be somewhat more benign than the above data suggest, as a comparison with the labour force in 1996 may not be appropriate given that the labour force contains a large number of unemployed whose educational attainment level is much weaker than the employed labour force.

OTHER CONTRIBUTIONS AND INTERNATIONAL COMPARISONS

Fitz Gerald (1997) constructed measures of human capital for Ireland over a much longer time period. Comparisons can be made with

Germany and Austria, countries for which human-capital similar measures have been constructed. Koman and Marin (1997) have constructed an index of human capital in the labour force, and of human capital per worker for both these countries. These suggest that in 1992, Irish workers had on average fewer years of education than German workers, and that the Irish population had on average less education than the population of Germany and Austria. Ireland performed well relative to Austria in terms of both total human capital accumulation and improvement in labour quality. Performance relative to Germany was less impressive, particularly in terms of total human capital accumulation.

Koman and Marin also supply data on growth rates of output and physical capital over the period 1960–92. The tables below compare these growth rates with the corresponding growth rates for Ireland for the period 1961–93. Over this period as a whole, in terms of output

Table 6.10   Average annual growth rate of output

Period	Austria	Germany	Ireland
1960–65	4.16	4.82	3.73
1965–70	4.79	4.05	3.99
1970–80	3.64	2.72	3.80
1980–85	1.31	1.14	0.34
1985–92	2.83	3.37	3.47
1960–92	2.82	2.76	2.49

Source: Koman and Marin (1997); *Statistical Abstract* (CSO).

Table 6.11   Average annual growth rate of physical capital

Period	Austria	Germany	Ireland
1960–65	2.68	6.20	2.15
1965–70	−0.72	5.23	3.79
1970–80	4.08	4.07	5.02
1980–85	2.48	2.77	3.59
1985–92	2.87	2.62	1.82
1960–92	2.58	4.06	2.67

Source: Koman and Marin (1997); ESRI – Dept. Finance Databank.

Table 6.12   Percentage contribution of factors to growth (1960–92)

	Physical capital	Labour quality	Raw labour	TFP
Austria	21.01	8.93	3.67	66.39
Germany	36.36	17.48	8.74	37.42
Ireland	35.08	18.88	7.00	39.04

Source: Koman and Marin (1997).

growth, Ireland was outperformed by both Austria and Germany. The pattern of growth is different in Ireland, however; it is highest at the end of the period rather than at the beginning. Physical capital stocks grew fastest in Germany, and slowest in Austria over the period of 30 years. The rate of physical capital accumulation has tended to fall over time in Germany, while in Austria and in Ireland it has fluctuated.

The authors also report a total factor productivity decomposition of output growth. The TFP decompositions for the period 1960–92 are reproduced below, with the corresponding decomposition for Ireland for the period 1961–94. The relative contributions of physical capital, raw labour, labour quality and total factor productivity in Ireland and Germany are remarkably similar, although this hides a different pattern over the different periods.

These comparisons show that in 1960, Ireland had lower levels of human capital than in the US, Germany and Austria. In the period 1961–71, the Irish rate of human capital accumulation was low by the standards of these countries. From 1971, the rate of human capital accumulation in Ireland was more respectable due to an increase in the numbers employed and in the labour force during the 1970s, and to significant improvements in labour quality in the 1980s and early 1990s.

CONCLUSIONS

This chapter has examined the relationship between economic growth and education. The first part has drawn a link between education and earnings, and established that higher levels of educational attainment are associated with increased earnings. The second part has linked differences in earnings to differences in output, and hence introduced the concept of the education-adjusted labour force – an attempt to capture a measure of human capital. This measure indicates that over the period of most rapid growth in the economy (1986–96), the effective

working population grew by 2.7 per cent per annum, compared with a growth of 1.7 per cent per annum in the measured working population. The education-adjusted labour force is projected forward to the middle of the next decade, and the results show that there will be continued rapid growth in the adjusted labour force, though not at the rate of the period 1986–96. The economy can continue to grow rapidly. A comparison with Austria and Germany suggests that even with the rapid growth in the level of educational attainment in Ireland it is still below Austria and Germany, so that there remains the potential for further development. This may well be not just in participation, but in educational content, and perhaps duration of courses. The OECD *Economic Survey: Ireland* (1995) suggested, on the basis of comparisons with other countries, that lengthening the school year, reducing the length of the school day, and reducing class size would all contribute to enhanced performance. This is an area of further research.

Notes

1. Thanks to the editor of this volume and to John Fitz Gerald for their helpful comments on this research. The usual disclaimer applies. The work of Harmon into research on schooling returns is supported under the auspices of the President's Award scheme of UCD which is gratefully acknowledged.
2. These measures do not measure the effect of education on unemployment in any definite way. To do so requires specification of a full structural model which encompasses a broader definition of the return to education that incorporates the impact of schooling on labour market transitions. Breen (1991) makes some attempt to examine unemployment/education interactions, and shows broadly that the probability and duration of unemployment is positively correlated with low levels of education.
3. The Group/Intermediate certificates have since been replaced by a single exam undertaken at the same point in the schooling cycle known as the Junior Certificate, but this reorganisation post-dates the data used in this chapter.

References

Ashenfelter, O., Harmon, C. and Oosterbeek, H. (1998) 'Estimating the Economic Return to Schooling', *Labour Economics*, forthcoming.
Barrett, A., Callan, T. and Nolan, B. (1997), 'The Earnings Distribution and Returns to Education in Ireland 1987–1994', unpublished paper, Economic and Social Research Institute, Dublin.

Barro, R. (1991) 'Economic Growth in a Cross-section of Countries', *Quarterly Journal of Economics*, 106, pp. 407–45.

Becker, G. S. (1964) *Human Capital* (New York: Columbia University Press).

Breen, R. (1991) *Education, Employment and Training in the Youth Labour Market* (Dublin: Economic and Social Research Institute).

Callan, T. and Harmon, C. (1998) 'The Economic Return to Schooling in Ireland', *Labour Economics*, forthcoming.

Callan, T. and Wren, A. (1994) *Male–Female Wage Differentials: Analysis and Policy Issues* (Dublin: Economic and Social Research Institute).

CSO (various years) *Statistical Abstract* (Dublin: Central Statistics Office).

Durkan, J., Sheehan, J. and Walsh, B. M. (1993) *Education and Training*. Report prepared for the Department of Education.

Fitz Gerald, D. (1997) Human Capital Indices', unpublished dissertation, Department of Economics, University College Dublin.

Koman, R. and Marin, D. (1997) 'Human Capital and Macroeconomic Growth: Austria and Germany, 1960–92', Centre for Economic Policy Research, discussion paper no. 1551.

Mankiw, N. G., Romer, D. and Weil, D. (1992) 'A Contribution to the Empirics of Economic Growth', *Quarterly Journal of Economics*, 107(2), pp. 407–37.

Mulligan, C. B. and Sala-i-Martin, X. (1995b) 'Measuring Aggregate Human Capital', National Bureau of Economic Research, working paper no. 5016.

OECD (1995) *Economic Survey: Ireland* (Paris: Organisation for Economic Cooperation and Development).

Psacharopoulos, G. (1973) *Returns to Education: An International Comparison* (Amsterdam: Elsevier).

Mincer, J. (1974) *Schooling, Experience and Earnings* (New York: Columbia University Press for the NBER).

Reilly, B. (1987) 'Wages, Sex Discrimination and the Irish Labour Market for Young Workers', *Economic and Social Review*, 18, pp. 271–305.

Romer, P. M. (1990) 'Human Capital and Growth: Theory and Evidence', *Carnegie-Rochester Conference Series on Public Policy*, 32, pp. 251–86

Sexton, J. and O'Connell, P. (eds) (1997) *Labour Market Studies: Ireland* (Luxembourg: Office for Official Publications of the European Communities).

Sexton, J., Whelan, B. and Williams, J. (1988) *Transition from School to Work and Early Labour Market Experience* (Dublin: Economic and Social Research Institute).

Tussing, A. D. (1978) *Irish Educational Expenditures – Past, Present and Future* (Dublin: Economic and Social Research Institute).

Walsh, B. M. (1993) 'The Contribution of Human Capital Formation to Post-War Economic Growth in Ireland', Centre for Economic Research, Department of Economics, University College, Dublin, working paper 93/8.

Walsh, B. M. (1996) 'The Contribution of Education to Irish Economic Growth: A Survey', unpublished paper, Department of Economics, University College, Dublin.

Walsh, B. M. and Whelan, B. J. (1976) 'A Micro-economic Study of Earnings in Ireland', *Economic and Social Review*, 7, pp. 199–207

Whelan, C. T., Smyth, E. and Hannan, D. (1996) 'Educational Inequality in the Republic of Ireland', paper presented at the British Academy Symposium on *Ireland: North and South*, Nuffield College, Oxford, December.

7 Wage Formation and the Labour Market

John Fitz Gerald

INTRODUCTION

The Irish labour market over the last fifty years has enjoyed some unusual features; in particular the extent to which labour mobility was legally possible and culturally accepted. Ireland moved from having a very high level of protection at the end of the 1950s to being highly integrated into the wider European economy as a member of the EEC after 1973. While the goods market was very closed up to 1960, Ireland had been part of a wider labour market with the United Kingdom for over a century, with very limited restriction on the outward movement of labour to the UK over the 75 years since independence in 1922. This has made possible very considerable migration and, as a result, the supply of labour in Ireland has been unusually responsive to external circumstances, giving rise to a more elastic supply of labour than in many other EU countries.

Over the last decade the economy has seen a rapid convergence in living standards towards the EU average. To what extent has this convergence been a product of a transformation in the operation of the labour market and to what extent is the labour market merely reflecting wider change in the economy? The evolving external environment and the changing structure of the domestic economy are all reflected in the evolution of the domestic labour market and, in particular, in wage formation. This chapter considers the changes in the wage formation process in Ireland since 1960, the forces which have produced this transformation, and what these changes can tell us about the operation of the labour market as a whole.

The second section of this chapter examines the development of wage rates since the period of protection in the 1950s. They are considered in the context of the wider labour market of these islands and the EU. This section also considers a number of factors which have been very important in affecting labour supply and demand over the period, in particular the role of migration. We then set out a framework to help

137

explain these stylised data, applying it to the available data to draw
conclusions concerning wage formation and the labour market.

THE IRISH LABOUR MARKET SINCE 1960

Ireland made relatively little progress in raising output per head (GNP)
towards the EU average over the 30 years up to 1990. However,
there has been a sudden transformation since that date as shown in
Figure 7.1. As discussed in Chapter 1, an important factor in the current
rapid rate of economic progress is the changing pattern in economic
dependency.

The economic dependency ratio (the population which is not in
employment divided by the numbers employed) reached a peak in the
mid-1980s and this put a major burden on the working population
(Figure 7.2). The rise in dependency due to purely demographic factors
was aggravated in the 1980s by the rise in unemployment. While output
continued to increase, especially in the second half of the decade, the
benefits had to be shared over an increasing number of non-workers.
Since the late 1980s the situation has reversed and now the dependency
rate is falling, both because of the changing demographic structure and
the fall in unemployment. The rise in dependency meant that while output (and income) per person employed converged on the EU average
gradually from 1970 onwards (from 76 per cent in 1970 to 86 per cent

Figure 7.1   Ireland compared to EU: GNP per head and per person
employed at PPS

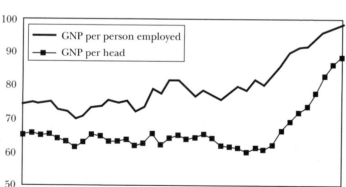

Source: Duffy, Fitz Gerald, Kearney and Shortall, 1997.

Figure 7.2   Economic dependency ratio: dependants per person
employed

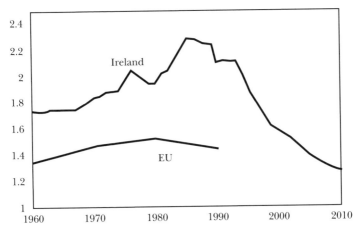

Source: Duffy, Fitz Gerald, Kearney and Shortall, 1997.

by 1990), measured as output per head there was little change between
1960 and 1990. Since 1990 both measures show a much more rapid rate
of convergence.

The relatively steady convergence since 1960 in income per person
employed was closely related to developments in the labour market and
to movements in relative wage rates. These developments were affected
by the openness of the labour market and it is important to consider
them in the context of developments in the wider UK labour market.

When Ireland became independent in 1922 it remained part of a
common labour market with no restriction on movement between
Ireland and Britain. With the exception of the years of the Second
World War, this was to remain the case (for Irish citizens) right up to
the present. By contrast, from the end of the 1920s tariffs were introduced in Ireland (and the UK) so that by the mid-1930s the goods
market was subject to very considerable restrictions. The exceptionally
high tariff barriers remained in place until the end of the 1950s, unlike
the situation in most other European countries where trade barriers
were rapidly reduced in the immediate postwar years.

Because of the historical ties with the United Kingdom, many of the
institutional features of the Irish labour market were shared: many of
the trade unions in Ireland were branches of UK trade unions and the
approach to wage bargaining owed much to developments in Britain.
These common features were reinforced by the movement of many

workers from Ireland to the UK, as well as through wider cultural influences, including the influence of shared media – newspapers, books, radio and, later, television.

This is the background to the main story of this chapter, the development of wage formation and the labour market since 1960. As shown in Figure 7.3, wage rates in Ireland in the early 1940s were only around 40 per cent of those in the UK.[1] They remained in the range 40 to 50 per cent of the UK level until 1960. Between 1960 and the late 1970s there was a very sharp rise in wage rates in Ireland relative to those in the United Kingdom. However, from the end of the 1970s wage rates in Ireland fluctuated around 80 to 90 per cent of the UK level. The fluctuations around this trend were largely due to changes in the bilateral exchange rate rather than to changes in the rate of growth of wage rates from one year to the next.

If other labour costs, in particular employers' social insurance contributions, are taken into account, the pattern is very similar (Figure 7.3). In this case the stabilisation in the graph occurs around the level where Irish costs are 90 to 100 per cent of the UK level, with them exceeding the UK level in years when sterling was abnormally weak. As shown in Figure 7.4, when viewed within a wider EU context in 1992, labour costs in Ireland and the UK were well below those in most other members of the EU (with the exception of Portugal and Greece). This relatively favourable position on labour costs has been true for at least the last decade.

Figure 7.3 Relative labour costs: Irish industry compared to UK

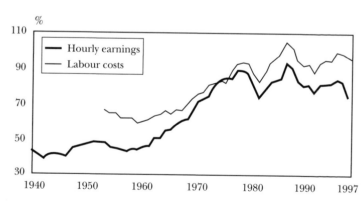

Source: Duffy, Fitz Gerald, Kearney and Shortall (1997).

Figure 7.4 Hourly labour costs in manufacturing, 1992

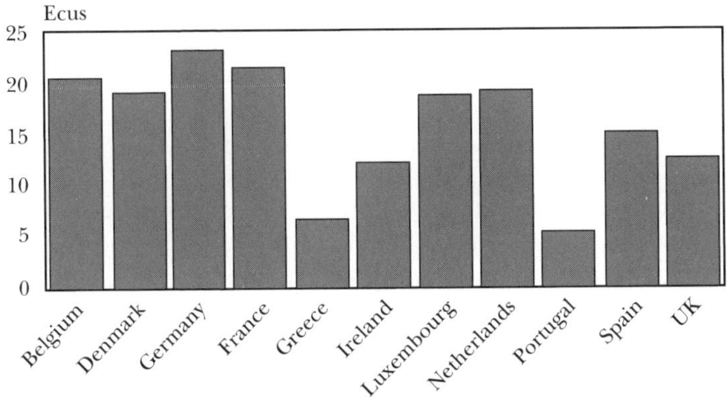

Source: Duffy, Fitz Gerald, Kearney and Shortall (1997).

Questions to be Answered

The timing and pattern of the convergence of Irish wage rates to UK wage rates over the last 40 years raises a number of interesting questions about the Irish labour market. Is it an accident or, as seems more likely, are there economic forces that can explain the convergence? What economic mechanisms could have given rise to the process and how can the timing of the convergence throw light on the underlying factors?

On the supply side there has been free movement of labour over a very long period so, on its own, it cannot explain the convergence in factor prices. However, if the costs of migration had changed over time this factor could have resulted in a shift in the equilibrium gap in unemployment rates (or expected earnings) between Ireland and the UK.[2] Falling travel and communications costs have undoubtedly made the decision to emigrate much less traumatic than in the era of the 'American wake'. In addition, the falling cost of labour mobility has made possible the situation where much of the emigration since 1960 has been temporary in character.

If the explanation for the convergence lay in reduced costs of migration it should be evident in the modelling of the migration decision or, equivalently, of the equilibrium difference in unemployment rates (Honohan, 1992). However, due to data problems, most of the studies of the migration decision use data from the post-1960 period, after the convergence process had begun, which makes it difficult to identify a change in behaviour.

A second possible supply-side explanation for the convergence is the effect of the opening up of the economy and society to the outside world from the late 1950s onwards, typified by EU entry in 1973. In earlier decades expectations in Ireland were much lower relative to those in the UK reflecting, among other things, a more closed society. The opening up of the economy, the impact of radio and television and foreign travel, may all have served to raise expectations of the labour force. If they could not get a satisfactory standard of living at home they had the option of moving.[3]

A third supply-side factor might be the investment in human capital resulting in rising earnings per person. However, as discussed in Chapter 6, the investment began in the late 1960s long after the convergence in wage rates had begun, and its full effects on the labour market are only maturing in the 1990s. As a result, the timing of this factor tends to rule it out as a major force in the convergence process.

The opening up of the goods market post-1960 provides a fourth possible mechanism whereby the convergence in wage rates took place. The coincidence of the rapid growth in wage rates in Ireland post-1960, commencing at the same time as the goods market was liberalised, may be just that – a coincidence. However, there remains the possibility that the entry of many multinationals into the Irish market, investing in new sectors of manufacturing, may have had a direct influence on the domestic labour market (Barry and Hannan, 1995). Prior to 1960 Irish firms were producing small production runs for a limited domestic market with a low marginal productivity of labour; the freeing of trade and the introduction of new technology in firms producing for a wider European market greatly increased labour productivity. As a result, foreign firms could afford to pay much higher wage rates than in the past (and higher rates than in existing domestic firms). The resulting upward pressure on wage rates undoubtedly contributed to the demise of much of the traditional manufacturing sector of the 1950s (see Barry and Hannan, 1995).

A final factor which may have played a role in the stabilisation of labour costs in Ireland around the UK level after 1980 may have been the development of a 'partnership approach' to incomes policy. While Irish labour costs rose continuously compared to costs in other EU countries over the 1960–80 period, there appears to have been a stabilisation since then. The new more consensual approach to wage bargaining could have played a role in this development; by changing expectations and bringing order to the labour market it may have resulted in a more moderate growth in wage rates in recent years.

The rest of this chapter considers the evidence on the combination of factors which explains the pattern of growth in Irish labour costs over the last 40 years.

FRAMEWORK FOR ANALYSIS

Observed wage rates over the last 40 years represent the outcome of a complex interaction between forces driving the supply and demand for labour. On their own these data cannot explain the behaviour of the labour market as they represent the reduced form of a complex set of relationships. In this section we consider the factors driving the structural model – the supply and demand for labour in Ireland. This analysis gives some clues as to how the questions, set out above, may be answered.

Labour Supply

There is a wide range of factors which have affected the supply of labour and its price over the years, the most obvious being the rate of inflation in consumer prices. Taxation also affects labour supply, both through the effects of indirect taxes on consumer prices, and also through taxes on labour income, which affect the spending power of wages.

A second set of variables which affects labour supply is the natural increase in the labour force, migration, and changing patterns of female participation. A third set of factors operates through the productivity of labour. Among the latter are the changing level of education and training of the labour force, which affects its productivity. A final set of factors broadly affects labour's expectations in terms of living standards. These include the degree of unionisation, which also influences market power, and external factors such as the standard of living available elsewhere, and incomes-policy initiatives.

In a world with perfect competition, rational individuals will make their decisions on labour supply on the basis of the real wage rate. This implies that in the long run, unless individuals suffer from money illusion, there will be a unitary elasticity with respect to consumer prices. In addition, the level of taxation on labour may well affect labour supply. If labour sees the availability of publicly provided goods as representing 'good value' for taxes paid, then changes in taxation might not necessarily be seen as representing changes in the reward to labour. However, if these benefits are discounted by labour, so that changes in labour taxation impact on the perceived return to work, then such taxes can be expected to affect the supply of labour, affecting wage rates. It remains an empirical question how taxes on labour affect wage rates in individual countries. The evidence from Drèze and Bean (1990) for a number of European labour markets is mixed, though a series of studies of the Irish labour market suggest that the tax wedge exerts a significant influence on wage bargaining (Bradley, Whelan and Wright, 1993; Curtis and Fitz Gerald, 1994).

Because of a high birth rate in the 1960s and the 1970s, which only went into serious decline in the 1980s, the numbers of young potential labour market entrants each year substantially exceeds the numbers retiring. This has the effect of shifting outwards the supply curve for labour in the Irish economy.

The second demographic variable influencing the supply of labour is migration. The free movement of labour has resulted in a huge outflow of Irish-born young adults over the last 200 years. Since the Second World War the numbers leaving Ireland have varied greatly from year to year (Figure 7.5, left scale). In the late 1950s net emigration reached 60 000 a year, roughly equal to the annual number of births, and again in the late 1980s emigration reached 40 000 a year.

Figure 7.5   Emigration and unemployment

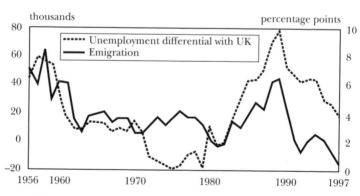

Source: CSO, *Labour Force Survey*.

By contrast, in the 1970s and again in the late 1990s there has been some net immigration. The potential importance of this mechanism is illustrated by recent research which examines the convergence in wage rates and living standards between the Irish and the British economies over the second half of the nineteenth century and the early years of the twentieth century. O'Rourke and Williamson, 1995, show that migration, by reducing the supply of labour in Ireland and increasing it in Britain, played a key role in promoting this convergence.

A number of studies of the factors driving emigration in Ireland in the postwar period have found that it is significantly affected by the differential in unemployment rates between Ireland and the UK (Walsh, 1968; Honohan, 1992). Honohan found that the equilibrium gap in unemployment rates between Ireland and the UK was around 4 percentage points; at that difference in unemployment rates there would be no net flow of migrants out of (or into) the country. Figure 7.5 shows both emigration in recent years (left scale) and the actual gap in unemployment rates between Ireland and the UK (right scale), which reached a peak in the late 1980s, around the time that the latest bout of emigration was at its maximum.

The propensity of Irish citizens to migrate changes the nature of the labour supply curve in Ireland, making it more elastic. Changes in domestic economic circumstances, through their effect on migration, directly influence the domestic labour force. In addition, the important role of migration makes the unemployment rate a poor indicator of tensions in the Irish labour market. When economic circumstances are particularly unfavourable in Ireland this may not be reflected in unemployment if there are simultaneously good job opportunities outside the country. As a result, the Irish unemployment rate may not be the appropriate variable to include in a wage rate equation. The UK unemployment rate may prove at least as good an indicator of domestic labour market tensions in Ireland if, as Honohan and others suggest, it ultimately drives the Irish rate through the migration mechanism.

There must be some uncertainty about the stability of the past relationship between unemployment rates in Ireland and the UK. In the 1950s the emigrants from Ireland were predominantly unskilled; by emigrating to the UK or the US they escaped an environment where unemployment was higher than in the destination country, wage rates lower and a welfare system which was much less developed. Since the early 1980s the emigrants have shifted from being predominantly unskilled to being largely skilled (Figure 7.6) (Fahey and Fitz Gerald, 1998). If they remained at home they would be unlikely to have faced

Figure 7.6   Education of emigrants: males and
females, aged 15–29

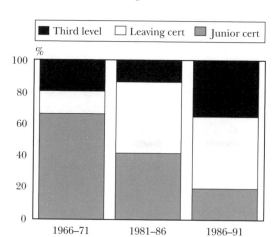

Source: Duffy, Fitz Gerald, Kearney and Shortall (1997).

unemployment,[4] though their earnings might have been somewhat lower than if they had moved to the UK (or elsewhere in the EU). It is only if the unemployment rate continues to reflect tensions in the market for skilled labour that it will be a good predictor of future migration. In addition, in recent years when there has been significant immigration, some of those entering the Irish labour market were not returning Irish citizens. Instead a significant minority were skilled workers from other EU countries and the factors driving their entry into the Irish labour market may well prove different from those which drove migration by Irish citizens in the past.

In the 1980s there was a big shift in the educational attainment of those who emigrated. By the second half of the decade at least two-thirds of emigrants had at least a leaving certificate level of education. The improvement in the education of the young labour force entrants enhanced their mobility. This was reflected in a very small gap in the unemployment rates for skilled workers between Ireland and the UK, while there was a much bigger gap for unskilled workers (Figure 7.7). The improved educational attainment of the labour force made individuals more mobile, increasing the elasticity of labour supply.

As discussed in Chapter 6, Ireland in recent decades has made a rather belated investment in human capital. While much of the rest of

Figure 7.7   Comparative unemployment rates by educational
attainment: Ireland vs UK, 1994

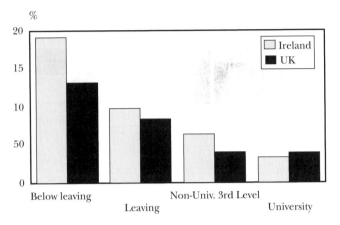

Source: OECD, *Education at a Glance*, 1996.

Northern Europe improved their educational systems in the immediate
postwar years, it was not until the end of the 1960s that Ireland followed
suit, and the impact of that investment since the late 1960s has taken
many years to trickle through into the labour market. However, in the
late 1980s and the 1990s the impact of past investment in education on
current productivity is probably at its peak (Chapter 6 and Bradley,
Fitz Gerald, Honohan and Kearney, 1997). Figure 7.8 shows the
educational attainment of the female population by age.[5]

The rising educational attainment of the female population has had
a direct effect on the labour supply through its effects on the female
labour force. Labour force participation by women is highly correlated
with educational attainment, and the rising average level of education
probably accounts for up to a third of the rise in the participation rates
in recent years (Fahey and Fitz Gerald, 1997). The effect has been to
shift outwards the supply curve for labour, especially for skilled labour.
In addition, female labour supply is more elastic than male labour
supply (Callan and Wren, 1994; Walsh, 1993) so that the changes which
have taken place in female participation have probably made the
supply of labour, especially of skilled labour, more elastic than in
the past.

Many of the models of wage behaviour assume that individuals, or
groups of individuals, bargain for a share of the output they produce.

Wage Formation

Figure 7.8   Educational attainment, females, 1994, by age, % of population

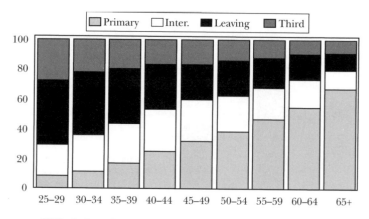

Source: CSO, *Labour Force Survey*.

If, for example, labour were to obtain a constant share of productivity growth (output per person), then labour's share of value-added would remain constant over time. As discussed in Chapter 6, the gradual replacement of unskilled workers in the labour force by those with a good education has enhanced the productivity of labour and of the economy as a whole. In a competitive labour market where labour was paid its marginal product this would be reflected in rising earnings per hour and rising output per head. The effect of this boost to productivity from investment in education probably played a small part in the convergence in average earnings in the 1970s. By the time the rising human capital was having its biggest impact on productivity, after 1980, the process of convergence in wage rates was largely completed.

A further major factor in determining the outcome of wage bargaining is the impact of unionisation. By raising the bargaining power of labour, unionisation can be expected to raise wage rates above the level they might reach in a perfectly competitive market. A popular model for understanding labour market outcomes is one where unions may be viewed as bargaining in terms of wage rates while employers set employment conditional on agreed wage rates. To the extent that unions' primary concern is their employed members, the bargaining process may attenuate the impact of unemployment on wage inflation. In particular, where a limited subset of the labour force experiences most of the unemployment, often because they have been failed by the education system, changes in unemployment may not affect the expectations of those who are already employed. This is particularly true of the Irish labour market since 1980; successive studies have shown that those with a very limited education face a very high probability of unemployment, while those with a good education generally experience few, if any, spells of unemployment (Sexton and O'Connell, 1996).

The effect of rising unionisation in the 1960s and the 1970s (Figure 7.9) may be expected to have affected the supply of labour, both through modifying its responsiveness to changes in unemployment, and also through changing union members' expectations about future earnings. All individuals, to a greater or lesser extent face a trade-off between leisure and work and their preferences in this regard will be conditioned by cultural factors, and by the return they expect to get from employment. Murphy and Thom (1987) considered labour supply in the context of just such a model. It is possible that these expectations could be directly affected by changes in external circumstances, such as the opening up of the Irish economy and society. Knowledge of the standard of living obtained abroad by relatives and friends may well directly affect expectations of domestic labour market participants.

These expectations may also be affected by institutional changes and incomes policy initiatives. 1987 saw the introduction of the Programme

Figure 7.9 Union membership, percentage of total employees

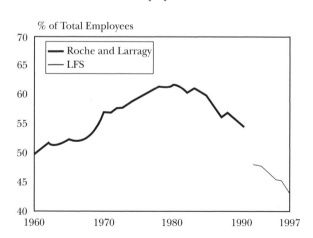

Source: Roche and Larragy, 1993; CSO, *Labour Force Survey*.

for National Recovery (PNR), where employers, trade unions and the government bargained simultaneously about national wage rates and taxes on labour. The inclusion of taxes (and other public services) in the national bargaining process gave recognition to the fact that labour was concerned with after-tax wage rates. This was the first of a series of agreements which developed what is referred to as a 'partnership approach' to wage bargaining (Sexton and O'Connell, 1996). These agreements may well have had an impact on expectations and, therefore, on the wage bargaining process. It is a widespread perception that the change in industrial relations procedures, occurring at a time of serious economic difficulty for the economy, did contribute significantly to the resolution of those problems. This partnership approach has been pursued up to the present day, with a series of multi-year agreements covering not only wage rates but also a range of other matters, such as the rate of taxation on labour.

Demand for Labour

In a standard neo-classical world, where firms are maximising their profits, the demand for labour is a function of the price of labour, the price of other inputs, the price of output and technical progress, with technical progress affecting the productivity of individual factors of production. The prices of the other factors of production will be relevant arguments in the firm's demand for labour where labour is substitutable by these factors. If there is very limited substitutability between factors of production they may not prove significant. In a competitive labour market the result will be that wages are equal to the marginal product of labour.

For firms it is the price of output, not consumer prices, which represents their reward for output and drives labour demand. The difference between consumer prices and output prices reflects the impact of indirect taxes and changes in the terms of trade, driving a wedge between the prices faced by the two parties to the bargaining process. For example, in the case of rising indirect tax rates labour will try to protect its purchasing power by raising nominal wage rates, while firms facing unchanged prices for their output will be very reluctant to concede such a wage rise. In this case the outcome, in terms of wage inflation, must depend on the strength of the different parties to the bargaining process.

Taxation also drives a wedge between the price of labour paid to the employer and the disposable wage received by the employee. Thus the measure of the real cost of labour to the employer and the real return to the employee is affected by a tax wedge that consists of both direct and indirect taxes (as well as the effects of the terms of trade). In the late 1970s and the first half of the 1980s rates of taxation rose rapidly in Ireland, greatly increasing this tax wedge. Its importance in the wage bargaining process was recognised in the development of the 'partnership approach' in the late 1980s where employees and employers sought to influence the tax wedge.

Over the last 40 years the Irish economy has been subjected to a series of shocks which have potentially affected the demand for labour. The opening up of the economy after 1960 had a major impact on labour demand. Between the early 1930s and 1960 Irish firms had a highly protected home market. Many firms had grown up just to serve that market. Typically they were very small-scale producers with no exports to the more competitive outside world. Due to the limited scope for exploiting scale economies and the absence of external stimuli, the marginal productivity of labour was probably quite low, helping explain the low wage rate compared to the UK.

The removal of trade barriers effected a radical transformation of the economy over the following 20 years with many of the older low-productivity firms closing. Simultaneous with the removal of trade barriers a long-term policy of encouraging foreign multinational investment in manufacturing was introduced. This relied on a zero or low rate of corporation tax to attract foreign firms. These firms brought new technologies to the manufacturing sector, substantially raising labour productivity.

For many businesses today, both Irish and foreign, the major competition comes from outside Ireland. In particular, for the very important multinational sector the decision facing the firm is first and foremost what country is likely to prove the most competitive in which to locate production. For smaller Irish-owned firms the question is whether they or foreign competitors will serve the same EU market. Under these conditions it might be expected that, as well as the cost of domestic factors of production, the representative firm would take into account the expected cost of production elsewhere. For such firms the demand for labour will be a function of both the cost of labour in Ireland and the cost of labour in competing countries, in particular in the UK (Bradley and Fitz Gerald, 1988; Bradley, Fitz Gerald and Kearney, 1993).

Technical progress over the years has enhanced the productivity of business so that the marginal product of labour, and other factors, has been increased. In recent years there is evidence that in the developed economies technical progress has enhanced the demand for skilled labour. This has been reflected in countries such as the US and the UK by an increasing differential in wage rates payable for skilled labour compared to unskilled (Nickell and Bell, 1995). Operating in a global market Ireland has not been immune to this factor. In fact, the very important role played by foreign multinationals in the economy has been a significant factor in shifting the demand for skilled labour through the introduction of new products and new technologies.

Labour Market Outcomes

The discussion of the factors affecting the supply of labour indicated that there has been a major outward shift in the supply of labour, especially skilled labour, over the last 30 years. This increase is ascribable to a number of factors, some of which are specific to Irish circumstances. The fact that the vast bulk of new labour force entrants now have at least a leaving certificate, compared to the 1960s when only a minority did so, has also probably changed the shape of the supply curves for both skilled and unskilled labour. However, the ultimate impact of this major investment in human capital also depends on the demand for both kinds of labour.

As shown in Figure 7.10 such an outward shift in the supply curve from S^0 to S^1, in the absence of a shift in the demand curve D^0, could be expected to lead to a fall in wage rates from W^0 to W^1. In addition, if as suggested above there has been structural change in the labour market making the supply of labour more elastic (S^2), then the expected reduction in wage rates could be even greater to W^2.

If the demand curves for the two kinds of labour had remained unchanged over time, the wages of skilled employees relative to unskilled would have fallen. This fall would have been particularly acute if many of the skilled were unable to find skilled employment and were forced to work in unskilled jobs. However, Barrett, Callan and Nolan (1997) have examined the effect of increasing human capital on earnings for two years, 1987 and 1994; these findings are discussed in Chapters 6 and 8. This study shows that the returns to education for the individual, as reflected in their earnings, are considerable and that the average differential in earnings for different educational levels for men and women in 1987 and 1994 showed little change (Figure 7.11). When other factors are controlled for they actually find that the returns to education increased.[6] In the light of the outward shift in the supply curve, this

Figure 7.10   Skilled labour: effects of increase in supply and
demand

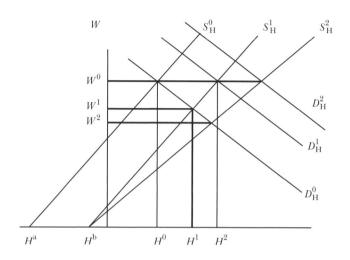

Figure 7.11   Returns to education: female,
earnings by educational attainment

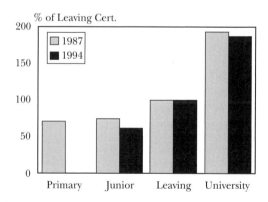

Source: Callan and Wren, 1994; Barrett, Callan and Nolan, 1997.

indicates that the demand curve must also have shifted out from D^0 to
D^1 or D^2.

The impact of the investment in education was also to reduce the
supply of unskilled labour. By changing the composition of the labour

force, with unchanged returns to education, the investment in human capital will have raised average earnings. The very big increase in the supply of skilled labour, and the big shift in demand for such labour, which is consistent with the observed behaviour of skilled wage rates, is also consistent with the very big increase in employment of skilled labour which is apparent in recent years.

MODELLING WAGE DETERMINATION

In seeking to understand the behaviour of the labour market in Ireland there are a range of possible behavioural models, some of which have been applied in the past. Certain elements are common to all of them. Three studies which adopted a bargaining model maintained rather different assumptions about the factors driving supply and demand in the Irish labour market. In Bradley, Fitz Gerald, Hurley, O'Sullivan and Storey (1993) and Bradley, Whelan and Wright (1993) a more traditional closed-economy model was adopted. More recently, Curtis and Fitz Gerald (1996) adopted a model which explicitly acknowledged the openness of the labour market. Both models assumed that wage rates were determined in the tradable sector (industry) with the rate of wage inflation being passed on to the rest of the economy (Lindbeck, 1979).[7] In this section we re-examine these models in the light of the latest data.

The models can be nested within a single encompassing model for the purpose of testing. The closed-economy model adopted the following specification for the demand and supply of labour (see Curtis and Fitz Gerald, 1996, for a formal derivation of the two models):

$$L^d = f(Q, w-p) \tag{7.1}$$

$$L^s = g(w, z, t, Q/L, U, N) \tag{7.2}$$

where L represents employment (L^d the demand for labour, and L^s the supply of labour); Q output in Ireland; w wage rates; p the output price; z consumer prices; t the tax wedge; Q/L productivity; U the unemployment rate; and N unionisation.

The demand for labour is a function of output and the real wage, where the price is the price of industrial output (equation (7.1)). Wage rates and consumer prices, the tax wedge, productivity, the unemployment rate and unionisation, determine the supply of labour, equation (7.2). Lower case variables represent the natural log of upper-case variables. The wage rate and output data are for the industrial sector and the data are described in more detail in Curtis and Fitz Gerald (1996).

The open-economy model took account of the fact that the tradeable sector was operating in a wider EU market and the representative firm had a choice between producing in Ireland or elsewhere. Labour supply is also assumed to be affected by conditions in the UK labour market, both directly through migration, and indirectly through changes in expectations. The resulting open-economy model is:

$$L^d = f(Q_w, w, w_u) \tag{7.3}$$

$$L^s = g(w, z, t, w_u, z_u, t_u, U, U_u, N) \tag{7.4}$$

where the subscript u indicates the appropriate variable for the UK and Q_w is a measure of world output.

In the open-economy model the demand for labour in Ireland is a function of world output, with the process of competition determining what share of that output is produced in Ireland (equation (7.3)). In this model competitiveness is measured in terms of relative labour costs between Ireland and the UK. In addition to the variables that appeared in the closed-economy labour-supply equation (7.2), the open economy equation (7.4) includes the UK wage rate, tax wedge and unemployment rates, reflecting the integration of the labour markets in the two countries.

Assuming a log-linear form for the labour supply and demand equations, representing the objectives of the representative employer and employee, they can be solved for the desired or 'equilibrium' wage rate w^*. The resulting specifications for wage rates from the two models, closed and open economy, can be nested within a single equation:

$$W^* = a_0 + a_1 q_w + a_2(z - t) + a_3 p + a_4 w_u + a_5(z_u - t_u)$$
$$+ a_6 e + a_7(q - 1) + a_8 U + a_9 U_u + a_{10} N \tag{7.5}$$

where e is the expected bilateral sterling/Irish pound exchange rate (proxied by a 4-period moving average).

For the closed-economy model the following restrictions apply:

$$a_1 = 0; \quad a_3 = 1 - a_2; \quad a_4 = a_5 = a_6 = 0$$

When these restrictions are implemented the equation to be estimated takes the form:

$$W^* - p = a_0 + a_2(z - t) - p + a_7(q - 1) + a_8 U + a_9 U_u + a_{10} N \qquad (7.6)$$

For the open economy model the following restrictions apply:

$$a_3 = 0; \quad a_5 = 1 - a_2 - a_4; \quad a_6 = 1 - a_2; \quad a_7 = 0$$
$$\Delta \log(w_i) = b_1 \Delta \log(w^*) + b_2(\log(w^*_{-1}) - \log(w_{-1})) \qquad (7.7)$$

In implementing this specification it is assumed that actual wage rates adjust to their optimal or 'equilibrium' level over time. In testing between the different specifications the adjustment process is specified as an error correction mechanism, equation (7.7). The closed and open-economy models are applied to data for Ireland covering the period 1962 to 1994. This sample spans a period of major change in the Irish economy as the process of integration into the EU proceeded and as the supply and demand curves for labour suffered the shocks discussed in the previous section. The dependent variable in the models estimated in this section is average annual earnings in the industrial (tradable) sector. This variable reflects the full costs to the employer of employing a unit of labour.

In estimating the model the unionisation variable is dropped because it did not prove possible to obtain a consistent series spanning the whole period. The variable used by Curtis and Fitz Gerald (1996) in estimating their model for the period to 1990 is not available for the later period. In spite of this omission, the tax wedge variable ensures that the parameters of the supply and demand curves are separately identified (with the exception of the intercepts).

The model also differs from the specification shown above in that the difference between the unemployment rates in Ireland and the UK is used to measure the extent of labour market pressure. This involves restricting $a_8 = -a_9$ in equation (7.5). In experimentation this proved the most satisfactory unemployment variable. As explained earlier, this is consistent with the models of migration where the difference in the unemployment rates was found to be an important driving force in the past.

Finally, we tested alternative definitions of productivity. The standard definition used in earlier work is output in industry divided by employment in that sector. We tried two alternative definitions which adjust for the distortionary effects of transfer pricing on the volume of industrial output. In the first we subtracted the volume of profit repatriations, deflated by the national accounts deflator for factor flows, from the volume of industrial output, essentially as discussed in Chapter 2. In the second we deflated the value of profit repatriations by the deflator for GDP arising in the industrial sector. The traditional definition unadjusted for profit repatriations performed better in the general equation (7.5). While in the restricted closed economy equation (7.6) the adjusted productivity variables performed slightly better, since the results for the other tests were unaffected by the choice of productivity variable, for consistency with previous studies we have continued to use the traditional definition throughout the results presented below.

In testing between the different restrictions on the general specification (7.5) the Error Correction Mechanism (ECM) was maintained. However, to maintain comparability with earlier work, the results shown below for the closed economy model use the partial adjustment scheme employed in the studies cited above. The results of estimating the three models: the unrestricted model, the closed-economy model and the open-economy model are all shown in Table 7.1. The results indicate that both sets of restrictions, the closed-economy and the open-economy models, are rejected by the data. While the open-economy model performs better than the closed-economy model, it does not dominate it.

In the case of the open-economy model, estimated for the full period, the coefficient on the UK wage rate is significant. The results imply a very high elasticity of labour supply with respect to wage rates of 4.4. The effect of a rise in UK wage rates of 1 per cent is to reduce domestic labour supply by around 2.5 per cent as enhanced conditions in the UK attract emigrants. The implied own elasticity of demand for labour is around -0.6. This is within the range suggested by Bradley, Fitz Gerald and Kearney (1993). The tax wedge is also significant, implying that a major part of the burden of taxation is passed on to employers. The coefficients determining the speed of adjustment indicate very rapid adjustment of wage rates to changes in the 'optimal' wage rate. The ECM term is small and insignificant.

In the closed economy model, estimated over the whole sample period, the coefficient on productivity comes out at just under 0.2, significantly different from unity (as imposed in Bradley, Whelan and Wright, 1993).[8] The coefficient on the tax wedge is also quite low, though still significant. The coefficient on the unemployment rate differential is not significant, though correctly signed. Finally, the

Table 7.1 Alternative Models of Wage Determination

Coefficient	Model						
	General	Closed economy			Open economy		
	1962–94	1962–94	1962–79	1980–94	1962–94	1962–79	1980–94
a_0	−4.1018				−3.0746	−2.0343	1.1273
	(2.6)				(1.9)	(1.5)	(0.1)
a_1	0.0711				0.2021	0.2644	0.3735
	(0.7)				(1.5)	(2.1)	(0.5)
a_2	0.5155	0.1836	0.5444	0.2331	0.8865	0.7226	0.5878
	(2.2)	(2.1)	(4.4)	(1.4)	(4.5)	(2.8)	(0.9)
a_3	0.1768						
	(2.0)						
a_4	0.5769				0.6098	0.4866	0.1549
	(2.6)				(3.7)	(3.1)	(0.2)
a_5	−0.3736						
	(1.7)						

a_6	−0.1164 (0.7)						
a_7	0.2957 (3.0)	0.2464 (2.3)	0.6046 (6.4)	0.2673 (1.5)			
a_8	−0.0042 (1.4)	−0.0051 (1.1)	−0.0332 (2.2)	0.0062 (1.5)	−0.0034 (0.7)	−0.0173 (2.1)	−0.0110 (0.9)
b_1	1.2764 (3.8)	0.6600 (6.8)	0.3527 (4.2)	0.4593 (2.4)	1.0132 (12.6)	1.1381 (6.7)	0.5206 (1.6)
b_2	0.0550 (0.5)				0.0636 (1.2)	−0.0250 (0.4)	0.4181 (1.3)
St. error	0.0154	0.0318	0.0201	0.0222	0.0208	0.0144	0.0206
Sum sq. errors	0.00522	0.0284	0.0052	0.0049	0.0113	0.00227	0.00341
Elasticities:							
own-demand					−0.6	−1.0	−1.1
own-supply					4.4	2.7	1.6
UK wage-supply					−2.5	−0.8	0.7

Note: *t*-statistics are given in brackets.

coefficient on the lagged dependent variable is significant, implying a relatively slow speed of adjustment. Further tests were carried out to check for a break in the sample. These tests proved significant at the 5 per cent level suggesting a break in sample in both equations. The results of tests for the timing of the break between 1975 and 1986 are shown in Table 7.2. The statistics for the Chow test suggests that the break took place around 1980 in the closed-economy equation rather than later in the 1980s. In the open-economy equation it seems to occur later, though still probably before the 'partnership' approach to wage bargaining was adopted. It will need data for a number of additional years before any firm conclusions can be drawn on when a change in behaviour occurred. While the limited data post-1986 still leave room for uncertainty in the case of the open-economy equation, this suggests that the impact of the 'partnership' approach to wage formation has been less significant than many have assumed.

Table 7.1 also shows the results for the two specifications assuming a break in sample at 1980. In the case of both the closed and the open-economy models a Chow test proved significant, indicating a break in sample at that point. In the open-economy equation the coefficient on the domestic tax wedge was also fairly consistent in terms of magnitude across the regressions, though for the latter sub-period it was not significant. The major change when the equation was estimated over separate sub-periods occurred in the speed of adjustment. It was significantly slower for the latter sub-period than for the earlier sub-period or for the regression over the whole sample.

Table 7.2 Chow test for break in sample

Break	*Closed economy*	*Open economy*
1975–76	4.25	2.31
1976–77	4.11	2.31
1977–78	8.70	2.26
1978–79	8.48	2.18
1979–80	8.26	2.67
1980–81	9.20	2.50
1981–82	6.10	2.95
1982–83	3.42	2.92
1983–84	2.62	2.66
1984–85	1.92	3.01
1985–86	1.78	2.33

In the case of the closed economy model the equation performed well when estimated over the sub-period to 1979. However, when estimated for the full period the tax wedge and productivity variables were barely significant and for the latest sub-period the equation proved totally unsatisfactory. A key factor in the difference between the two sub-periods is the coefficient on productivity, which has a value of 0.6 for the period to 1979, but is not significantly different from zero for the post-1979 period.[9]

These results suggest that the open-economy model is better than the closed-economy model but that it does not adequately handle the changing circumstances of the Irish labour market over the full period. The specification does not allow for the likely outward shift in the supply curve, discussed earlier (p. 145 ff). It also assumes that the elasticity of labour supply is constant over time whereas changes in migration and in female labour force behaviour may have affected it making it more elastic. The results suggest a very high elasticity of labour supply, which may well be due to the effects of ignoring the changes in the nature of the supply curve giving rise to specification error.

CONCLUSIONS

Turning to the questions posed earlier (p. 143) as to why convergence in wage rates between Ireland and the UK occurred when it did, these results do not provide a clear-cut answer. The results from the open-economy model strongly suggest that external forces have influenced the domestic labour market – in particular the standard of living (cost of labour) in the UK.

While the cost of migration may have fallen in the sample period, it seems unlikely that it could have had a major role in explaining the extent and speed of the convergence. To test this hypothesis formally it would be necessary to consider the very limited data available for the earlier period 1930 to 1960. If the explanation were a falling cost of migration then this would have had an impact on the unemployment rate differential between Ireland and the UK. This, in turn, could affect the economy through the Phillips curve. However, the unemployment differential between Ireland and the UK has been greater in the years since 1960 than it was in the 1950s.

The second possibility, that European integration affected expectations causing a rapid rise in wage rates, remains just that, a possibility.

If this were the case it would have the effect of shifting inwards the supply curve for labour. However, as already discussed, there were a number of factors that led to a rapid outward shift in the labour supply curve, especially for skilled labour. The high elasticity of supply of labour thrown up by the open-economy model would, if anything, tend to contradict this hypothesis, though this result is probably due to a failure to fully model the factors driving labour supply in the sample period.

This leaves the effect of European integration on the demand for labour as probably the most important single factor driving convergence. The timing of the adjustment process is consistent with this hypothesis. The opening up of the economy did not happen instantaneously in 1960 but it involved a series of different measures culminating in EU membership in 1973. For firms facing this changing environment their reaction time was slow. They first of all had to be convinced that the change was irreversible and then the implementation of new investment took many years to achieve. This could explain a slow outward shift in the demand curve for labour as firms gradually implemented their decisions to expand production in Ireland. If the only factor were a shift in expectations shifting the supply curve, then the adjustment process should have been much more rapid. The costs to individuals of raising their labour costs and adjusting their lifestyle would have been small!

However, if it had been purely a demand shift, then wage rates should not have run ahead of the ability of the economy to absorb the change. The pricing out of existence of many unskilled jobs in the early 1980s as a result of the convergence in labour costs would suggest that other factors must have played a contributory role (possibly including changes in the social welfare system).

While institutional change – the 'partnership approach' – could explain the apparent slow down in real wage growth after 1980, it can not explain the earlier process of convergence. The tests for the timing of the change in behaviour suggest that it may have occurred before the Programme for National Recovery of 1987. Even though the change in behaviour in the 1980s and the 1990s could be consistent with the story of 'partnership' being important in moderating wage demands, the nature and the extent of the change in behaviour would suggest that much more is going on in the Irish labour market. While helping to bring about a more orderly labour market, with fewer industrial disputes than in the 1970s, the partnership approach served more to validate the results which market forces had made inevitable.

The significant differences in the growth in wage rates in individual industrial sectors in recent years reflect the importance of market forces in determining wage rates.

The convergence in labour costs between Ireland and the UK over the period 1960 to 1980 was almost certainly a manifestation of the wider process of integration. On balance it seems likely that it owes more to a shift in demand for labour, resulting from European integration, than to any of a range of supply-side shocks. However, it is also clear that no single factor can account for the observed phenomena and that changes in the supply side have also contributed to the change, especially to the reduction in the rate of increase in real wage rates since 1980. It seems likely that the favourable developments in the field of industrial relations since the mid-1980s have favoured this transformation, even if it was not its root cause.

Notes

1. The first series in Figure 7.3 compares hourly wage rates in Ireland with those in the UK. This takes no account of labour taxes and other costs of employment. The second series takes account of differences in labour costs by using national accounting series for the wage bill (divided by employment). This latter series is used later in the chapter when estimating different models.
2. The differential in expected earnings between Ireland and the UK at which emigration would be expected to be zero. See Harris and Todaro, 1970, for a model of migration decisions.
3. Another aspect of this convergence was the development of the Irish social welfare system, from a situation where it was very much inferior to that of the UK in 1960, to one where benefit rates are more generous in Ireland in the 1990s (Callan and Sutherland, 1997).
4. Instead, they might have taken less skilled jobs at home squeezing the least skilled out of work into unemployment.
5. The picture for males is very similar to that for females.
6. The figures for men are rather similar.
7. An alternative specification was examined here using non-agricultural wage rates (average earnings) rather than average earnings in the industrial sector, but the results were very similar.
8. If the productivity variable is adjusted for profit repatriations (deflated by the national accounts deflator for factor income) the coefficient is 0.45.
9. Using the alternative measure of productivity (note 8) the coefficient on productivity in the period to 1979 is 0.61, while it is 0.38 and insignificant for the period 1980–94.

References

Barrett, A., Callan, T. and Nolan, B. (1997) 'The Earnings Distribution and Returns to Education in Ireland, 1987–1994', The Economic and Social Research Institute, Dublin, working paper no. 85.

Barry, F. and Hannan, A. (1995) 'Multinationals and Indigenous Employment: An Irish Disease?', *Economic and Social Review*, 27(1), pp. 21–32.

Bradley, J. and Fitz Gerald, J. (1988) 'Industrial Output and Factor Input Determination in an Econometric Model of a Small Open Economy', *European Economic Review*, 32, pp. 1227–41.

Bradley, J., Fitz Gerald, J., Honohan, P. and Kearney, I. (1997) 'Interpreting the Recent Irish Growth Experience', in D. Duffy, J. Fitz Gerald, I. Kearney and F. Shortall (eds), *Medium-Term Review: 1997–2003*, The Economic and Social Research Institute, Dublin.

Bradley, J., Fitz Gerald, J., Hurley, D., O'Sullivan, L. and Storey, A. (1993) 'HERMES: A Macrosectoral Model for the Irish Economy', in Commission of the European Communities (ed.), *HERMES: Harmonised Econometric Research for Modelling Systems* (Amsterdam: North Holland).

Bradley, J., Fitz Gerald, J. and Kearney, I. (1993) 'Modelling Supply in an Open Economy', *Economic Modelling*, 10(1), January, pp. 11–21.

Bradley, J., Whelan, K. and Wright, J. (1993) *Stabilization and Growth in the EC Periphery: A Study of the Irish Economy* (Aldershot: Avebury).

Callan, T. and Sutherland, H. (1997) *Income Support and Work Incentives: Ireland and the UK*, The Economic and Social Research Institute, Dublin, Policy Research series, no. 30.

Callan T. and Wren, A. (1994) *Male–Female Wage Differentials: Analysis and Policy Issues*, The Economic and Social Research Institute, General Research series, no. 163.

CSO (19XX) *Labour Force Survey* (Dublin: Central Statistics Office).

Curtis, J. and Fitz Gerald, J. (1994) 'Real Wage Convergence in an Open Labour Market', *The Economic and Social Review*, 24(4), pp. 321–40.

Drèze, J. H. and Bean, C. R. (1990) *Europe's Unemployment Problem* (Cambridge, Mass.: MIT Press).

Duffy, D., Fitz Gerald, J., Kearney, I. and Shortall, F. (1977) *Medium-Term Review 1997–2003* (Dublin: Economic and Social Research Institute).

Fahey, T. and Fitz Gerald, J. (1997) *Welfare Implications of Demographic Trends*, Dublin, Combat Poverty Agency, Research Report series.

Fahey, T. and Fitz Gerald, J. (1998) 'The Economic and Social Implications of Population Change', *Journal of the Statistical and Social Inquiry Society of Ireland*, forthcoming.

Harris, J. and Todaro, M. (1970) 'Migration, Unemployment and Development: A Two-Sector Analysis', *American Economic Review*, 84, pp. 259–88.

Honohan, P. (1992) 'The Link Between Irish and UK Unemployment', *Quarterly Economic Commentary*, The Economic and Social Research Institute, Spring, pp. 33–44.

Lindbeck, A. (1979) 'Imported and Structural Inflation and Aggregate demand: The Scandinavian Model Reconstructed', in A. Lindbeck (ed.), *Inflation and Employment in Open Economies* (Amsterdam: North-Holland), pp. 13–40.

Murphy, A. and Thom, D. R. (1987) 'Labour Supply and Commodity Demands: An Application to Ireland', *The Economic and Social Review*, 18(3), pp. 149–58.

Nickell, S. and Bell, B. (1995) 'The Collapse in Demand for the Unskilled and Unemployment Across the OECD', *Oxford Review of Economic Policy*, 11(1), pp. 40–62.

OECD (1996) *Education at a Glance*. (Paris: Organisation for Economic Cooperation and Development).

O'Rourke, K. and Williamson, J. G. (1995) 'Around the European Periphery 1870–1913: Globalization, Schooling and Growth', University College Dublin, working paper WP95/17.

Roche, B. and Larragy, J. (1993) 'Data Series on Trade Unions', Department of Industrial Relations, University College, Dublin.

Sexton, J. J. and O'Connell, P. (1996) *Labour Market Studies: Ireland* (Luxembourg: European Commission).

Walsh, B. M. (1968) *Some Irish Population Problems Reconsidered*, The Economic and Social Research Institute, General Research series paper no. 42.

Walsh, B. M. (1993) 'Labour Force Participation and the Growth of Women's Employment in Ireland', *The Economic and Social Review*, 24(4).

8 Income Inequality in Ireland in the 1980s and 1990s

Tim Callan and Brian Nolan

INTRODUCTION

The 1980s and 1990s have seen Ireland on a macroeconomic roller-coaster ride, as described and analysed in other papers in this volume, with stagnation through much of the 1980s, economic growth accelerating from 1987, stop-starting in the early 1990s, and then reaching and sustaining exceptionally high levels each year from 1994. Recent research internationally has highlighted the fact that income and earnings inequality increased very sharply during the 1980s and into the 1990s in a number of industrialised countries, notably the UK and the USA. Against the background of dramatic changes in the macroeconomy, has Ireland seen such an increase in inequality? Here we examine how earnings dispersion, the distribution of income, and household poverty evolved in Ireland during the 1980s and 1990s, and seek to place Ireland in comparative perspective.

Studies of the distribution of income in Ireland rely on household surveys rather than administrative tax/social security records.[1] Two large-scale household surveys carried out by the Economic and Social Research Institute (ESRI), the 1987 Survey of Income Distribution, Poverty and Use of State Services (see Callan, Nolan *et al.*, 1989) and the 1994 Living in Ireland Survey (see Callan *et al.*, 1996), have served as the basis for a body of research on poverty and related topics surveyed in Nolan and Callan (1994). The Household Budget Survey (HBS) carried out by the Central Statistics Office is primarily an expenditure survey, but contains detailed income data and has been carried out at seven-year intervals – in 1973, 1980, 1987 and 1994/95 (see Murphy, 1984). Here we draw on, without attempting to review, previous research on income inequality in Ireland[2] based on these surveys and also present new findings for 1994. (The distribution of household wealth has been analysed in Nolan (1992) using data from the 1987 ESRI survey, but there is no point of comparison to assess trends over the period.)

We look first at trends in the distribution of earnings among employees, the subject of so much attention elsewhere. We then examine the level of income inequality in Ireland, how it changed over the period and how it compares with other Western countries. This is followed by a similar analysis of household poverty. Finally, the factors underlying these trends in earnings dispersion, income inequality and poverty are explored, and some implications considered.

THE DISTRIBUTION OF EARNINGS

Measuring Earnings Dispersion

Sharply widening inequality in the distribution of earnings among employees in the United Kingdom and the United States in the 1980s and 1990s has been a major preoccupation in recent research on inequality in those countries, and to it has been attributed much of the responsibility for rising inequality in the distribution of total income among households there. Some industrialised countries have experienced much smaller increases in earnings inequality, however, while others again have maintained stability in their earnings distributions (OECD, 1993 and 1996). In this light it is particularly interesting to focus first on what has been happening on this front in Ireland.

Unfortunately, a detailed profile of the overall earnings distribution is not available for 1980, and so we have to concentrate on the comparison of 1987 and 1994. We use data from the household surveys carried out by the ESRI in each of those years, covering employee earnings and hours worked. We follow conventional practice in the earnings distribution literature in analysing gross earnings, and summarising the shape of the earnings distribution by expressing various percentiles as proportions of the median – for example the bottom decile (the earnings level below which 10 per cent of earners fall), bottom quartile decile (the level below which 25 per cent of earners fall), and so on. It is customary to focus on either hourly earnings, or on weekly earnings for full-time employees only. Various definitions and measures of what constitutes 'full-time' are used in different countries or datasets: here we follow most common practice in counting as full-time those reporting at least 30 hours usual work per week. Almost 16 per cent of employees in 1994 worked part-time on this basis, up from 9 per cent in 1987.

Trends in the Distribution of Earnings in Ireland

Table 8.1 shows the distribution of gross hourly earnings and weekly earnings among full-time employees in Ireland in 1987 and 1994. This shows that from 1987 to 1994 there was a consistent widening in dispersion at the top of the distribution for both weekly and hourly earnings: the earnings cut-off above which the top 10 per cent of earners lie moved further away from the median. For hourly earnings the bottom decile was the same proportion of the median in each year, whereas for weekly earnings among full-time employees it fell. For both hourly and weekly earnings the bottom and the top quartile each moved further away from the median over the period. The ratio of the top to the bottom decile, commonly used as a single summary inequality measure in this context, rose from 4.2 to 4.8 for hourly earnings, and for weekly earnings among full-time employees from 3.7 to 4.1. Overall, then, a considerable widening in earnings dispersion, particularly at the top of the distribution, is seen.[3]

Earnings Dispersion in Ireland in Comparative Context

A comparative perspective on both the Irish earnings distribution in 1994 and on the way it has changed since 1987 can be obtained using measures of earnings dispersion for a range of developed countries

Table 8.1   Distribution of earnings, Ireland 1987 and 1994
(as proportion of median)

	1987	1994
All employees, hourly earnings:		
bottom decile	0.47	0.47
bottom quartile	0.73	0.68
top quartile	1.37	1.50
top decile	1.96	2.24
top/bottom decile	*4.17*	*4.77*
Full-time employees, weekly earnings:		
bottom decile	0.50	0.48
bottom quartile	0.75	0.72
top quartile	1.35	1.43
top decile	1.82	1.97
top/bottom decile	*3.65*	*4.10*

recently brought together by the OECD (1996). These figures generally refer to full-time employees, and to weekly, monthly or annual rather than hourly gross earnings. There are potentially important differences in definition and coverage across countries (including the period over which earnings are measured, how 'full-time' is defined and measured, and whether all sectors are covered), so these comparisons should be treated with extreme care, but they can serve to highlight some key features of the Irish results. Table 8.2 shows the ratio of the top to the bottom decile in 1987 and 1994 for Ireland and other OECD countries, for weekly pay among full-time employees.

We see that in 1987, Ireland had a particularly high level of earnings dispersion, only Canada having a higher top/bottom decile ratio among the countries then covered. (OECD, 1996, gives these figures for the USA only from 1993.) What is even more striking is that between 1987 and 1994, the increase in earnings dispersion by this measure was greater in Ireland than any of the other OECD countries for which these figures are available for both points in time. In 1994, then, the top/bottom decile was much higher in Ireland than in most of the other countries,

Table 8.2   Earnings dispersion in Ireland and other OECD countries, 1987 and 1994

Country	Top/bottom decile 1987	Top/bottom decile 1994	Change in top/ bottom decile, 1987–94
Sweden	2.09	2.13	0.04
Italy*	2.42	2.80	0.38
Belgium*	2.44	2.24	−0.20
Finland	2.52	2.38	−0.14
Netherlands	2.53	2.59	0.06
Germany	2.54	2.32	−0.22
Australia	2.81	2.87	0.06
New Zealand**	2.92	3.05	0.13
Japan	3.15	3.02	−0.13
France	3.19	3.28	0.09
United Kingdom	3.20	3.31	0.11
Austria	3.47	3.66	0.19
Ireland	3.67	4.06	0.39
Canada**	4.44	4.20	−0.24
United States	—	4.35	—

Note: *1993; **1988.
Source: OECD (1996), Table 3.1, pp. 61–2.

with only Canada and the USA having a higher degree of dispersion. So the scale of the increase in earnings dispersion which has been taking place in Ireland is striking in comparative perspective.

INCOME INEQUALITY

Measuring Income Inequality

What impact has this been having on the distribution of total income from all sources – not just earnings – accruing to households? *Disposable income* is now the core concept, that is income from the market plus social welfare payments less income tax and employees' social security contributions; we also use *gross income*, before deduction of tax and contributions. The time-period these cover is important. Both the ESRI surveys and the HBS obtained information for most sources of income (earnings, social security transfers, pensions) in respect of the amount received in the current pay period (week, fortnight, month and so on). For income from self-employment, farming, rent or investment income details were recorded on the basis of the most recently available annual figures. In constructing household income all these are converted to a weekly average, which we will call *current* income. In some other countries and some of the main sources of international comparisons on income inequality, however, an *annual* accounting period for income from all sources is adopted. Data on that basis were also obtained in the 1994 ESRI survey, and estimates of annual income have been made from the 1987 ESRI survey in providing data for Ireland for the Luxembourg Income Study database, now widely employed in cross-country studies of income distribution.

A range of methodological issues arise in measuring income inequality (see for example Jenkins, 1991; Cowell, 1996; Atkinson, Rainwater and Smeeding, 1995). Here we cannot discuss these in any depth, but simply note the key ones and set out the approaches followed here. While the ultimate source of concern is the welfare of the individual, income is generally shared among members of a given family or broader household, and here we follow common practice and use the household as the income recipient unit.[4] The extent to which income is actually shared within the household so as to equalise living standards is an empirical question which has recently been receiving attention (see for example Lundberg, Pollak and Wales, 1997; Cantillon and Nolan, 1998) but is particularly difficult to address.

Since a given income will provide a different living standard to the individuals in a large versus a small household, equivalence scales are widely used to adjust income for differences in household size and composition, with actual household income being divided by the number of equivalent adults in the household to produce equivalent or equivalised income. There is no consensus as to which method for estimating these scales is most satisfactory, and studies such as Buhman *et al.* (1988) and Coulter, Cowell and Jenkins (1992) have shown the extent to which the scale used can affect the measured income distribution. A variety of equivalence scales has been used in research on the Irish income distribution and in cross-country studies, and here we make reference to three. One is the square root of household size, without distinguishing between adults and children. The second is widely known as the OECD scale: where the first adult in the household is given a value of 1, each other adult is attributed a value of 0.7 and each child is attributed a value of 0.5. The third is the 'modified OECD' scale, where each additional adult is attributed a value of 0.5 and each child 0.3.[5]

A further issue is whether one focuses on the distribution of income among households, which attributes each household equal weight in the analysis, or on the distribution among individuals. As noted by Atkinson, Rainwater and Smeeding (1995), it makes sense to treat each household as a single unit if no adjustment is made to income for household size, but when equivalent income is used counting persons rather than households (by weighting each household by the number of persons it contains) seem more appropriate.

The distribution of income among households and/or persons may be portrayed and summarised in a number of different ways. Following conventional practice we present decile shares – the share of total income going to the bottom 10 per cent, the next 10 per cent, ... top 10 per cent. As summary measures of inequality we employ the Gini coefficient and Theil's entropy measure.[6] Comparison of Lorenz curves, showing the cumulative proportion of total income received by the bottom x per cent of persons, provides a way of ranking distributions in terms of social welfare. Comparing two distributions, the one with a higher proportion of total income going to the bottom x per cent of persons for all x 'Lorenz-dominates' the other and is associated with a higher level of social welfare (where the ranking is being made independently of the levels of mean income, and given certain assumptions about the social welfare function). Where Lorenz curves cross, no such unambiguous welfare ranking is possible (Atkinson, 1971). Generalised Lorenz curves provide a convenient way of incorporating information about average living standards into the comparison of the level of social welfare yielded by different distributions: cumulative mean incomes instead of cumulative income shares are plotted against cumulative population shares (see Shorrocks, 1983; Jenkins, 1991).

Trends in Income Inequality in Ireland

Table 8.3 shows the decile shares in disposable income among households, without adjustment for size or composition, from the 1980 and 1987 HBS and from the ESRI surveys for 1987 and 1994. First, comparing 1980 and 1987 HBS the share of the bottom two deciles rose substantially and that of the top decile fell. However, the middle deciles experienced a decline in share while those of the second and third deciles from the top had increased, so there was only a marginal redistribution from the top half of the distribution to the bottom half. Thus, although the Lorenz curve for 1987 lies inside that for 1980 at most points, the curves cross. Nonetheless, the Gini and Theil coefficients show a decline in inequality in disposable income between 1980 and 1987. For gross income, by contrast (not shown in the table), both Gini and Theil summary measures rose, so the redistributive impact of income tax and

Table 8.3   Ireland: decile shares in disposable household income, 1980, 1987 and 1994

Decile	HBS		ESRI	
	1980	*1987*	*1987*	*1994*
Bottom	1.7	2.2	2.0	2.2
2	3.5	3.7	3.4	3.2
3	5.1	5.0	4.8	4.6
4	6.6	6.3	5.9	5.8
5	7.9	7.6	7.3	7.3
6	9.3	9.2	8.8	8.9
7	11.0	11.0	10.7	10.9
8	13.0	13.4	13.2	13.3
9	16.2	16.6	16.5	16.4
Top	25.7	25.0	27.4	27.2
All	100.0	100.0	100.0	100.0
Gini	0.360	0.352	0.377	0.377
Theil	0.211	0.200	0.233	0.230

social insurance contributions grew over the period – a point to which we return.

Between 1987 and 1994, on the other hand, Table 8.3 shows that in the ESRI surveys the overall shape of the disposable income distribution was stable, as reflected in very similar (intersecting) Lorenz curves and virtually unchanged Gini and Theil coefficients. The gross income distribution was also more stable than between 1980–87. It is to be noted that the 1987 ESRI survey has a considerably larger shape of total income going to the top decile than the HBS. This may partly reflect differences in timing, particularly in 1987 when the ESRI survey measured farm income for 1986, a particularly bad year, whereas the HBS used accounts for 1987 when farm incomes were on average over 25 per cent higher. There is also a handful of households in each ESRI survey with very high incomes from self-employment, and estimates of the share of income going to the top are very sensitive to the sampling and subsequent treatment of such high-income 'outliers'.

It is important to place these trends in inequality in the context of the evolution of average real incomes, because the pattern of real income growth was very different in the two sub-periods 1980–87 and 1987–94. Between 1980 and 1987, average disposable household incomes rose by 87 per cent in nominal terms but the Consumer Price Index (CPI) was 91 per cent higher by the end of the period, so mean income actually fell in real terms. With mean income slightly lower (in real terms) but the income share of the bottom deciles slightly higher, generalised Lorenz curves for the distribution of disposable income in the 1980 and 1987 HBS cross: no unambiguous ranking is possible on this basis. Between 1987 and 1994, on the other hand, average household income rose by 42 per cent in nominal terms and consumer prices rose by 22 per cent, so incomes rose substantially in real terms and generalised Lorenz curves show an increase in social welfare.

Proceeding to the analysis of income after adjustment for household size and composition, unfortunately only very limited results on this basis are available from the 1980 HBS which suggest that overall trends between 1980 and 1987 were broadly similar to those in unadjusted income.[7] For the 1987–94 period equivalised distributions can be derived from the micro-data, and Table 8.4 shows the distribution of equivalised disposable income in the 1987 and 1994 ESRI surveys using the three sets of scales described earlier. (In focusing on equivalised income we now count persons rather than households.) The share of the bottom decile increases, and both the middle of the distribution and the top

Table 8.4   Decile shares in equivalised disposable income anong persons,
Ireland, 1987 and 1994 ESRI surveys

Decile	Square root scale		OECD scale		Modified OECD scale	
	1987	1994	1987	1994	1987	1994
			%			
Bottom	3.1	3.6	3.1	3.6	3.3	3.8
2	4.5	4.5	4.6	4.6	4.7	4.7
3	5.5	5.4	5.7	5.5	5.7	5.5
4	6.6	6.4	6.6	6.4	6.7	6.3
5	7.7	7.6	7.6	7.4	7.7	7.4
6	9.0	9.1	8.9	8.7	9.0	8.9
7	10.5	10.6	10.3	10.4	10.4	10.5
8	12.6	12.5	12.3	12.5	12.4	12.6
9	15.3	15.4	15.1	15.4	15.1	15.3
top	25.2	24.8	25.8	25.6	25.1	24.9
all	100.0	100.0	100.0	100.0	100.0	100.0
Gini	0.322	0.317	0.323	0.322	0.315	0.314
Theil	0.169	0.163	0.173	0.170	0.163	0.160

decile now consistently have falling shares. As a result both the Gini
and Theil measures show a decline in overall inequality: this is very
slight with the OECD and modified OECD scales, though slightly greater
with the square-root scale. The Lorenz curves for 1987 and 1994 inter-
sect with the OECD and modified OECD scales, though with the square-
root scale 1994 Lorenz-dominates 1987. The two OECD scales take into
account both the number of people in the household and how many
of these are children, unlike the square-root scale, so one might give
more weight to them. Our overall conclusion is that after adjusting for
household composition, the distribution of equivalised disposable income
was little different in 1987 and 1994, with no evidence of increasing
inequality.

Income Inequality in Ireland in International Perspective

How does the distribution of income in Ireland compare with other
industrialised countries? It has become clear in recent years that great
care is needed in making such cross-country comparisons. Without care-
ful attention to maximising the degree of comparability of the estimates
in terms of income concept, income unit, time period, nature and coverage of data source, equivalence scale (where relevant) and so on,

misleading conclusions can be reached. The income distribution database assembled by the Luxembourg Income Study (LIS) is designed to overcome these obstacles to the greatest extent possible. The preferred income concept in the LIS is annual rather than weekly, but the 1987 ESRI survey has been used to estimate the distribution of annual income in Ireland, and that data is included in the LIS database. The recent comprehensive comparative study of income inequality based (mostly) on LIS data by Atkinson, Rainwater and Smeeding (1995) for the OECD thus provides a reference point for the mid–late 1980s.

Their results for the late 1980s on inequality in the distribution of equivalised disposable income (using the square-root equivalence scale and with person weighting), as summarised in the Gini coefficient, are shown in Table 8.5. Ireland is seen to have an exceptionally high level of inequality compared with the other OECD countries covered, with only the USA having a higher Gini coefficient. This reflects the fact that the lower parts of the Irish income distribution have a relatively low share of total income, but even more important is the fact that the top decile has a larger share in Ireland than in any of the other countries.

Table 8.5   Distribution of equivalised disposable income among persons, mid/late 1980s

Country	Year	Gini
Australia	1985	0.295
Belgium	1988	0.235
Canada	1987	0.289
Finland	1987	0.207
France	1984	0.296
Germany	1984	0.250
Ireland	1987	0.330
Italy	1986	0.310
Luxembourg	1985	0.238
Netherlands	1987	0.268
Norway	1986	0.234
Portugal	1998/90	0.310
Spain	1990/91	0.310
Sweden	1987	0.220
UK	1986	0.304
USA	1986	0.341

Source: Atkinson, Rainwater and Smeeding (1995) Table 4.4, except Spain from Table 5.21 and Portugal from Table 5.20.

This is subject to the caveat that, as we have seen, the top decile has a larger share in the 1987 ESRI survey (used by Atkinson *et al.*) than in the HBS, but even so the Irish distribution was clearly among the more unequal in the LIS dataset in the mid-late 1980s.

A more up-to-date comparative picture can be obtained from data from the European Community Household Panel (ECHP) survey, which got under way in 1994. In the ECHP survey, like the LIS, the reference period is annual for all income sources, in the case of Wave 1 relating to the calendar year 1993. The ESRI Living in Ireland Survey constitutes the Irish element of the ECHP, and collected income information on both a (largely) current and an annual basis: the former was used earlier in making comparisons with the HBS, but the latter will be used here for comparability with other countries in the ECHP. Table 8.6 shows the Gini coefficient for the distribution of equivalised disposable income, now using the modified OECD scale, produced by Eurostat from wave 1 of the ECHP.

The picture this conveys about Ireland's relative position in 1993 is quite different: Ireland now looks to be among the more equally-distributed of the countries covered (which because we are drawing on the ECHP are now confined to the European Union, and exclude France and Germany because of data-related complications). The level of inequality in Ireland is now, for example, lower than in the UK, whereas in Atkinson *et al.*'s results the opposite was the case. In Ireland, as we have seen, the level of inequality was stable between the mid-1980s and

Table 8.6   Distribution of equivalised disposable income among persons, 1993 from ECHP

Country	Gini
Belgium	0.285
Denmark	0.219
Greece	0.352
Ireland	0.320
Italy	0.297
Luxembourg	0.300
Netherlands	0.316
Portugal	0.391
Spain	0.334
UK	0.343

Source: Verma (1998), Table 3.1.

the mid-1990s, whereas it rose quite sharply in some other EU countries, notably the UK (as confirmed by national studies such as Goodman, Johnson and Webb, 1997). It would, however, be surprising if inequality had increased in some of the countries – notably Luxembourg and Portugal – by as much as these results suggest, and a good deal of work on reconciling data from different sources remains to be done. We can, however, conclude that Ireland's relative position has certainly improved between 1987 and 1993, because inequality in the distribution of disposable equivalised income increased in some other OECD countries but not in Ireland. While Ireland appeared as something of an outlier in 1987, by 1993 this was less obviously the case.[8]

POVERTY

Measuring Trends in Poverty

Various approaches to the measurement of poverty in developed countries have been proposed and applied, involving, for example, poverty lines based on subjective views about adequacy, on social security rates, on budget standards, on proportions of average or median income or expenditure, and on deprivation indicators (see Callan and Nolan, 1991, for a review). A series of studies using the 1987 and 1994 ESRI surveys has applied a number of different approaches to measuring poverty, including relative income lines, subjective lines based on the Leyden approach, and the combination of information on income and on the type of indicators of deprivation developed by Townsend (1979) and Mack and Lansley (1985) (see Callan *et al.* 1989, 1996).

Here our primary interest is in trends over time, however, and for this purpose it is again necessary to rely on the HBS for 1980 as the starting point for comparison. We therefore focus first on results which can be replicated from that survey, which did not include information on subjective views about adequacy or the range of deprivation indicators employed in the specially-designed ESRI survey. We therefore employ straightforward relative income poverty lines, constructed as a given percentage of average equivalent income in the sample. This approach has in any case a number of advantages in making comparisons over time or across countries, in that the identical procedure can be readily applied in each case, and the sensitivity of the results to the particular line or equivalence scale chosen can be examined. Having presented results on this basis we then look at how real incomes, and therefore the absolute rather than relative position of those on low incomes, evolved over the period.

Trends in Poverty in Ireland

We look at the numbers falling below relative income poverty lines constructed as 40, 50 and 60 per cent of mean equivalent household income. The equivalence scale employed at this stage is the OECD one, and these lines were applied to the HBS for 1980, to both the HBS and the ESRI sample for 1987, and to the ESRI Living in Ireland Survey 1994. Table 8.7 presents the percentage of households and persons falling below each line.

Comparing the results from the 1980 and 1987 HBS, the percentage of households falling below each of the three lines fell but the average size of these households rose, so that there was an increase in the percentage of persons below the 50 per cent and 60 per cent lines while the percentage in households below the 40 per cent line remained unchanged. The ESRI sample for 1987 has a higher percentage of households and persons falling below each of the relative lines than the HBS. The fact that the ESRI survey measured income from farming in 1986, when it was particularly low, appears to be the principal factor producing this difference. Over the more recent sub-period, between 1987 and 1994, the poverty rate for households and persons fell with the 40 per cent line, was broadly stable with the 50 per cent line, and rose quite sharply with the highest, 60 per cent line.

Simply counting the number of persons below an income threshold takes no account of how far below it they fall, and as highlighted by

Table 8.7   Percentages below relative poverty lines, Ireland, 1980, 1987 and 1994

	1980 HBS	*1987 HBS*	*1987 ESRI*	*1994 ESRI*
40% line:				
% of households	8.5	7.3	8.9	7.0
% of persons	10.4	10.4	11.8	10.7
50% line:				
% of households	17.2	16.2	17.6	16.9
% of persons	19.2	20.9	21.8	22.7
60% line:				
% of households	27.9	26.6	27.7	33.3
% of persons	29.7	31.6	32.2	35.2

Sen (1976) can thus give a misleading picture. We therefore also use the summary poverty measures developed by Foster, Greer and Thorbecke (1984): the per capita income gap and the depth- and distribution-sensitive measure of poverty (which gives more weight to the poorest). Between 1980 and the 1987 ESRI survey these both fell with the 40 per cent line, were little changed with the 50 per cent line, and rose with the 60 per cent line – similar trends to the headcount. Over the most recent period from 1987 to 1994, however, these measures give a rather different picture to the headcount, falling with all three lines. While the numbers falling below the highest line rose, then, they were a good deal nearer the poverty line in 1994.

Low income on its own may not be an entirely satisfactory measure of *exclusion* arising from lack of resources. This is not primarily because of the (real) difficulties in measuring income accurately, but more because a household's command over resources is affected by much more than its current income. Long-term factors, relating most importantly to the way resources have been accumulated or eroded over time, as well as current income play a crucial role in influencing the likelihood of current deprivation and exclusion. An approach which combines information on income and on indicators of deprivation to provide an alternative identification of those who are poor has therefore also been developed and applied to data from the 1987 and 1994 ESRI surveys (as described in detail in Nolan and Whelan, 1996; and Callan *et al.*, 1996). A set of eight items or activities was identified from a more extensive list as representing basic deprivation and suitable to serve as an indicator of underlying generalised deprivation (for example, being able to afford new rather than second-hand clothes or a warm overcoat). In 1987, 16 per cent of households were experiencing such deprivation, stated this was because of lack of resources, and had income falling below the 60 per cent relative income poverty line. By 1994, the corresponding figure had fallen marginally to 15 per cent. This may be a better indicator of the scale of, and trends in, generalised deprivation or exclusion due to lack of resources than the numbers below income lines alone.

As noted earlier, the pattern of real income growth in Ireland was very different in the two sub-periods analysed here, with a slight fall between 1980 and 1987 followed by rapid growth between 1987 and 1994. This means that poverty lines held constant in real terms, rather than changing *pari passu* with average income, would show very different patterns in the two sub-periods. In the 1980–87 period, the number below lines held constant in real terms increased slightly more than with relative lines. Between 1987 and 1994, a substantial fall in the numbers below such lines was seen. While it makes sense to see poverty primarily in relative terms, concentrating entirely on relative income poverty lines will miss the difference between these periods. It will also fail to highlight the seriousness of a situation where the real incomes of the poor actually fall, as apparently occurred in the UK during the 1980s, in contrast to the substantial rise in real incomes for the poor in Ireland between 1987 and 1994.

It is worth pointing out that, although some specific areas and types of areas have very high poverty rates, poor households are not spatially concentrated. Households living in public sector housing do have a relatively high poverty risk, and this increased particularly for those located in Dublin between 1987 and 1994. Even so, public housing in the major urban centres contains only a minority of all poor households (Nolan, Whelan and Williams, 1998).

Poverty in Ireland in International Perspective

To see the extent of relative poverty in Ireland compared with other EC member states in the mid–late 1980s, one can draw on a number of cross-country studies carried out for the EC Commission or Eurostat, by O'Higgins and Jenkins (1990), ISSAS (1990), and Hagenaars, de Vos and Zaidi (1994). Key results from the comprehensive analysis presented in Hagenaars *et al.* are summarised in Table 8.8. The relative

Table 8.8   Relative income poverty rates in the mid–late 1980s (modified OECD scale)

Country	% below relative line		
	40%	*50%*	*60%*
Denmark (1987)	3.3	8.8	17.6
Netherlands (1988)	2.2	7.1	18.1
Luxembourg (1987)	1.9	5.7	14.9
France (1989)	7.1	14.4	23.4
United Kingdom (1988)	8.8	19.0	28.1
Ireland (1987)	6.7	16.9	27.6
Italy (1988)	5.6	13.0	23.7
Greece (1988)	10.2	17.3	26.7
Spain (1988)	7.0	13.7	22.3
Portugal (1989)	8.8	17.2	26.8

Source: Hagenaars, de Vos and Zaidi (1994).

position of the different countries varies somewhat with the line chosen. The European Commission tends to place most emphasis on the half-average-income standard, and on that basis Ireland is shown as having about the same percentage of households in poverty as Greece, Portugal and the UK, with Denmark, The Netherlands and Luxembourg having much lower rates. As far as non-EC countries are concerned, the study by Atkinson *et al.* (1995) using the LIS dataset also includes the percentage falling below various proportions of the median in the mid–late 1980s. Their results suggested that around 1987 the proportion of persons below half or 60 per cent of median income was higher in Ireland than most of the European countries covered, about the same as Australia and Canada, and lower than the USA.[9]

More recent results are now available from the first wave of the ECHP, for income in the calendar year 1993. Table 8.9 shows Ireland with a particularly low percentage below 40 per cent of mean income. With half or 60 per cent of mean income as the standard, Ireland has a rate similar to the UK, Greece and Spain, lower than Portugal but higher than the other EU members covered.

An interesting perspective on the implications of taking differences in real incomes into account in such cross-country poverty comparisons is provided by Hagenaars, de Vos and Zaidi (1994), who also present results for the percentages in each member country below a Community-wide poverty line set at half average expenditure. The divergence in poverty

Table 8.9   Relative income poverty rates in wave 1 ECHP, 1993 (modified OECD scale)

Country	% below relative line		
	40%	*50%*	*60%*
Denmark	2.6	6.6	13.9
Netherlands	10.0	14.2	22.9
Belgium	9.3	14.0	20.3
Luxembourg	5.4	14.9	25.3
UK	13.0	21.6	30.8
Ireland	6.9	19.9	30.7
Italy	11.3	15.8	23.2
Greece	15.1	21.9	29.7
Spain	11.4	20.1	29.1
Portugal	18.7	26.0	33.0

Source: Verma (1998) Table 3.2.

rates across countries is then very much wider than with relative lines, since the countries with low poverty rates on a purely relative basis also tend to be those with relatively high income per capita (adjusted for purchasing power), and vice versa.

EXPLAINING TRENDS IN INEQUALITY

The results we have presented show that between 1987 and 1994 the distribution of earnings among employees in Ireland became a good deal more unequal; the distribution of disposable income among households was little changed having become more equal between 1980 and 1987; and the change in relative income poverty varied with the poverty line and summary measure used having gone up between 1980 and 1987. In seeking to identify the factors behind these trends, here we can only point to the likely impact of developments in the macroeconomy and in tax and social security policy, without trying to quantify these with any precision. The central features of the Irish economic landscape in the 1980s and 1990s from this perspective were the trends in economic growth, unemployment, direct personal taxation and social welfare income support.

The direct impact of the acceleration in economic growth towards the end of the period is most obvious in the case of the earnings distribution. Attempts to explain increasing earnings dispersion in the USA and UK have highlighted rising returns to education and skill,[10] which have in turn been attributed to a shift in demand towards more skilled labour due to factors such as skill-biased technical change (Katz and Murphy, 1992) and globalisation and competition from developing countries (Wood, 1994).[11] Most other OECD countries have not seen earnings dispersion increase to the same degree, and it has been argued that institutional factors such as centralised wage bargaining and more highly regulated labour markets have been limiting the growth in earnings inequality in these countries, and that differential trends in the supply of skilled workers are also important. However, over the 1987–94 period Ireland has had highly centralised wage bargaining through a social partnership structure and a very rapid increase in the supply of highly-educated workers. On both counts, a relatively modest increase in earnings inequality in Ireland compared with other countries might have been expected, rather than the exceptionally large increase which we have seen actually occurred.

Barrett, Callan and Nolan (1997) explore how this came about, in terms of changes in returns to education and skills and changes in the education profile of the workforce. Estimated wage equations for the sample of employees in 1987 and 1994 showed increased returns to higher levels of education, especially university education, over the period. Decomposition analysis (along the lines of Juhn, Murphy and Pierce, 1992) shows that this accounts for a substantial proportion of the increase in earnings dispersion. Centralised wage setting is clearly not enough in itself to limit the growth in earnings inequality.[12] In the Irish case, high levels of economic growth and demand for skilled labour appear to have led many employers to give increases in wages well above those agreed centrally. The commonly maintained assumption in comparative studies of trends in earnings and returns to skills, that OECD countries experienced similar changes in the structure of demand, may be called into question. A small and very open economy such as Ireland, with growth fuelled by foreign direct investment concentrated in specific sectors requiring highly-skilled labour, may find the returns to those skills rising substantially even with a relatively rapid increase in supply – indeed that increase in supply may be one of the crucial factors in attracting such investment in these sectors.

Why then did increasing earnings dispersion not feed through to greater inequality in the distribution of disposable income by 1994? Direct taxation clearly plays a major role here. In the earlier part of the period studied, between 1980 and 1987, total tax revenue rose from 34 per cent to 40 per cent of GDP, and within that taxes on personal income plus employees' social security contributions became more important. This reflected not only the growing burden of unemployment on the public purse, but also the working through of the debt over-hang from the ill-fated expansionary fiscal policy of the late-1970s (as discussed in the chapter by Honohan). Income tax and employees' social insurance contributions had an increasing redistributive impact, as reflected in the fact that the Gini coefficient for disposable income was 94 per cent of that for gross income in 1980, but by 1987 it was only 88 per cent. Table 8.10 shows that this was attributable to both the growing importance of income tax and employees' social insurance contributions and their increasing degree of progressivity. The Suits measure of progressivity for income tax plus social insurance contributions together rose by 35 per cent over the period,[13] helping to explain why overall inequality fell for disposable income although it had risen for gross income.

Table 8.10   Average tax rate and Suits progressivity index for income tax and PRSI contributions, 1980, 1987 and 1994

	1980	1987	1994
Average tax rate %			
income tax	12.9	15.4	14.1
PRSI contributions	2.2	3.5	3.7
total	15.1	18.9	17.8
Suits progressivity index			
income tax	0.207	0.275	0.282
PRSI contributions	0.056	0.133	0.148
total	0.185	0.249	0.254

The impact of taxation was much more stable over the 1987–94 period. The proportion of gross income going in income tax and employee social insurance contributions fell marginally, while both income tax and social insurance contributions became only slightly more progressive. Thus the gap between the level of inequality in gross and disposable income distributions, as reflected in the Gini and Theil summary measures, was about the same in 1994 as it had been in 1987. Direct taxation will have smoothed out the impact of increasing dispersion in gross earnings over this period on disposable household incomes, but even for gross household incomes that impact was not as pronounced as might perhaps have been expected. One contributory factor here – 'a dog that did not bark' – is that, in contrast to the UK and the USA, the substantial increase in labour force participation by married women does not appear to have had much impact on the household income distribution in Ireland, at least between 1987 and 1994 (Callan, Nolan, O'Neill and Sweetman, 1998). As elsewhere, a good deal of work remains to be done in understanding the relationship between trends in the earnings distribution and the household income distribution.

As for the lower half of the household income distribution and household poverty, trends in unemployment together with changes in the level of social welfare payments relative to other incomes had the most direct impact. Between 1980 and 1987 unemployment increased very rapidly, rising from 8 per cent to over 18 per cent of the labour force, contributing to falling gross income shares for the second and third quintiles. In assessing the impact on household incomes, it is worth noting that in the Irish case an unusually high proportion of the unemployed are married men living in families, who would conventionally be termed 'household heads', rather than secondary earners. Despite the fact that social security support rates were increased in real terms over the period, unemployment in general resulted in a substantial decline in income for those affected.[14] Again in the Irish case a particularly high proportion of the unemployed have also been away from work long-term, and have therefore exhausted unemployment insurance entitlements, relying on means-tested social assistance payments which during the 1980s were considerably lower.

The impact of increasing unemployment on poverty during the 1980s is also clear. Classifying households on the basis of the labour force status of the household head, in 1980 15 per cent of those below the 50 per cent relative income poverty line had a head who was unemployed, but by 1987 the figure was 37 per cent. The *risk* of poverty for households headed by an unemployed person did not in fact rise, their increasing importance among the poor was due simply to the dramatic rise in the numbers unemployed in the population. At the same time, relatively rapid increases in social security support levels for the elderly compared with others depending on social welfare, improved provision for widows and other lone parents, and increased coverage of occupational pensions, contributed to a marked decline in the proportion of the poor coming from those groups during the 1980–87 period. As a result, by 1987 less than one in ten households below the 50 per cent relative poverty line were headed by a retired person, compared with almost one in five in 1980. With households having an unemployed head effectively replacing some of the elderly among the poor and much more likely to contain children, the risk of poverty for children also rose markedly.

Between 1987 and 1994, on the other hand, unemployment fell to below 16 per cent and there was also a significant shift in the strategy adopted towards different types of social welfare recipient. By 1987, payment rates varied considerably between contributory and non-contributory schemes, and between the elderly, widows and the unemployed.[15] The government-appointed Commission on Social Welfare (1986) focused on the inadequacy of the lowest payment rates and set an adequacy standard approximating the higher rates of payment. Thus the rates of payment for the lowest paid schemes, principally the means-tested safety net for the unemployed, were increased a good deal more rapidly than average incomes, and this sufficed to bring them much closer to half average income by 1994. As Figure 8.1 brings out, this also brought means-tested payments to the unemployed closer to average take-home pay.

Figure 8.1   Trends in unemployment benefit and long-term unemployment assistance for a single adult as a percentage of take-home pay corresponding to average industrial earnings

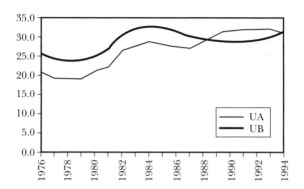

Notes: UA = Long-term unemployment assistance. UB = Unemployment benefit.

Source: Callan *et al*. (1996).

At the same time support rates for other groups, notably the elderly and widows, rose by a good deal less than mean incomes (though still ahead of inflation). As a result, by 1994 many of those relying on old age or widow's pensions were on incomes at or about the 50 per cent line, whereas in 1987 they had been comfortably above that line. This convergence of social welfare rates helps to explain the fact that the headcount of numbers below half average income rose slightly between 1987 and 1994, while poverty measures taking into account the depth of their poverty fell and so did the numbers below relative income lines and experiencing basic deprivation.

Finally, it should be emphasised that throughout this chapter we have concentrated on inequality and poverty in terms of cash incomes, without attempting to broaden the focus to include state expenditure on health, education and housing and its distributional impact. Estimates of the way such expenditure affects different parts of the income distribution are currently available only for 1980 and 1987. They played a particularly important part in debates about the distributional impact of Ireland's fiscal adjustment from 1987, with some arguing that restraining public expenditure in these areas hit the poor particularly hard. It is thus worth summarising briefly here the conclusions we reached in an earlier assessment of this issue (Callan and Nolan, 1992b).

A counter-factual which assumes no fiscal adjustment does not appear particularly helpful, so the real argument is about the balance between expenditure reduction and tax increases, and about where the expenditure cuts were made. Tax increases in fact made a major contribution to the adjustment achieved, as documented in Honohan's chapter in this volume. As for where the cuts were made, over the 1987–90 period current social spending on health, education and housing did not bear a disproportionate share of the burden of restraining expenditure relative to other spending areas, but that this still meant that health spending fell significantly and education spending was held constant in real terms. Public capital spending on social infrastructure, notably on housing, was where the most substantial reductions were made. In general, it was not the case that the cuts were most severe in those areas of social spending from which the poor benefit most, though the curtailment of the public housing programme in particular may have adverse long-term distributional consequences.

CONCLUSIONS

The tax/transfer system in Ireland has played a central role in mediating the impact of trends in the macroeconomy on the distribution of disposable income among households. It helps to explain why that distribution has remained rather stable over the 1980s and 1990s in the face of substantial macroeconomic fluctuations, and of the recent sharp increase in the dispersion of gross earnings. What is at this stage very difficult to assess is the impact of the combination of continued rapid growth and falling unemployment on the Irish income distribution. Is the USA and UK experience of sharply increasing earnings dispersion feeding directly through to rising overall income inequality and poverty rates the inevitable product of shifting patterns of demand? There has not been a general trend towards greater inequality in other OECD countries in the 1980s and 1990s (though few saw inequality fall as it had generally done in the preceding decades),[16] but these countries – including Ireland – could simply be lagging behind the USA and the UK. Alternatively, tax and social protection systems, together with other institutional factors such as collective bargaining arrangements, may provide mechanisms enabling these countries to offset the adverse impact of shifting demand patterns on post-tax and transfer incomes. Given the remarkable levels of economic growth currently being sustained, Ireland will be a particularly interesting test case.

Notes

1. See Nolan (1978) and Callan (1991) on the relationship between survey and administrative income data.
2. Nolan (1978) and Rottman *et al.* (1982) analysed income distribution in the 1973 HBS; Murphy (1984, 1985) and Rottman and Reidy (1988) in 1973 and 1980. Callan and Nolan (1992a) used the 1987 ESRI survey. Callan and Nolan (1997) examined inequality in the household income distribution in the 1973, 1980 and 1987 HBS. Micro-data from the 1987 and 1994 HBS have just been released by the CSO.
3. This is not attributable simply to changing numbers of male versus female, or 'young' versus adult employees: a sharp widening also took place in the distribution of hourly earnings among men or among women only, and among full-time adult men or women.
4. Persons living at the same address with common housekeeping count as a household even if not related.
5. As in studies for Eurostat such as Hagenaars, de Vos and Zaidi (1994), we take adult here to be age 14 years or over.
6. These and other commonly-used summary inequality measures are fully described in e.g. Cowell (1996).
7. Equivalent gross and disposable income distributions for 1980 using scales derived from social security rates are in Roche (1984); the 1980 micro-data are not available for analysis.
8. In a broader comparative perspective, income inequality is generally higher in developing countries than in the industrialised countries discussed here, though there are exceptions and the relationship between inequality and level of development is a subject of considerable debate (see Callan and Nolan, 1992; Anand and Kanbur, 1993).
9. Atkinson, Rainwater and Smeeding (1995), Table 4.2.
10. See for example Gosling, Machin and Meghir (1994) and Schmitt (1995) for the UK, Levy and Murnane (1992) and Juhn, Murphy and Pierce (1992) for the USA.
11. US studies assessing such explanations include Bound and Johnson (1992), Borjas and Ramey (1994), and Burtless (1995).
12. Gottschalk and Joyce's (1997) seven-country study shows that some countries with centralised bargaining in fact saw substantial increases in returns to skill, but these were offset by factors such as declining age premia or declining inequality within age or education groups.
13. Progressivity increased overall by less than for each component because contributions became a more important element in the total and remained less progressive than income tax.
14. Callan, Nolan and O'Donoghue (1996) show that in most cases the cash replacement rate for the unemployed is below 80 per cent, and this did not rise between 1987 and 1994.
15. The lowest rates of payment were close to the 40 per cent relative income line, while the highest rates were close to the 60 per cent relative income standard.
16. See for example Atkinson (1996), Gottschalk and Smeeding (1997).

References

Anand, S. and Kanbur, S. (1993) 'Inequality and Development: A Critique', *Journal of Development Economics*, 41, pp. 19–43.

Atkinson, A. B. (1971) 'On the Measurement of Economic Inequality', *Journal of Economic Theory*, 2, pp. 244–63.

Atkinson, A. B., Rainwater, L. and Smeeding, T. M. (1995) *Income Distribution in OECD Countries: Evidence from the Luxembourg Income Study* (Paris: OECD).

Barrett, A., Callan, T. and Nolan, B. (1997) *The Earnings Distribution and Returns to Education in Ireland, 1987–1994*, Centre for Economic Performance, working paper.

Borjas, G. and Ramey, V. (1994) 'Time-Series Evidence on the Sources of Trends in Wage Inequality', *American Economic Review*, Papers and Proceedings, 84, pp. 10–16.

Bound, J. and Johnson, G. (1992) 'Changes in the Structure of Wages During the 1980s: An Evaluation of Alternative Explanations', *American Economic Review*, 82, pp. 371–92.

Buhman, B., Rainwater, L., Schmaus G. and Smeeding, T. (1988) 'Equivalence Scales, Well-being, Inequality and Poverty: Sensitivity Estimates Across Ten Countries Using the Luxembourg Income Study Database', *Review of Income and Wealth*, Series 34, pp. 115–42.

Burtless, G. (1995) 'International Trade and the Rise in Earnings Inequality', *Journal of Economic Literature*, 33(2), pp. 800–16.

Callan, T. (1991) *Income Tax and Welfare Reform: Microsimulation Modelling and Analysis*, General Research Series no. 154 (Dublin: The Economic and Social Research Institute).

Callan, T. and Nolan, B. (1991) 'Concepts of Poverty and the Poverty Line: A Critical Survey of Approaches to Measuring Poverty', *Journal of Economic Surveys*, 5, pp. 243–62.

Callan, T. and Nolan, B. (1992a) 'Income Distribution and Redistribution: Ireland in Comparative Perspective', in J. H. Goldthorpe and C. T. Whelan (eds), *The Development of Industrial Society in Ireland* (Oxford: Oxford University Press).

Callan, T. and Nolan, B. (1992b) 'Distributional Aspects of Ireland's Fiscal Adjustment', *Economic and Social Review*, 23, pp. 319–42.

Callan, T. and Nolan, B. (1997) 'Income Inequality and Poverty in Ireland in the 1970s and 1980s', in P. Gottschalk, B. Gustafsson and E. Palmer (eds), *Changing Patterns in the Distribution of Economic Welfare: An International Perspective* (Cambridge: Cambridge University Press).

Callan, T., Nolan, B. and O'Donoghue, C. (1996) 'What Has Happened to Replacement Rates?', *Economic and Social Review*, 27, pp. 439–56.

Callan, T., Nolan, B., O'Neill, D. and Sweetman, O. (1998) *Female Labour Force Participation and Household Income Inequality in Ireland*, paper for Irish Economics Association Annual Conference, April.

Callan, T., Nolan, B., Whelan, B. J., Hannan, D. F. with Creighton, S. (1989) *Poverty, Income and Welfare in Ireland*, General Research Series no. 146 (Dublin: The Economic and Social Research Institute).

Callan, T., Nolan, B., Whelan, B. J., Whelan, C. T. and Williams, J. (1996) *Poverty in the 1990s: Evidence from the Living in Ireland Survey*, General Research Series paper 170 (Dublin: Oak Tree Press).

Cantillon, S. and Nolan, B. (1998) 'Are Married Women More Deprived than their Husbands?', *Journal of Social Policy,* forthcoming.

Coulter, F., Cowell, F. and Jenkins, S. P. (1992) 'Equivalence Scale Relativities and the Extent of Inequality and Poverty', *Economic Journal*, 102, pp. 1067–82.

Cowell, F. (1996) *Measuring Inequality*, LSE Handbooks on Economics (Hemel Hempstead: Prentice Hall/Harvester Wheatsheaf).

Foster, J. E., Greer, J. and Thorbecke, E. (1984) 'A Class of Decomposable Poverty Measures', *Econometrica*, 52, pp. 761–6.

Goodman, A., Johnson, P. and Webb, S. (1997) *Inequality in the UK* (Oxford: Oxford University Press).

Gosling, A., Machin, S. and Meghir, C. (1994) 'What has Happened to Men's Wages since the Mid-1960s?', *Fiscal Studies*, 15(4), pp. 63–87.

Gottschalk, P. and Joyce, M. (1997) *Cross-National Differences in the Rise in Earnings Inequality: Market and Institutional Factors*, LIS working paper no. 160 (Luxembourg: CEPS/INSTEAD).

Gottschalk, P. and Smeeding, T. (1997) 'Cross-National Comparisons of Earnings and Income Inequality', *Journal of Economic Literature*, XXXV, pp. 633–87.

Hagenaars, A., de Vos, K. and Zaidi, M. A. (1994) *Poverty Statistics in the Late 1980s: Research Based on Micro-data* (Luxembourg: Office for Official Publications of the European Communities).

Institute of Social Studies Advisory Service (1990) *Poverty in Figures: Europe in the Early 1980s* (Luxembourg: Eurostat).

Jenkins, S. (1991) 'The Measurement of Income Inequality', in L. Osberg (ed.), *Economic Inequality and Poverty: An International Perspective* (New York: M. E. Sharpe).

Juhn, C., Murphy, K. and Pierce, B. (1992) 'Wage Inequality and the Rise in Returns to Skill', *Journal of Political Economy*, 101(3), pp. 410–42.

Katz, L. and Murphy, K. (1992) 'Changes in Relative Wages, 1963–1987: Supply and Demand Factors', *Quarterly Journal of Economics*, 107(1), pp. 35–78.

Levy, F. and Murnane, R. (1992) 'US Earnings Levels and Earnings Inequality: A Review of Recent Trends and Proposed Explanations', *Journal of Economic Literature*, 30(3), pp. 1333–81.

Lundberg, S., Pollak, R. A. and Wales, T. J. (1997) 'Do Husbands and Wives Pool Their Resources?', *Journal of Human Resources*, 32(3), pp. 463–80.

Mack, J. and Lansley, S. (1985) *Poor Britain* (London: Allen & Unwin).

Murphy, D. (1984) 'The Impact of State Taxes and Benefits on Irish Household Incomes', *Journal of the Statistical and Social Inquiry Society of Ireland*, XXV, pp. 55–120.

Murphy, D. (1985) 'Calculation of Gini and Theil Inequality Coefficients for Irish Household Incomes in 1973 and 1980', *Economic and Social Review*, 16, pp. 225–49.

Nolan, B. (1978) 'The Personal Distribution of Income in the Republic of Ireland', *Journal of the Statistical and Social Inquiry Society of Ireland*, XXIII, pp. 91–139.

Nolan, B. (1992) *The Wealth of Irish Households* (Dublin: Combat Poverty Agency).

Nolan, B. and Callan, T. (eds) (1994) *Poverty and Policy in Ireland* (Dublin: Gill & Macmillan).

Nolan, B. and Whelan, C. T. (1996) *Resources, Deprivation and Poverty* (Oxford: Clarendon Press).

Nolan, B., Whelan, C. T. and Williams, J. (1998) *Where Are Poor Households Found? The Spatial Distribution of Poverty and Deprivation in Ireland* (Dublin: Oak Tree Press).

O'Higgins, M. and Jenkins, S. P. (1990) 'Poverty in the EC: Estimates for 1975, 1980 and 1985', in Teekens, R. and Van Praag, B. M. S. (eds), *Analysing Poverty in the European Community* (Luxembourg: Eurostat).

OECD (1993) *Employment Outlook* (Paris: OECD).

OECD (1996) *Employment Outlook* (Paris: OECD).

Roche, J. (1984) *Poverty and Income Maintenance Policies in Ireland* (Dublin: Institute for Public Administration).

Rottman, D. B., Hannan, D. F., Hardiman, N. and Wiley, M. (1982) *The Distribution of Income in the Republic of Ireland: A Study in Social Class and Family-Cycle Inequalities*, General Research Series paper 109 (Dublin: The Economic and Social Research Institute).

Rottman, D. and Reidy, M. (1988) *Redistribution Through State Social Expenditure in the Republic of Ireland 1973–1980*, report no. 85 (Dublin: National Economic and Social Council).

Sen, A. (1976) 'Poverty: An Ordinal Approach to Measurement', *Econometrica*, 44, pp. 219–31.

Schmitt, J. (1995) 'The Changing Structure of Male Earnings in Britain, 1974–88', in R. Freeman and L. Katz (eds), *Differences and Changes in Wage Structures* (Chicago: University of Chicago Press).

Shorrocks, A. F. (1983) 'Ranking Income Distributions', *Economica*, 50, pp. 3–17.

Townsend, P. (1979) *Poverty in the United Kingdom* (Harmondsworth: Penguin).

Verma, V. J. (1998) *Robustness and Comparability in Income Distribution Statistics*, paper to EU high-level think-tank on Poverty Statistics, Stockholm, January.

Wood, A. (1994) *North–South Trade, Employment and Inequality: Changing Fortunes in a Skill-driven World* (Oxford: Clarendon Press).

9 The Persistence of High Unemployment in a Small Open Labour Market: The Irish Case

Brendan Walsh[1]

INTRODUCTION

This chapter contains an overview of the Irish unemployment problem. It starts with a review of existing research and presents further analysis of unemployment in a small, open labour market. The reasons for the persistence of high unemployment and the recent improvement in the labour market situation are discussed.

BACKGROUND

Ireland has many of the characteristics of a regional economy. Accounting for less than 1 per cent of the EU's output, it is smaller than most of the regions of the larger European nations. The Irish economy is also like a region in its heavy dependence on external trade and the exceptional role played by mobile capital and labour in its development. This has important implications for the study of Irish unemployment.

The importance of external migration is shown by the fact that in the late 1980s, when the UK economy boomed and the Irish economy was in the doldrums, average annual net emigration amounted to 0.75 per cent of the population. During the current economic boom there has been a significant net inflow of population. The impact of migration on the labour market is much greater than on the whole population. Over the period 1986–91, emigration depleted the male cohort aged 15–19 in 1986 by 20 per cent. This outflow fell to just half that level over the following five years, and there was a significant net inflow in the 25–34 year age group (Figure 9.1).

Figure 9.1   Impact of net external migration by age cohort, 1986–91 and
1991–96

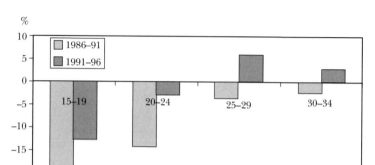

The data on usual residence in the 1996 census show one-year gross inflow rates of between 2 and 3.5 per cent among the population aged 20–34. However, immigration is still on a relatively small scale. The net inflow rate amounted to only 0.25 per cent of the population aged 15–44 in 1996–97, compared with an annual average rate of net emigration of 1.6 per cent a year between 1986–91.

The dependence of the Irish industrial sector on foreign direct investment (FDI) is evident from the fact that much of the current export boom is due to foreign-owned companies. The share of new, 'high-tech' industries, such as pharmaceuticals, electronic machinery, office and data processing equipment, and health care products in total exports rose from 18.2 per cent in 1979 to 49.1 per cent in 1995. While the overall investment ratio declined during the 1980s, there was a marked change in its composition, with a growing share accounted for by FDI. This has been cited as the principal reason for the dramatic decline in the marginal capital/output ratio (Walsh, 1996). Traditional industrial sectors, such as food and livestock, clothing, and textiles, have recorded modest increases in employment, output and exports, but they have become proportionately much less important in the national economy. The expanding 'modern' sectors are predominantly foreign-owned and have exceptionally high valued-added per employee.[2]

After years of relative stagnation, Ireland became the star performer in the EU and indeed the OECD during the 1990s. Of relevance to this chapter is the fact that the rapid rate of output growth has been translated into an impressive rate of job creation. Figure 9.2 shows

Figure 9.2   Level of employment

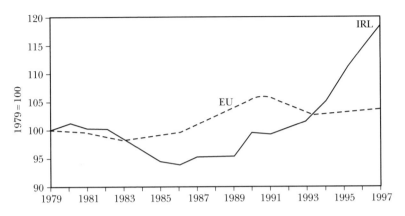

Source: OECD, *Employment Outlook.*

how much more rapidly employment has grown in Ireland than in the
EU since the mid-1980s. Growth at the pace that has been recorded
in Ireland is more characteristic of a booming region than of a separate
national economy (Krugman, 1997). The rapid growth of employment
has been facilitated on the supply side by the rapid growth of the labour
force, which in turn reflects the age structure of the population, rising
women's labour force participation rates, and net immigration. In a
later section the role of FDI in the growth of the demand for labour
is highlighted.

THE RISE AND PERSISTENCE OF UNEMPLOYMENT

High unemployment and the related phenomenon of heavy emigration
have traditionally been major policy issues in Ireland. The poor performance of the Irish labour market in the 1980s left us with the lowest
employment/population ratio and the highest net emigration rate in
the OECD and the second highest unemployment rate (after Spain).

The graph of Irish unemployment clearly resembles the 'European'
rather than the 'American' paradigm (Figure 9.3). Starting from an
average of about 6 per cent during the 1960s, the unemployment rate
rose to unprecedented levels in the wake of the global recessions of the
1970s. In a characteristic European pattern it declined only slowly
during subsequent economic expansions and despite the recent period

Figure 9.3   Irish unemployment rates

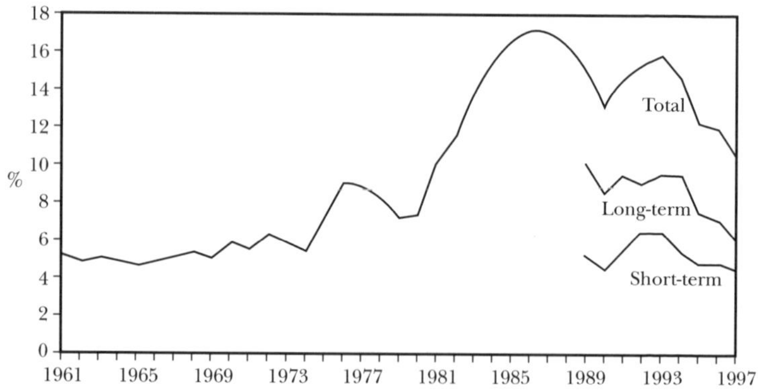

Source: Leddin and Walsh (1998).

of unprecedented employment growth it remains almost twice the average level of the 1960s.[3]

The duration of unemployment is of great economic and social significance. The demoralisation associated with long-term unemployment is one of the main social costs of unemployment. Furthermore, the long-term unemployed become 'outsiders' in the sense of losing touch with the labour market and ceasing to exert a moderating pressure on the wage bargain. There are marked differences between countries in the share of long-term unemployment in total unemployment. There is much less relative international variation in short-term unemployment rates, as may be seen from the coefficients of variation in Table 9.1. The countries with high overall unemployment – Ireland and the main continental European countries – are by and large countries with very high rates of long-term unemployment. The low overall rates of unemployment in countries like the United States and Japan are due to the virtual non-existence of long-term unemployment.

Figure 9.3 shows separate long- and short-term unemployment rates since 1989 (a consistent ILO series on unemployment by duration is not available for earlier years). By 1997 Ireland's rate of short-term unemployment had fallen to just over 4 per cent, which compares favourably with the rate of short-term unemployment in the US and many other OECD countries (Table 9.1). A comparison of short- and long-term unemployment rates across countries shows that they are almost unrelated phenomena: the correlation between the two rates in

Table 9.1 is only +0.41, and when Spain is excluded it falls to a non-significant +0.06 (Figure 9.4). Despite the very large differences in overall unemployment rates, the short-term unemployment rates in Ireland, the UK and the US are similar. One explanation that has been

Figure 9.4   Long- and short-term unemployment rates, 1996

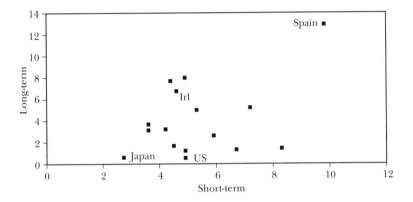

Table 9.1   Unemployment rates by duration, selected countries, 1996

	Short-term	Long-term	Total
Ireland (1997)	*4.6*	*6.7*	*11.3*
Australia	5.9	2.6	8.5
Austria	4.5	1.7	6.2
Belgium	4.9	8.0	12.9
Canada	8.3	1.4	9.7
France	7.2	5.2	12.4
Germany	5.3	5.0	10.3
Italy	4.4	7.7	12.1
Japan	2.7	0.6	3.3
Netherlands	3.6	3.1	6.7
New Zealand	4.9	1.2	6.1
Portugal	3.6	3.7	7.3
Spain	9.8	12.9	22.7
Sweden	6.7	1.3	8.0
United Kingdom	4.2	3.2	7.4
United States	4.9	0.5	5.4
Coefficient of variation (%)	33.5	81.2	46.3

Note: 'Long-term' refers to durations of a year or more.
Source: OECD, *Employment Outlook*, July 1997, Tables 1.3 and H.

offered for the low rate of long-term unemployment in the US is that while the rate of inflow to unemployment is just as high as in the main European countries, the outflow rate is also high. There is a tendency for people to churn through recurrent short spells of unemployment rather than, as in Europe, remaining more or less permanently unemployed (Cohen, 1997). In Ireland and several other OECD countries a relatively high incidence of both short- and long-term unemployment points to high inflow rates and low outflow rates. The recent decline in Irish long-term unemployment indicates that the outflow rate has increased.

Relatively little information is available on labour market flows. A flow analysis of the registered unemployment data concluded that there was a decline in hazard rates in the first half of the 1980s, followed by a reversal of this trend in more recent years (Harrison and Walsh, 1994). The authors state that the flows into and out of unemployment 'are predominantly pushed and pulled by growth in the working-age population, rather than flows created by employment flows' (p. 57). Further light is shed on the dynamics of the Irish labour market by an analysis of the responses to the Labour Force Survey, which provide more reliable information on labour market outcomes than does the series on registered unemployment. Table 9.2 presents the results of a tabulation of economic activity – principal economic status (PES) – of respondents at the time of the survey and a year earlier for two years, 1993 and 1996. More detail is provided for women than for men in order to explore the sources of the rapid increase in women's employment. A comparison of the flows for these two years shows a clear improvement in labour market outcomes. For both men and women the probability of remaining employed increased, and the probability of remaining unemployed decreased. The large jump in the flow from unemployment to employment among women is striking. There is no evidence of an increased outflow from either employment or unemployment to 'other', but there was a significant increase among both men and women in the flow from 'other' to 'employed'. Overall, these data reveal a general tightening of the labour market, with increasing flows from unemployment and inactivity into employment.

DEMOGRAPHIC INFLUENCES ON UNEMPLOYMENT

Participation rates have been changing for numerous reasons. As unemployment became a growing policy concern, governments have tended to encourage non-participation in the labour force as a way of

Table 9.2   Principal economic status (PES) in 1995, cross-tabulated with PES in 1996 and, in brackets, 1992 status cross-tabulated with 1993

PES in t − 1 (%)	PES in t (%)			
	Employed	*Unemployed*	*Other*	*Total*
Employed	95.5 (93.5)	4.0 (5.7)	0.6 (0.7)	100 (100)
Unemployed	17.3 (15.8)	81.2 (82.6)	1.5 (1.5)	100 (100)
Other	10.0 (7.5)	2.9 (3.7)	87.0 (88.8)	100 (100)

Females aged 20–54

PES in t − 1 (%)	PES in t (%)					
	Employed	*Unemployed*	*Student*	*Home duties*	*Other*	*Total*
Employed	93.7 (92.2)	3.0 (4.2)	0.3 (0.5)	2.5 (2.7)	0.4 (0.3)	100 (100)
Unemployed	26.9 (21.9)	69.3 (72.2)	0.4 (0.8)	2.8 (4.1)	0.6 (1.0)	100 (100)
Student	19.2 (17.7)	3.5 (6.0)	76.2 (74.5)	0.6 (1.0)	0.5 (0.8)	100 (100)
Home duties	3.5 (2.4)	0.4 (0.3)	0.1 (0.1)	95.8 (97.2)	0.1 (0.0)	100 (100)
Other	12.4 (7.9)	2.6 (0.6)	0.3 (0.2)	2.4 (0.5)	82.3 (90.4)	100 (100)

Note: The first row of the table shows, for example, that 95.5 percent of those employed in 1995 were still employed in 1996.
Source: *Labour Force Survey*, 1993 and 1996, special tabulations.

reducing the headline statistics. The trend towards longer participation in the educational system was probably accentuated by the poor labour market situation in the 1980s, while the decline in labour force participation rates among older males (Figure 9.5) has been encouraged by a policy of reclassifying the long-term unemployed as 'retired' or 'permanently invalid'. The non-employment rate among men in this age group has risen from 23.9 per cent in 1983 to 30.6 per cent in 1997. The factors that raise the probability of inactivity among men in this age group are similar to those that raise the probability of unemployment. Inactive men of working age who state that they are not looking for work and have no interest in a job,

> tend to be older, poorly educated men, of whom 86 per cent had been unemployed a year ago ... for almost half of this group no information was available on their last job and a majority of those for whom information was available had been labourers or production workers.   (Murphy and Walsh, 1997, pp. 99 100)[4]

Even though the vast majority of those who were not economically active expressed no interest in employment, the decline in the labour force participation rate among men aged 45–64 during the past 15 years nonetheless suggests that the persistence of long-term unemployment among older men may be understated in the conventional measure of unemployment. Over the period when male labour force participation rates have been falling, women's labour force participation rates have risen dramatically (Figure 9.5). The contrasting trends in male and female participation rates suggest that the problem of poor labour market outcomes among older males is not simply due to an overall dearth of employment opportunities. There is evidence of a mismatch between the skills and experience of older males and the requirements of the available job opportunities.

Figure 9.5   Labour force participation rates

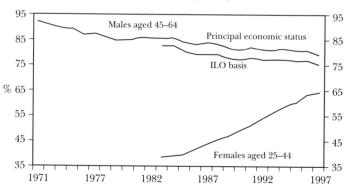

Source: Labour Force Survey; Census of Population.

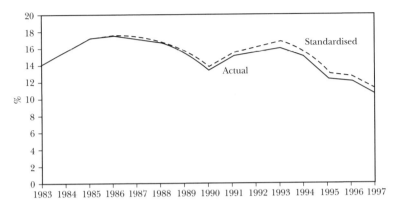

Figure 9.6   Actual and standardised unemployment rates

Note: Standardised rate based on six age-sex labour force groups.
Source: *Labour Force Survey*.

Early in the debate on the natural, or non-accelerating, inflation rate of unemployment attention was focused on the changing structure of the labour market and the working-age population. It was believed that demographic changes, especially the increase in the proportion of young adults in the population, could account for some of the apparent increase in the rate of equilibrium unemployment in the US (Perry, 1970). This topic merits examination in an Irish context.

A standardised unemployment rate (based on the share of six demographic groups in the 1983 labour force) allows us to see how the changing demographic structure of the labour force has affected the aggregate unemployment rate. The actual and standardised rates are shown in Figure 9.6. The differences between them are small: the unemployment rate would be only marginally higher had the demographic structure of the labour force remained unaltered since 1983. While the gap between the actual and hypothetical unemployment would be higher if account were taken of the rise in the labour force's average education level, it nonetheless seems safe to take the unadjusted unemployment rate as a guide to underlying labour market conditions.

EQUILIBRIUM UNEMPLOYMENT

There is no agreed definition of equilibrium unemployment. In large economies the concept is usually defined as the rate of unemployment at which no inflationary pressures emanate from the labour market. The non-accelerating inflation rate of unemployment, or NAIRU, is defined as the rate consistent with a stable rate of inflation in the absence of supply shocks (Gordon, 1997). But the role of unemployment in the inflationary mechanism of a small open economy such as Ireland is far from clear, making the definition of equilibrium unemployment problematic.

We can use the conventional Phillips curve as a starting point. Figure 9.7 shows Irish wage inflation and the rate of unemployment over the past 35 years. The Phillips curve shifted upwards in the 1970s, indicating a deteriorating wage adjustment process in the wake of the supply-side shocks of the energy crises. The behaviour of unemployment and inflation over the period 1980–86 is consistent with a short-term trade-off between unemployment and inflation, but no such trade-off is detectable in the data after 1986. Wage inflation remained very stable in the face of falling unemployment (1986–90), rising unemployment (1990–93) and finally as unemployment fell to a 17-year low over the years 1993–97.

The instability of the Phillips curve has led to attempts to estimate a time-varying NAIRU. These are usually based on expectations-augmented Phillips curves. Estimates of equilibrium unemployment based on this approach tend to track actual unemployment very closely. Layard, Nickell and Jackman (1991), for example, provide estimates of equilibrium unemployment for 19 OECD countries for three periods (the 1960s, the 1970s and the 1980s). The cross-sectional correlation between the actual and equilibrium unemployment rates are 0.94, 0.85

Figure 9.7   Phillips curve

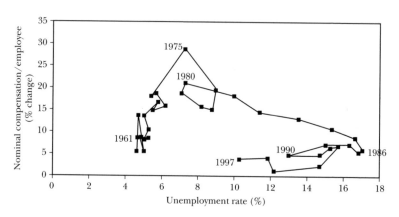

and 0.97 for the three periods, respectively. The correlation between actual and estimated equilibrium unemployment rates is even closer under alternative approaches to the estimation of equilibrium unemployment (Gordon, 1997). It seems that these constructs add little to the information already contained in the actual unemployment data.

The concept of equilibrium unemployment is central to the estimation of the 'sacrifice ratio', that is the cost associated with a disinflation. A temporary increase in unemployment may be regarded as the cost of squeezing inflation out of the economy. Between 1981 and 1994 the number of 'point-years' of excess unemployment[5] totalled 73 in Ireland. Over the same period inflation fell by 15 percentage points. If the excess unemployment is regarded as the price of the disinflation, the sacrifice ratio was 4.9. This compares, for example, with a ratio of 2.8 for the US during the Volcker disinflation (Mankiw, 1997, p. 355).[6] It therefore seems that excess unemployment would be a very costly mechanism for reducing inflation in an Irish context. But there is actually little evidence to believe that causality ran from rising unemployment to falling wage and price inflation, which renders the concept of the sacrifice ratio questionable.

The hypothesis underlying the NAIRU is that price inflation reflects pressure originating in a tightening labour market. Larger wage increases are conceded as workers become scarcer. Higher labour costs are reflected in higher prices. Both the links in this chain of events appear weak in Ireland. The link between wage and price inflation in a small open economy is much weaker than it would be in a large closed one. The evidence on this point is discussed below. The evidence supporting a relationship between unemployment and wage inflation is also weak. When unemployment rises due to adverse shocks there appears to be little downward pressure on real wages that would move the economy back to a full-employment equilibrium. This is borne out by the findings of numerous previous econometric studies. For example, a recent comparative analysis used annual data to estimate wage-formation equations for 21 countries (including Ireland) over the period 1970–95 (OECD, 1997). With the rate of change in the real wage as dependent variable, variables on the right-hand side included the GDP deflator, trend productivity, and the rate of unemployment and its change. The specification may be regarded as a consensus view of how to model wage–price inflation. The Irish equation has the second lowest $\bar{R}^2$ in the study, 0.37 compared with an average of 0.66. The coefficient on the rate of unemployment in the Irish equation is also the second smallest reported, indicating low responsiveness of real wages to unemployment.

Table 9.3 Regression of after-tax real wage (w) on the unemployment rate, u, and productivity (x): annual data 1974–96 (t-ratio in parentheses)

Intercept	Δu	Δx	w_{-1}	x_{-1}	u_{-1}	$\bar{R}^2$	D.W.
1.34	−0.28		−0.27		−0.02	0.50	1.88
(2.2)	(4.2)		(2.3)		(0.6)		
−0.80		0.02	−0.44	0.63		0.53	1.29
(1.4)		(0.1)	(3.5)	(4.5)			
0.22	−0.19	0.13	−0.46	0.44	−0.20	0.70	2.20
(0.4)	(3.1)	(0.7)	(3.9)	(3.4)	(0.8)		

Note: Dependent variable = Δw. All variables in logs.

Table 9.3 shows regressions of real after-tax wage rates on the unemployment rate and a measure of productivity.[7] The null hypothesis of no long-run relationship between unemployment and take-home pay is not rejected, but the null hypothesis of no long-run relationship between take-home pay and productivity is.[8] These findings confirm the weak link between unemployment and wage bargaining in Ireland. The interpretation of the relationship between productivity and pay is discussed further in a later section.

An alternative approach to the process of Irish wage determination also leads to scepticism about the role of Irish unemployment. Curtis and FitzGerald (1996) argue that the links between the Irish and UK labour market directly affect the process of wage formation in Ireland. They claim that

> [Over the past thirty years] economic integration has affected domestic labour cost developments through changing conditions for both the demand and supply of labour. The effect of these changes has been to promote a convergence in wage rates between the two economies.
>
> (p. 335)

They support this conclusion by appealing to the significance of a UK wage variable in a wage equation that also includes domestic variables such as prices, the tax wedge, unemployment, productivity and union density. In the closed-economy version of their model the coefficient on the unemployment variable has the expected negative sign but barely reaches statistical significance. When the UK wage rate is included, the Irish unemployment rate ceases to be significant. The coefficient on the UK wage rate is highly significant (and not significantly different from unity), suggesting that Irish wage rates adjust fully to changes in the target UK wage rate. Irish wages can be explained in terms of UK wages, UK unemployment, and a world productivity variable. The authors argue that this approach provides a better explanation for Irish wage behaviour than one based on measures of domestic labour market conditions. This conclusion reinforces the scepticism about the relevance of the NAIRU concept in an Irish context.

Several studies have shown that domestic costs are not a major factor in Irish price inflation. A recent study of Irish price inflation confirms the widely held view that the main influences are foreign inflation and the exchange rate (Kenny and McGettigan, 1996b). Excessive wage pressures can be reflected in higher domestic inflation but this inflation is eventually reflected in a lower exchange rate. Wages and prices have tracked each closely over time, with strong evidence of causality running in both directions. Following a review of 13 different econometric studies of Irish inflation in the post-EMS period, the authors conclude that

> The significance of domestic 'demand' conditions is found to be mixed, with some support for the role of output, *but no role being found for unemployment.*   (p. 146, emphasis added)

The authors favour a hybrid model of Irish inflation, mixing elements of a wage mark-up model and a price-taking small, open-economy model. Wage increases that exceed the growth of productivity and are accommodated by nominal exchange rate depreciation result in inflation, and a PPP relationship is preserved. An overvalued exchange rate has a direct disinflationary impact on nominal wages. While they do not rule out the possibility that indirect channels operate through, for example, rising unemployment leading to downward pressure on wages, they do not explicitly model a link between unemployment and wage inflation. No guidance is provided as to how the rate of unemployment could be used to gauge labour market conditions. However, they note that following the reintroduction of centralised wage bargaining in the mid-1980s, 'the contribution of domestic inflationary impulses, relative to foreign ones, has been largely subdued' (Kenny and McGettigan, 1996a, p. 89).

To summarise, the evidence from the extensive available research on Irish wage and price inflation indicates that the role of the unemployment rate in the Irish wage formation process is weak. While undoubtedly a 'low' unemployment rate would lead to inflationary pressure in the labour market and higher prices of non-traded goods and services, the relevance of this to the broad evolution of Irish wage and price inflation over the past 25 years appears to be slight. However, the future role of unemployment cannot be extrapolated from the evidence of the past. The current tightening of the Irish labour is moving the economy into uncharted waters. But when Ireland becomes a participant in the European monetary union to be launched at the start of 1999, the scope for independent variation in the rate of inflation in traded goods will be eliminated. An overheating Irish labour market could only affect the overall rate of inflation through its effect on the non-traded components of the price index.

THE ANGLO-IRISH LABOUR MARKET AND IRISH UNEMPLOYMENT

The openness of the Irish labour market and its close links with the UK suggest that it might be possible to define the equilibrium rate of Irish unemployment with reference to the level of unemployment in Britain. The equilibrium rate of unemployment in Ireland could be thought of as that which reflects full adjustment to the corresponding rate in the UK. A visual comparison of the two unemployment rates (Figure 9.8) shows that between 1961 and the mid-1970s the gap between them was very stable.[9] This relationship weakened, if it did not

Figure 9.8   Irish and British unemployment rates

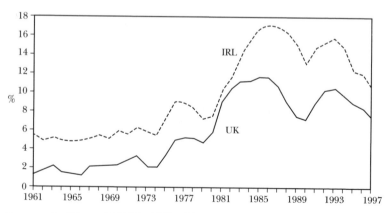

Source: Leddin and Walsh (1998); OECD, *Employment Outlook*.

completely break down, in the second half of the 1970s and early 1980s, to be re-established over the past ten years.

A possible explanation of the similarity in the behaviour of Irish and British unemployment rates is that the two countries' business cycles are in phase; both experienced similar shocks in the 1970s and 1980s. But there have also been significant differences between the influences on the two economies. The energy price shocks of the 1970s had a differential impact due to the fact that Britain became a net exporter of energy in the 1980s, whereas Ireland is almost totally dependent on imported energy. Ireland has pursued independent fiscal and monetary policies: there was a major fiscal expansion during the late 1970s and since we joined the exchange rate mechanism of the European Monetary System in 1979 the Irish pound has been loosely pegged to the DM but volatile relative to sterling. This allowed us to escape the major real appreciation experienced by sterling in the early 1980s. Finally, Ireland, unlike Britain, has been a major net beneficiary of transfers from the EU. These factors lead us to expect considerable independent variation in the Irish unemployment rate.

A mechanism that would preserve a stable long-run relationship between the two unemployment rates is migration. The sensitivity of migration from Ireland to relative labour market conditions in Ireland and Britain is well-established. It has been modelled using a Harris–Todaro framework (Walsh, 1974; Keenan, 1981; Kirwan, 1982). These models predict that migration is a response to the difference in *expected* wages in the two countries, where the expected wages reflect the differences in actual wage rates and in the probability of finding employment (1 minus the unemployment rate). As wage rates in the two countries have converged, relative unemployment rates have become the dominant influence in the migration decision. As the employment situation deteriorated in Ireland, the availability of employment opportunities in Britain triggered large-scale emigration, which tended to curb the rise in Irish unemployment. However, as is evident from Figure 9.9, the gap between the two unemployment rates has varied significantly, falling sharply at the end of the 1970s, rising rapidly during the 1980s and falling back to the levels of the 1960s during the 1990s. It appears, nonetheless, that after the disturbances of the late 1970s the gap has tended to revert to its long-run mean.

Previous work on Irish labour market flows used the following simple framework. Starting from labour market accounting identities:

$$\Delta P \equiv NI + NM \equiv \Delta E + \Delta U + \Delta NA$$

where P is the population of working age, E the numbers employed, NI the natural increase of population of working age, NM the net migration of population of working age, U the unemployed, and NA the non-active population of working age.

Applying these identities to the labour force involves approximations – we do not have exact estimates of 'natural increase' (the excess of the inflow over the withdrawals from the labour force), and our migration data do not distinguish between those of working age and others. Nonetheless, this provides a useful framework for tracking the relationship between changes in unemployment, employment and net migration. When estimated in the form:

$$\Delta U = \alpha_0 + \alpha_1 NM + \alpha_2 \Delta E$$

We expect that $\alpha_0 > 0$, α_1, $\alpha_2 < 0$.

The intercept term, α_0, includes the natural increase of the labour force, that is the difference between NI and ΔNA.

This *ad hoc* relationship has been refined to allow for differences in the responses of the short-term unemployed (U_{st}) and long-term unemployed (U_{lt}), and to distinguish between periods of net inward and outward migration. Walsh (1987) found that this model provided a better account of changes in short-term than long-term unemployment, and that net-out migration (NM_{out}) had a much bigger impact on unemployment than net in-migration (NM_{in}). The following equations were estimated with annual data 1966–86 (absolute t ratios in parentheses):

$$\Delta U_{st} = 11.25 - 0.94 NM_{out} - 0.66 \Delta E - 0.04 NM_{in} \quad (\bar{R}^2 = 0.51; \ D.W. = 2.0)$$
$$\qquad (2.8) \quad (3.0) \qquad\quad (4.6) \qquad (0.1)$$

$$\Delta U_{lt} = 6.45 - 0.12 NM_{out} - 0.26 \Delta E + 0.04 NM_{in} \quad (\bar{R}^2 = 0.33; \ D.W. = 1.7)$$
$$\qquad (2.7) \quad (0.7) \qquad\quad (3.1) \qquad (0.2)$$

Long-term unemployment is relatively unresponsive to growth of employment and the outflow of migrants does not appear to contain long-term unemployed. This finding identifies a source of hysteresis in unemployment.

The data on long- and short-term unemployment in this study were derived from the claimant count (or 'Live Register'). As noted above, in recent years the discrepancy between these figures and the LFS measure of unemployment has widened. Rather than updating a study based on the registration data, which are considered unreliable as an indicator of the recent trend in unemployment, the relationship between Irish and UK unemployment has been explored using the ILO unemployment rates for the two countries.

Honohan (1992) argues that the influence of migration is so strong that Irish unemployment can be regarded as determined primarily by UK labour market conditions. His general approach is to fit an error-correction model in Irish and UK unemployment and a trend. On the basis of the behaviour of the numbers of registered unemployed over the period 1971–91 he concludes that

> trends and fluctuations in UK unemployment ... have a decisive long-term influence on Irish unemployment.   (p. 33)

A strong correlation between the Irish and UK claimant counts is still found with more recent data.[10] This provides us with a starting point in accounting for Irish unemployment, namely the notion that it maintains a stable relationship with UK unemployment, with migration serving as the mechanism linking the two rates.

An econometric problem exists, however, with the interpretation of Irish unemployment as somehow 'anchored' in UK unemployment. The two series in Figure 9.9 are not cointegrated. Even though the gap appears now to be reverting to the mean level of the 1960s, formal tests do not reject the hypothesis that no cointegrating vector exists between the two unemployment rates over the period 1961–97.

Figure 9.9   Gap between Irish and UK unemployment rates

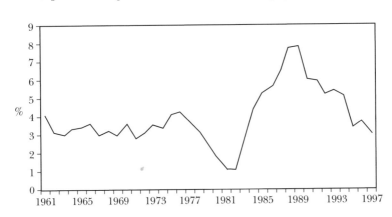

On economic grounds, too, the idea that variations in Irish unemployment can be explained entirely by the level of unemployment in the UK is obviously incomplete. In particular it ignores the empirical finding that the Irish unemployment rate is very responsive to changes in the growth rate of output in Ireland. This relationship – known as Okun's law – fits the Irish data surprisingly well in view of the openness of the labour market (see Leddin and Walsh, 1998, and Figure 9.10). It would therefore seem necessary to include both UK unemployment and the growth rate of Irish GNP (g_y) among the influences on the Irish unemployment rate.[11]

Among the other possible influences on the Irish unemployment rate, and the gap between Irish and British unemployment, the most important is the relative generosity of the social welfare system. This has received considerable attention in previous studies, dating back to Walsh (1978). In a recent study Scarpetta (1996) claims that 4.9 percentage points of the 9.7 percentage points increase in Irish structural[12] unemployment over the period 1971–93 was due to the increased generosity of the Irish unemployment benefit system. Similarly, Burda (1997) argues that the reason for the deterioration in Ireland's employment record relative to the UK during the 1980s was the growth of the 'unemployment trap' – the lack of incentive for the unemployed to take jobs at wage rates that do little more than replace benefits.

These arguments have obvious parallels with the Card and Riddell (1993) account of the divergence of Canadian and US unemployment rates. They emphasise the 'entitlement effect' of the more generous

Figure 9.10   Okun's law: growth of GNP and changes in unemployment rate, 1974–97

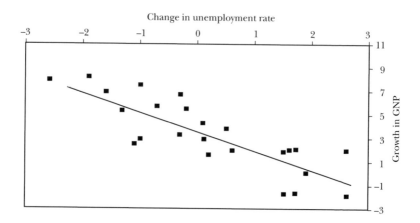

Canadian unemployment insurance system, claiming that the easing of the Canadian benefit qualification conditions resulted in higher participation and unemployment rates. This argument is very sensitive to the measure of unemployment that is used. Walsh (1993) and Murphy and Walsh (1997) found a significant entitlement effect among Irish females. But, on the other hand, they also found that a significant proportion of older Irish males are registered as unemployed (and classify themselves as such in terms of 'principal economic status') but are not included in the ILO measure of unemployment because they do not report any active job search. If this phenomenon has been increasing it would work against the entitlement effect found amongst women.

Before presenting the results of formal econometric tests of this hypothesis, we may note that the evidence does not, at first sight, seem to support the interpretation that the relative generosity of the Irish social welfare system helps to explain the gap between Irish and British unemployment rates. The sharpest increase in the Irish replacement ratio relative to the UK ratio occurred between 1979 and 1984, when the gap between the Irish and UK unemployment rates *narrowed* as UK unemployment rose rapidly. It is also implausible to suggest that the recent narrowing of the Irish–UK unemployment gap should be attributed to an increased harshness of the Irish, relative to the British, social welfare system.

To test the importance of these considerations for the aggregate Irish unemployment rate and the Irish–UK gap it is necessary to have a measure of the relative generosity of the two social welfare systems. The best available measure is the ratio of the Irish to UK unemployment replacement ratio, *rrratio*.[13] This may be included in an equation that allows for other influences on the Irish–UK unemployment gap.[14] The regression results in Table 9.4 explore the alternative explanations of Irish unemployment discussed above. A range of results is reported in order to allow the reader to judge the relative merits of the alternative hypotheses.

Equation (1) in Table 9.4 is a simple estimate of Okun's law. It provides a good fit to the data according to standard statistical criteria. However, when the change in UK unemployment is added (equation 2), there is a marked improvement in the equation's fit.

Equation (3) shows the results of fitting an ECM model to Irish and British unemployment (3). In equation (4) the growth of GNP is included as a conditioning variable, while in equation (5) *rrratio* is included in the ECM. The interpretation of g_y should be *deviations of the growth rate from its long-run trend* g_y^*. The influence of g_y^* is subsumed in the intercept term.

The most satisfactory result is provided by equation (4):

$$\Delta u_{IRL} = \alpha + \beta_1 \Delta u_{UK} + \gamma_1 u_{IRL\,t-1} + \gamma_2 u_{UK\,t-1} + \delta g_y$$

The hypothesis that $\gamma_1 + \gamma_2 = 0$ is rejected, as indeed it is in all the equations in Table 9.4. This implies that the equilibrium gap between the two unemployment rates is not constant. The long-run equilibrium level of Irish unemployment implied by equation (3) is

$$u_{IRL} = -\alpha/\gamma_1 - \gamma_2/\gamma_1 u_{UK}$$

Since $\gamma_1 < \gamma_2$ in all the specifications, Irish unemployment is higher, and the gap between Irish UK unemployment is also higher, the higher the level of UK unemployment. This accords with the fact that the gap between the two unemployment rates widened as UK unemployment rose during the 1980s.

Table 9.4 Regression results for Irish unemployment rate (dependent variable Δu, t-ratios in parentheses)

	Equation number				
	(1)	*(2)*	*(3)*	*(4)*	*(5)*
Sample period 1961–97					
Intercept	1.33	0.82	0.54	1.00	1.32
	(5.6)	(4.0)	(1.5)	(3.0)	(3.5)
g_y	−0.33	−0.22		−0.17	−0.14
	(6.2)	(4.6)		(3.4)	(2.9)
Δu_{UK}		0.60	0.78	0.60	0.69
		(5.3)	(6.6)	(5.2)	(5.6)
$\Delta rrratio$					−0.0004
					(0.5)
$u_{IRL\,t-1}$			−0.25	−0.16	−0.06
			(3.0)	(2.0)	(0.6)
$U_{UK\,t-1}$			0.33	0.20	0.22
			(3.3)	(2.2)	(2.3)
$Rrratio_{t-1}$					−1.33
					(1.7)
$\bar{R}^2$	0.52	0.73	0.66	0.75	0.76
D.W.	2.1	2.0	1.4	1.9	2.2

Table 9.4 *(Continued)*

	Equation number				
	(1)	(2)	(3)	(4)	(5)
Sample period 1961–77					
Intercept	0.80	0.32	2.85	4.06	3.27
	(2.0)	(1.0)	(3.2)	(6.6)	(4.3)
g_y	−0.15	−0.08		−0.17	−0.12
	(1.6)	(1.1)		(4.4)	(2.4)
Δu_{UK}		0.80	1.18	1.13	0.98
		(3.8)	(6.5)	(9.8)	(7.0)
$\Delta rrratio$					0.83
					(0.7)
$u_{IRL\,t-1}$			−0.96	−1.21	−1.38
			(3.4)	(6.6)	(6.8)
$u_{UK\,t-1}$			1.12	1.52	1.46
			(3.3)	(6.7)	(6.4)
$Rrratio_{t-1}$					2.34
					(1.7)
$\bar{R}^2$	0.1	0.54	0.73	0.89	0.90
D.W.	1.9	2.3	1.7	2.3	2.5
Sample period 1978–97					
Intercept	1.41	0.97	−1.32	−0.34	−0.52
	(4.8)	(3.7)	(1.7)	(0.5)	(0.4)
g_y	−0.38	−0.27		−0.18	−0.18
	(6.1)	(4.4)		(2.7)	(2.5)
Δu_{UK}		0.50	0.86	0.64	0.64
		(3.5)	(5.9)	(4.3)	(3.9)
$\Delta rrratio$					−0.0003
					(0.4)
$u_{IRL\,t-1}$			−0.22	−0.12	−1.38
			(2.4)	(1.4)	(1.0)
$u_{UK\,t-1}$			0.49	0.29	0.29
			(3.9)	(2.3)	(2.1)
$Rrratio_{t-1}$					0.24
					(0.2)
$\bar{R}^2$	0.66	0.78	0.76	0.83	0.80
D.W.	2.6	2.3	1.8	2.6	2.5

The results for the specification including *rratio* in the ECM are not satisfactory. This variable does not perform well by the usual statistical criteria and the implied equilibrium relationship between UK and Irish unemployment is implausible: the estimate of $-\gamma_2/\gamma_1$ is 3.8, implying too high a *ceteris paribus* long-run responsiveness of Irish to UK unemployment. The results do not support the interpretation that the breakdown in the traditional link between Irish and UK unemployment that occurred in the late 1970s was due to the increasing relative generosity of the Irish social welfare system. In the following section, however, attention is drawn to some important changes in the social welfare code not adequately captured in the *rratio* variable that may have contributed to the decline in Irish unemployment.

Tests reveal a significant structural break in the relationship between Irish and British unemployment in the 1970s. The inclusion of g_y and *rratio* do not remove this problem. The equations have been estimated for two separate sub-periods, 1961–77 and 1978–97, and the results shown in the lower two sections of Table 9.4, even though it is obvious that the reliability of estimates based on only 20 annual observations is not high. Nonetheless, the results for the more recent sub-period, 1978–97 support the same conclusions about the relative merits of alternative models as those based on the full sample. In particular there is strong support for the importance of including g_y in the equation. The *rratio* variable is not significant. While the link between Irish and British unemployment is strong in both sub-periods, there is little evidence that Irish unemployment has been influenced by the social welfare regime in either.

To summarise, the following conclusions are warranted:
1. The two key influences on the Irish unemployment rate are:
    *   the rate of growth of the Irish economy, and
    *   the rate of unemployment in the UK.
2. There was, however, a structural break in the relationship between these variables and Irish unemployment in the late 1970s. This is not accounted for by changes in the relative generosity of the Irish social welfare system. It may have been brought about by a shift in the UK demand for labour away from unskilled workers.
3. A standard error-correction model captures the dynamics of the adjustment of Irish to UK unemployment and to the rate of growth of the Irish economy. In addition to a long-run relationship between these variables and Irish unemployment, the short-run influences are important.

Table 9.5   Irish unemployment rate as a function
of UK unemployment (u_{UK}), based on results for
1978–97 (Table 9.4)

u_{UK} (%)	8	6	4	2
u	11.6	7.2	2.8	*

Note: * = negative predicted value.

The estimates of equation (4) for the period 1977–97 in Table 9.4 have been used to estimate the equilibrium rate of unemployment in Ireland. This can be done first from the crude Okun relationship, which suggests that Irish unemployment will stabilise when the economy is growing at 3.7 per cent (close to its long-run average growth rate). Assuming that the rate of growth stabilises at its 'natural' rate, g_y^*, the equilibrium Irish unemployment rate can be expressed as a function of the rate of unemployment in Britain. The results are shown in Table 9.5.

This shows the interesting result that Irish equilibrium unemployment falls more rapidly than UK unemployment, causing the Irish–UK gap to change from positive to negative when UK unemployment is below 5 per cent. It is implied that if the Irish economy maintains its potential output growth rate, and UK unemployment falls to historically low levels, then Irish unemployment will fall to a very low level. It remains to be seen whether this is a realistic scenario.

The equilibrium rate of unemployment in Ireland would be lowered by a permanent increase in the 'natural' growth rate, g_y^*. In light of the fact that the annual average growth rate of real GDP was 6.1 per cent over the period 1987–98, compared with 4.7 per cent over the period for which the equation on which the estimates in Table 9.5 are, it is likely that the equilibrium unemployment rate is lower than the rates shown in Table 9.5.

THE STRUCTURE OF THE LABOUR MARKET AND EQUILIBRIUM UNEMPLOYMENT

To avoid misunderstanding, let me emphasize that by using the term 'natural' rate of unemployment, I do not mean to suggest that it is immutable and unchangeable. On the contrary, many of the market characteristics that determine its level are man-made and policy-made. (Friedman, 1968, p. 9)

A consensus emerged among economists in the 1990s that high unemployment persists in Europe because many features of the typical European labour market militate against adjustment to shocks. In contrast, it is believed that in North America and Japan labour market flexibility facilitates rapid adjustment (OECD, 1994). However, detailed study of labour market conditions reveals the difficulty of generalising across countries. A majority of the measures of labour market flexibility that have been developed are indices based on assigning a country to one of a few categories based on subjective assessments of labour market institutions. Some countries are classified as flexible on one dimension but inflexible on others. There is no satisfactory composite flexibility index. But the results of cross-section analyses of OECD unemployment rates support the belief that these indicators capture important features of the way economies reacted to the shocks of the 1970s, and help explain the degree of unemployment persistence in different countries (Scarpetta, 1996; Nickel, 1997). There is evidence that the following factors contribute to the persistence of high unemployment:

- Generous unemployment benefits that run on indefinitely.
- High unionisation combined with uncoordinated wage bargaining.
- High overall tax rates.
- Lack of training and skills among job seekers.

Two features of the Irish tax/social welfare system have consistently been identified as creating an increased incidence of long-term unemployment. These are:

- The indefinite duration of assistance.
- The payment of a social welfare child benefit and the absence of a child allowance from the income-tax system. This can result in very high replacement ratios for unskilled unemployed persons with large dependent families.

We have already explored the role of the Irish social welfare on Irish unemployment in a model that allows for other influences, such as the rate of growth of Irish GDP and the level of UK unemployment. The following broader considerations are also relevant to assessing its importance in the persistence of high unemployment in Ireland.

Compared with other OECD countries, payments to jobless persons are not high in Ireland. On an after-tax basis, the Irish replacement rate was 37 per cent in 1995 compared with an OECD average of 50 per cent (OECD, 1997, p. 81; Martin, 1996, Figure 1). It is, however, hazardous to base a comparison on a single index. Over the past three years changes in the administration of the housing benefit, the family income supplement, and means-tested medical benefits have been introduced with a view to reducing the disincentive effects of the unemployment benefit regime. The long-term unemployed returning to work may now retain a proportion of their benefits over a three-year period (the Job Search Scheme), and the unemployed can now take part-time employment without loss of benefit. It is virtually impossible to incorporate these changes in an index of the replacement ratio. Simulations of the replacement ratios facing the unemployed show little change in the distribution between 1987 and 1994 – the median was 63 per cent in both years (Callan, Nolan and O'Donoghue, 1996).[15] Longer-run time series show that the average replacement ratio rose sharply in the 1970s, peaked in the early 1980s, and declined slowly thereafter. The recent decline in the ratio has been more pronounced for the short-term than for the long-term unemployed.

The role of the indefinite duration of unemployment benefits and the relative rise in the replacement ratio facing the long-term unemployed in the persistence of high long-term unemployment in Ireland remains uncertain. A more important influence is likely to have been the prolonged recession of the 1980s, which destroyed many unskilled jobs and made it extremely difficult for unemployed men of mature years to be re-employed. The abundant supply of younger, better-educated job applicants would also have militated against this group. Murphy and Walsh (1997) have shown the contributions of low educational attainment and residence in inner city areas (and in local authority housing in particular) to the risk of unemployment. The highest replacement ratios are associated with large families, but this study found that the risk of unemployment is highest, *ceteris paribus*, among unmarried men and women. While the presence of dependent children in the household raises the risk of unemployment, the proportion of the unemployed with child dependants is small.[16]

To obtain a broader view of where the Irish labour market ranks on the flexibility/rigidity spectrum, Table 9.6 summarises the indicators contained in a recent comparative study. The picture of Ireland's labour market that emerges is mixed. The country is rated 'better' (that is, more flexible) than average on the benefit replacement ratio and the two tax measures, but 'worse' than average on employment protection, benefit duration, union coverage, spending on active labour market policies, and the coordination of wage bargaining.

The low index of corporatism assigned to Ireland in Table 9.6 does not reflect the re-introduction of centralised wage bargaining ('National Wage Agreements') in the 1980s. National wage agreements were adopted in the 1970s but abandoned during the 1981–87 period of rising unemployment and high inflation. The resumption of national pay bargaining in the late 1980s is believed by Irish policy-makers to have made an important contribution to the recent improvement in economic performance. A feature of these agreements was that in return for low nominal wage demands the government held out the promise of reductions in the rate of income taxation and improvements in social benefits (as well as a wide variety of other measures).

The return to corporatist wage bargaining has been widely credited – especially in official circles – for securing moderate wage demands over the past 10 years. Between 1988 and 1995 the central wage agreements allowed for nominal pre-tax wage rates would have increased by 25 per cent. This would have resulted in a mere 0.5 per cent rise in

Table 9.6   Measures of labour market flexibility/rigidity

	Ireland	*OECD average*
Employment protection index (20 = most rigid)	12.0	10.5
Labour standards index (10 = most strict)	4.0	4.0
Benefit replacement ratio (%)	37.0	56.7
Benefit duration (years)	4.0	2.3
Active labour market policies (spending per unemployed person as a percent of GDP per member of the labour force)	9.1	12.3
Union density (%)	49.7	41.5
Union coverage index (scale increasing from 1 to 3)	3.0	2.6
Coordination: union (scale increasing from 1 to 3)	1.0	1.9
Coordination: employer (scale increasing from 1 to 3)	1.0	2.0
Payroll tax rate (%)	7.1	19.0
Labour cost–take home pay tax wedge (%)	34.3	48.2

Note: The data relate to averages over the period 1989–94. The OECD average relates to 20 countries.
Source: Nickell, 1997.

real wages. However, real wage rates increased by almost 9 per cent, reflecting the additional effect of local pay negotiations, and reductions in income taxation caused real after-tax wages to increase by almost 20 per cent. Thus, much of the increase in workers' disposable income was due to tax reductions rather than pay increases.

The stated goal of Irish incomes policy in the 1980s was to stabilise nominal wages in order to allow the benefits of a stable nominal exchange rate and rising productivity to be reflected in employment growth. There was a consistent emphasis on improving international competitiveness in order to increase employment and lower unemployment. This wage policy – combined with two large devaluations of the Irish pound in the exchange rate mechanism of the European monetary system (in 1985 and 1993) – led to a reversal of the rise in relative hourly earnings, measured in a common currency, that occurred in the first half of the 1980s (Figure 9.11). An even more dramatic improvement in the competitiveness of manufacturing industry is revealed by an index of unit labour costs measured in a common currency. This index reflects changes in (i) nominal wages, (ii) productivity, and (iii) the nominal exchange rate, all relative to the country's trading partners. While it may be objected that this index reflects the fact that only efficient firms survive, and hence is endogenous, the main reason for its dramatic decline in Ireland since 1985 has been the inflow of

Figure 9.11   Indices of competitiveness

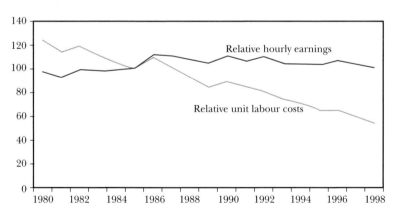

Note: Both series are expressed in a common currency.
Source: Central Bank of Ireland, *Quarterly Bulletin*, various issues.

FDI and its impact on the productivity of those employed in Irish industry. The rapid growth in productivity has not been captured by workers through higher wages. The evidence is unambiguous that a combination of low wage inflation, rapid gains in productivity, and a stable effective nominal exchange rate resulted in pronounced gains in competitiveness to industry since the mid-1980s. This operated like a successful devaluation, stimulating demand for Irish exports at a time when aggregate demand in Europe was stagnant (Krugman, 1997). Combined with the high initial level of unemployment and the rapid growth of the working-age population, it facilitated rapid growth of employment combined with low wage inflation.

These trends are also reflected in the changing distribution of national income. Figure 9.12 shows that the share of wages in GDP has declined sharply since the mid-1980s. Care must be exercised in the interpretation of this series. Both the numerator and the denominator include the effects of transfer pricing on the value added in the Irish subsidiaries of MNCs. While there are limits on the ability of these firms to located profits in Ireland's low-tax jurisdiction, it undoubtedly has influenced the share of profit in value added. The growth of FDI is part of the reason why Ireland's 'adjusted wage share' fell from 80.4 per cent of GDP (the highest in the EU) in 1980, to 62.2 per cent in 1997 (the lowest in the EU). When expressed as a proportion of GNP, the decline in the share of wages is less dramatic – from 83.75 to 71.7 per cent. While it

Figure 9.12   Adjusted wage share

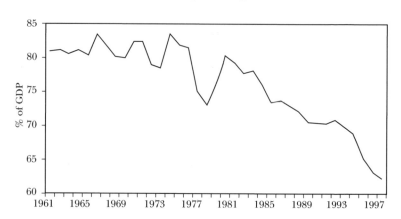

Source: *European Economy*, various issues.

is largely due to the influx of FDI to the country since the mid-1980s, it also reflects the impact of moderation in the wage bargaining process and may in turn be cited among the factors that have contributed to the inflow of FDI and the spectacular growth of employment.

AN INTERPRETATION

This chapter has explored various approaches to understanding the behaviour of Irish unemployment since the 1960s. It has been shown that the standard definitions of the natural, equilibrium, or non-accelerating inflation, rate of unemployment (NAIRU) are difficult to apply in the context of a small, open economy. A wealth of previous research has shown that the link between the rate of unemployment and wage and price inflation is weak in Ireland.

Numerous studies have shown the sensitivity of Irish migration to relative unemployment rates. A useful approach to accounting for the behaviour of Irish unemployment utilises the long-standing links between the small Irish and the larger UK labour markets to define an equilibrium rate of unemployment based on the gap between the unemployment rates in the two countries. But it is also important to take account of the influence of the rate of growth of the Irish economy on changes in Irish unemployment – the standard Okun's-law approach. Taking account of both internal and external influences it is possible to estimate an equilibrium rate of unemployment that increases as unemployment in Britain rises and falls as the Irish growth rate rises.

The relationship between Irish and UK unemployment that existed in the 1960s broke down in the 1970s. The reasons for this break are not clear. The econometric results contained here do not support the view that it was due to changes in the relative generosity of the Irish and UK social welfare systems. It is more plausible to argue that the enormous increase in British unemployment and the change in the composition of the demand for labour weakened the traditional Irish propensity to emigrate in response to rising unemployment in Ireland. It took some time for the migration mechanism to be re-established.

The most remarkable feature of the Irish labour market in the 1990s has been the exceptionally rapid rate of growth of employment. This has in due course led to falling unemployment, although the effect on unemployment has been modified by the highly elastic supply of labour. The moderate rate of growth of wages and the rising share of profit in national income have been a cause of Ireland's success in attracting

FDI and expanding exports. The changing composition of the Irish labour supply has also played an important role. The inflow to employment is heavily weighted with well-educated young people who have significantly improved the average quality of the labour force. The availability of a relatively abundant supply of educated workers at wage rates that are low by European standards has contributed to the profitability of FDI in Ireland. The inflow of high-productivity foreign capital has in turn reinforced the competitive gain.

The simple model outlined in Figure 9.13 shows a supply-of-labour schedule intersected by a demand for labour in the range where the elasticity of supply is infinite. As the demand for labour shifts outward due to competitive gains, employment grows and the employment/population ratio rises without an increase in the wage rate. Upward pressure on wage rates is held at bay by the availability of labour at the prevailing wage rate. The elastic labour supply reflects factors such as the high initial level of unemployment, the rapid growth of the population of working age, the rising rate of labour force participation among women, and the propensity of Irish emigrants living abroad to return home.

Figure 9.13   Effect of increase in productivity and change in wage bargaining

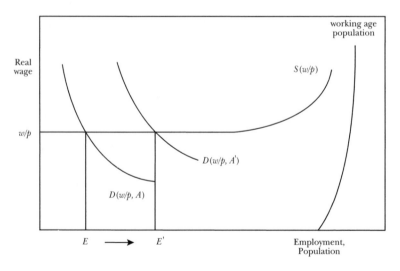

Note: *w/p* is the real wage, *D*( ) the demand for labour, *S*( ) the supply of labour, and *A* is a measure of productivity.

CONCLUSION

The evolution of the Irish labour market since the mid-1980s has been very impressive. Employment has grown more rapidly than at any previous period of the country's history. Between 1986 and 1997 the numbers at work increased at an annual average rate of 2.1 per cent, and the unemployment rate fell from 17.1 to 10.3 per cent. The Irish–UK unemployment gap narrowed from 8 to 3 percentage points, and at the same time the rates of price and wage inflation remained subdued.

These favourable outcomes have been made possible by the existence of a high initial level of unemployment and an elastic supply of labour. It is difficult to estimate with any precision for how long this high rate of employment growth can be maintained, or how low the unemployment rate can fall, before the labour market overheats and threatens the continuation of the boom.

Much credit is generally given to the role of corporatism, or centralised wage bargaining, in the performance of the Irish economy since the mid-1980s. It can, however, be argued that the initial slack labour market conditions and the very elastic supply of labour were the key moderating factors on the rate of wage inflation. A large inflow of FDI and the resultant gains in productivity, combined with favourable nominal exchange rate developments, were critical to the subsequent rapid growth of the economy. By 1998 the key issue had become whether centralised wage bargaining could continue to contain wage inflation in the face of low unemployment and increasing skill shortages.

Notes

1. Earlier versions of this paper were presented at a CEPR/ESRC workshop on 'Unemployment Dynamics' at the London Business School, 22 October 1997, and at a CEPR conference on 'Unemployment Persistence and the Long Run; Reevaluating the Natural Rate' at Vigo, Spain, on 30 November 1997. I would like to thank Frank Barry, Michael Burda, Joseph Durkan, Donal Garvey, Brian Henry, Anthony Leddin, John Martin, Anthony Murphy, Stephen Nickell, Dennis Snower and Rodney Thom for comments on earlier drafts. Responsibility for the views expressed is of course mine alone.
2. In 1993 net output per employee averaged Ir£36 500 in Irish-owned firms compared with Ir£96 133 in foreign-owned firms.
3. The unemployment data used in this paper are all based on ILO definitions from the Labour Force Survey (available since 1975) and earlier sources that have been adjusted for comparability. Until 1997 the Irish LFS was

conducted annually. A quarterly survey is now underway. There are large and growing discrepancies between the data on registered unemployment and unemployment as measured in the LFS. A significant proportion of older men who are 'ILO inactive' are on the Live Register. Women are likely to be on the Live Register if they have been recently employed and hence presumably entitled to unemployment benefit even if not actively seeking employment (Murphy and Walsh, 1997).

4. It was also found that the probability of being economically active is much higher among males living in rural areas. Some of the decline in labour force participation may therefore be due to the reduced importance of agricultural employment and a shift from underemployment on farms to more overt unemployment in the non-farm situation.

5. Defined simply as unemployment above its pre-recession level.

6. This estimate differs from that contained in Ball (1993) for Ireland. Balls' 'sacrifice ratio' is the ratio of the deviation of *output* (GDP) from its 'full employment' (trend) level to the reduction in inflation. He reports a value of 1.7 per cent for Ireland over the period 1980–87, compared with 7.7 per cent for the US over the years 1979–83. The switch from using unemployment to output to measure the social costs of disinflation is questionable. Under Irish circumstances, the growth of GDP quickly regained its trend path after 1979 but the response of employment and unemployment to the resumed growth was delayed.

7. The null hypothesis of no cointegrating vectors between these variables is rejected at the 95 per cent confidence level.

8. Based on the F-statistic for a cointegrating relationship.

9. Using the OECD's standardised unemployment rate for the UK. In recent years this rate has been almost one percentage point above the commonly used definition.

10. Personal communication from Patrick Honohan, October 1997.

11. The two unemployment rates are $I(1)$, while the growth rate is $I(0)$. It would be permissible to estimate an error-correction representation of the three series if there were a cointegrating relationship between the two unemployment rates. But this is not the case and we must be wary about drawing inferences from the results of an ECM.

12. That is the actual rate minus the component attributable to cyclical factors.

13. This variable is the ratio of the *gross* replacement ratios in the two countries. The methodology used in the calculation of these ratios is described in Martin (1996). John Martin of the OECD kindly supplied the original data for odd-numbered years. Missing year values have been linearly interpolated. *Net* replacement ratios for 1994 are shown in Table 2.1 of the OECD *Employment Outlook*. The Irish ratios are higher than the UK ratios in almost all situations.

14. This variable is $I(1)$ and the trace statistic of the cointegration LR test allows us to reject the hypothesis of no cointegrating vector between u_{Irl}, u_{UK}, and *rratio* at the 95 per cent confidence level (Johansen and Juselius, 1992), in favour of the alternative hypothesis of one cointegrating vector. This favours an explanation of changes in Irish unemployment based on the behaviour of UK unemployment and the relative levels of unemployment replacement ratios in the two countries.

15. A significant caveat attaches to these calculations, however, because they do not take account of benefits in kind or work-related expenses.
16. Department of Social Welfare statistics reveal that in 1996, 65.9 per cent of recipients of unemployment benefits (of all types) had no child dependants and the average number of child dependants per claimant with a child dependant was only 2.4.

References

Ball, L. (1993) 'What Determines the Sacrifice Ratio?', National Bureau of Economic Research, working paper no. 4306.

Blanchard, O. (1997) *Macroeconomics*, international edn (Englewood Cliffs, N.J.: Prentice-Hall).

Blanchard, O. and Katz, L. (1997) 'What we Know and do Not Know about the Natural Rate of Unemployment', *Journal of Economic Perspectives,* 11(1), pp. 51–72.

Burda, M. (1997) 'Persistently High Irish Unemployment: A Comparison with the UK', in A. Gray (ed.), *International Perspectives on the Irish Economy* (Dublin: Indecon), pp. 85–111.

Callan, T., Nolan, B. and O'Donoghue, C. (1996) 'What has Happened to Replacement Rates', *Economic and Social Review*, 27, pp. 439–56.

Card, D. and Riddell, W. Craig (1993) 'A Comparative Analysis of Unemployment in the United States and Canada', in D. Card and R. Freeman (eds), *Small Differences that Matter: Labour Markets and Income Maintenance in Canada and the United States* (Chicago: University of Chicago Press), pp. 149–89.

Central Bank of Ireland *Quarterly Bulletin*, various issues (Dublin: Central Bank).

Cohen, D. (1997) 'Patterns of Wage and Labour Flexibility: A Transatlantic Comparison', paper to CEPR Conference on Unemployment Persistence and the Long Run: Re-evaluating the Natural Rate, Vigo.

CSO (various years) *Census of Population* (Dublin: Central Statistics Office).

CSO (various years) *Labour Force Survey* (Dublin: Central Statistics Office).

Curtis, J. and FitzGerald, J. D. (1991) 'Real Wage Convergence in an Open Labour Market', *Economic and Social Review*, 27(4), pp. 321–40.

Friedman, M. (1968) 'The Role of Monetary Policy', *American Economic Review*, 58(1), pp. 1–17.

Gordon, R. J. (1997) 'The Time-Varying NAIRU and its Implications for Economic Policy', *Journal of Economic Perspectives*, 11(1), pp. 11–32.

Harrison, M. J. and Walsh, P. P. (1994) 'A Flow Analysis of the Irish Live Register', *Economic and Social Review*, 26(1), pp. 45–59.

Honohan, P. (1992) 'The Link between Irish and UK Unemployment', *Quarterly Economic Commentary*, (Spring), pp. 33–44.

Johansen, S. and Juselius, K. (1992) 'Testing Structural Hypotheses in a Multivariate Cointegration Analysis of the PPP and UIP for UK', *Econometrica*, 53(2), pp. 211–44.

Keenan, J. G. (1981) 'Irish Migration: All or Nothing Resolved?', *The Economic and Social Review*, 12(3), pp. 169–86.

Kenny, G. and McGettigan, D. (1996a) 'Non-traded, Traded and Aggregate Inflation in Ireland', Central Bank of Ireland, technical paper, 3/RT/96 (June).

Kenny, G. and McGettigan, D. (1996b) 'Inflation in Ireland: Theory and Evidence', Central Bank of Ireland, *Annual Report*, pp. 127–60.

Kirwan, F. X. (1982) 'Recent Anglo-Irish Migration – The Evidence of the British Labour Force Surveys', *Economic and Social Review*, 13(3), pp. 191–204.

Krugman, P. (1997) 'Good News from Ireland: A Geographical Perspective', in A. Gray (ed.), *International Perspectives on the Irish Economy* (Dublin: Indecon), pp. 38–53.

Layard, R., Nickell, S. and Jackman, R. (1991) *Unemployment: Macroeconomic Performance and the Labour Market*, (Oxford: Oxford University Press).

Leddin, A. and Walsh, B. (1998) *The Macroeconomy of Ireland*, 4th edn (Dublin: Gill & Macmillan).

Mankiw, N. G. (1997) *Macroeconomics*, 3rd edn (New York: Worth).

McGettigan, D. (1992), 'Irish Unemployment: A Review of the Issues', Central Bank of Ireland, technical paper 2/RT/92.

Martin, J. P. (1996) 'Measures of Replacement Ratios for the Purpose of International Comparisons: A Note', OECD *Economic Studies*, 26(1), pp. 99–115.

Murphy, A. and Walsh, B. (1997) *Aspects of Employment and Unemployment in Ireland*, Dublin: National Economic and Social Forum, report no. 13.

Nickell, S. (1997) 'Unemployment and Labor Market Rigidities: Europe versus North America', *Journal of Economic Perspectives*, 11(3), pp. 37–54.

OECD (1994) *The OECD Jobs Study* (Paris: OECD).

OECD (1996 and 1997) *Employment Outlook* (Paris: OECDC).

Perry, G. L. (1970) 'Changing Labour Markets and Inflation', *Brookings Papers on Economic Activity*, 3, pp. 411–88.

Scarpetta, S. (1996) 'Assessing the Role of Labour Market Policies and Institutional Settings on Unemployment: A Cross-Country Study', OECD *Economic Studies*, 26(1), pp. 43–98.

Walsh, B. (1974) 'Expectations, Information and Human Migration: Specifying an Econometric Model of Irish Migration', *Journal of Regional Science*, 14(2), pp. 107–20.

—— (1978) 'Unemployment Compensation and the Rate of Unemployment: The Irish Experience', in H. C. Grubel and M. A. Walker (eds), *Unemployment Insurance: Global Evidence of its Effects on Unemployment*, Vancouver, B. C., The Fraser Institute, pp. 172–201.

—— (1987) 'Why is Unemployment so High in Ireland Today?', *Perspectives on Economic Policy,* University College, Dublin: Centre for Economic Research, 1, pp. 3–42.

—— (1993) 'Labour Force Participation and the Growth of Women's Employment, Ireland, 1971–1991', *Economic and Social Review*, 24(4), pp. 369–400.

—— (1996) 'Stabilisation and Adjustment in a Small Open Economy: Ireland 1979–95', *Oxford Review of Economic Policy*, 12(3), pp. 74–86.

Index